Conversations with Maurice Sendak

Literary Conversations Series
Monika Gehlawat
General Editor

Conversations
with Maurice Sendak

Edited by Peter C. Kunze

University Press of Mississippi   Jackson

www.upress.state.ms.us

The University Press of Mississippi is a member of the Association of American University Presses.

First printing 2016

Library of Congress Cataloging-in-Publication Data

Names: Sendak, Maurice, author. | Kunze, Peter C. (Peter Christopher), editor.
Title: Conversations with Maurice Sendak / edited by Peter C. Kunze.
Description: Jackson : University Press of Mississippi, 2016. | Series:
    Literary conversations series | Includes index.
Identifiers: LCCN 2016007781 | ISBN 9781496808707 (hardback)
Subjects: LCSH: Sendak, Maurice—Interviews. | Authors, American—20th
    century—Interviews. | Children's stories—Authorship—Juvenile literature.
Classification: LCC PS3569.E6 Z46 2016 | DDC 813/.54—dc23 LC record available at http://
lccn.loc.gov/2016007781

British Library Cataloging-in-Publication Data available

Contents

Introduction

In the final year of his life, Maurice Sendak gave two prominent interviews that garnered considerable media coverage. The first was with Terry Gross, the mild-mannered host of NPR's *Fresh Air*, in September 2011. During this interview, many listeners heard something that must have taken them aback: a reflective and melancholy Sendak, one overwhelmed by the relatively recent deaths of friends and his partner of nearly fifty years, Eugene Glynn (in 2007), and the likely prospect that his own death was imminent. The sincerity Sendak exhibited in this interview resonated with many members of the audience, and, by *Fresh Air*'s count, inspired more responses than any other interview that year and even a 2012 "illustrated talk" by Christoph Niemann for the *New York Times Magazine* website. The second interview, with Stephen Colbert on *The Colbert Report* in January 2012, offered its audience quite a different Sendak: one who was cranky, acid-tongued, and mischievous. He both humored Colbert's faux conservative schtick on the one hand and eviscerated the comedian's feigned stupidity on the other. These two interviews, for their respective solemnity and playfulness, reveal two sides of Sendak's personality, revealing how incredibly thoughtful, spirited, and multi-faceted he was. *Conversations with Maurice Sendak* hopes to recapture much of his complexity and preserve it in one volume; in doing so, readers will hopefully gain a newfound appreciation for Sendak and the range and depth of his considerable oeuvre.

When Maurice Sendak died in 2012, Margalit Fox of the *New York Times* contended that he had "wrenched the picture book out of the safe, sanitized world of the nursery and plunged it into the dark, terrifying and hauntingly beautiful recesses of the human psyche." Similar sentiments echoed throughout the press, academia, and social media. Jules Feiffer told *Publishers Weekly* that Sendak "gradually redefined what a children's book should look like and what we were to think of the form from here on out. He was a game-changer" ("Maurice Sendak Remembered"). George R. Bodmer, writing in the academic journal *PMLA*, started off his tribute to Sendak by noting that he was "an artist who not only produced extraordinary art and memorable books but also expanded the range of children's literature, what it can portray. In doing so, he eagerly dealt with his own life, his anxieties and joys, and focused on the importance of art to a child's life" (101). On Twitter, John Green posted, "Maurice Sendak taught me and millions of others that it was no sin to be a child." The praise, quite understandably, knew no bounds. Sendak himself undersold his contribution to children's literature, and one can see that his take on children was largely informed by those literary figures he read, like William Blake, or collaborated with, particularly editor Ursula Nordstrom and writer Ruth Krauss.[1] Yet Sendak's contribution to children's literature may also be his refusal to take it as anything less than a serious artistic venture. Sendak was but one member of the vanguard of writers, illustrators, and editors who understood that children's literature was, first and foremost, literature and that children as an audience were sophisticated, intelligent, and capable readers.

Of course, to celebrate Maurice Sendak as a revolutionary artist of the twentieth century is somewhat ironic, given he was a man somewhat out of his time. Through his private studying and formidable collecting, Sendak demonstrated his serious admiration for the art of the past, especially of the nineteenth century. Sendak testifies again and again to his enduring admiration for Herman Melville and Emily Dickinson, George Cruikshank and Beatrix Potter, Wolfgang Amadeus Mozart and Gustav Mahler throughout the interviews that follow. This point should not imply Sendak was a cultural snob; he also had a great fondness for Mickey Mouse (though he preferred the Mickey of his youth to the later incarnations) and Hollywood cinema of the 1930s and 1940s. One sees these influences time and again, whether in Pierre's Bartleby the Scrivener–like indifference or the bakers who resembled Oliver Hardy in *In the Night Kitchen*. Sendak's work reveals a profound eclecticism that fused the popular culture of his youth with the folk culture of his Jewish ancestors as well as the mainstays of the Western canon. When one looks at the cartoons he drew for the physics textbook *Atomics for the Millions* in 1947, the iconic cross-hatching used for the *Wild Things* in 1963, and the baroque imagery of *Outside Over There* in 1981, one cannot help but marvel at the diversity of styles Sendak employed as his understanding and command of illustration developed. Considering both his approaches and his influences, one begins to see his body of work as both learned and nuanced, but still pleasing and accessible.

Yet to see Sendak as a "children's book author" alone greatly impairs one's understanding of his art. A brief look over the bibliography included in this volume shows a sharp decline in children's book illustration in the late

1970s, when Sendak began to work in other media and art forms, including television, theater, and opera. He wrote, with Carole King, an adaptation of *The Sign on Rosie's Door* and *The Nutshell Library* for the stage and, eventually, an animated television special. He designed sets, costumes, and posters for theatrical and operatic productions around the United States and Europe. He produced cover art for literary biographies and national magazines as well as promotional illustrations for American Express and the New York Is Book Country Festival. In 2003, he even collaborated with Tony Award–winning playwright Tony Kushner to adapt Hans Krása and Adolf Hoffmeister's *Brundibár*, a Czech opera famously put on by children in the Theresienstadt concentration camp to entertain visiting Nazi officials. To identify Maurice Sendak as "the author of *Where the Wild Things Are*" alone greatly underestimates the breadth and complexity of an artist who, for over fifty years, sought new challenges and broke new ground in his effort to produce and promote art for children and adults in the United States and abroad.

This volume, in some modest way, gestures toward a richer vision of Sendak and his work. The interviews herein explore his evolving ideas about childhood, literature, and art in general, but a good deal of attention is also paid to children's literature, which Sendak continued to theorize throughout his career. While talking with Bill Moyers on the show *NOW*, he recounted watching an interview with the accomplished opera singer, Christa Ludwig. The interviewer observed Ludwig's peculiar fondness for singing Franz Schubert, who he implied was a simple and insignificant composer of Viennese waltzes. Sendak fondly recalled,

> And she smiled and she said, "Ah, Schubert is so big, so delicate. But what he did was pick a form that looks so humble and quiet, so that he could crawl into that form and explode emotionally, find every way of expressing every emotion in this miniature form." And I got very excited, and I wondered, "Is it possible that's why I do children's books?" [. . .] But my thought was that's what I did. I didn't have much confidence in myself—never. And so I hid inside, like Christa was saying, this modest form called "the children's book" and expressed myself entirely. ("Maurice Sendak: *Where the Wild Things Are*")

Indeed, for Sendak, the picture book was more than words and pictures; it was a place for synthesizing his artistic influences, for philosophizing on the nature of childhood and life itself, for speaking candidly and honestly with both children and adults. Whereas some may perceive Sendak as a major figure in a minor field, he instead proved that the picture book—and children's literature more broadly—merited serious critical attention and performed the valuable social labor of interacting with the youngest and most impressionable of readers. For Sendak, though, the writer does not talk down to her or his child reader, but merely relates one's experience of the world as she or he knows it. Indeed the worlds within Sendak's books can be, at times, terrifying and unfamiliar, but they are also spaces where love, freedom, and authenticity are celebrated. Protagonists are not punished for their insolence; instead, they flourish.

The twelve interviews in *Conversations with Maurice Sendak* were selected for the range of topics they cover as well as their ability to illustrate Sendak's changing ideas about children's literature, illustration, and his own artistic identity. The opening piece is Nat Hentoff's 1966 profile of Sendak for the *New Yorker*. Written three years after the publication of *Where the Wild Things Are* and Sendak's only winning of the prestigious Caldecott Medal, the profile provides a portrait of Sendak at a turning point in his career. By now, he had illustrated a substantial number of children's books, but *Where the Wild Things Are* gave him greater prominence. In addition to hearing from Ursula Nordstrom, his legendary editor at Harper & Row, the interview also features a cameo by his beloved Sealyham Terrier, Jennie, who appears in several books, most prominently *Higglety Pigglety Pop! or, There Must Be More to Life*, which was published the following year. The interview also came out before Sendak's heart attack in 1967, which largely motivated his departure (on doctor's orders) from New York City for Connecticut in the early 1970s. "Among the Wild Things" not only captures a young artist finally receiving his due, but encapsulates some of Sendak's earliest thoughts on his craft.

The next piece, "Questions to an Artist Who Is Also an Author: A Conversation between Maurice Sendak and Virginia Haviland," reproduces a dialogue between Sendak and Virginia Haviland, a children's librarian and the founder of the Children's Literature Center at the Library of Congress. Originally published in the Library's quarterly journal and subsequently excerpted in Sendak's book of essays, *Caldecott & Co.: Notes on Books & Pictures*, the interview appears here in full. Only a few years after the Hentoff profile, this interview reveals a more reflective Sendak—one who has developed his ideas about children as readers of books and as an intended audience. He also speaks at length about his fondness for earlier writers, especially George MacDonald, as well as his command of the history and current state of illustration, both in the United States and abroad. (Many of these concerns appear again and again throughout this volume.) Of equal interest is his discussion of his style; as Haviland notes, critics compared the fine, engraving-like style employed in *Higglety Pigglety Pop!* to the "fat style" developed in his earlier illustrations, especially for Ruth Krauss. The latter approach was prominently used in his most recent book at the time, *In the Night Kitchen*, which Sendak also discusses here.

Unlike most interviews in this volume, which were conducted by journalists, librarians, or scholars, Muriel Harris, a schoolteacher, wrote "Impressions of Sendak." Harris, now Muriel Harris Weinstein, became a children's book writer herself in retirement, publishing *When Louis Armstrong Taught Me Scat* in 2008 and, two years later, *Play, Louis Play!: The True Story of a Boy and His Horn*. She visited with Sendak at his home in New York City soon after the publication of *In the Night Kitchen* and before his health would lead him to leave New York City permanently for rural Connecticut. Her profile captures him being relaxed and playful, and she draws attention to several themes and issues that come up throughout the later interviews: the influence of Judaism on his work, his collection of childhood toys, his fondness for nineteenth century literature and illustration, his family and his childhood. Unlike the more focused interviews that come later, "Impressions of Sendak" is informal and intimate, offering a welcome departure for readers and scholars alike.

Walter Lorraine's "A Conversation with Maurice Sendak," also excerpted in *Caldecott & Co.*, follows Harris's interview and features some of Sendak's most candid thoughts on illustration and the picture book. In particular, it demonstrates Sendak's ongoing concern that children's picture books are in an unremarkable period, fueled by a corrupting lack of talent, originality, and risk-taking. Sendak actively worked to redress this concern both through his university teaching and active mentorship of younger artists. In 2010 he established the Sendak Fellows program to rebuke the vapidity and stupidity he perceived as stifling the craft.

The fifth interview comes from the dissertation of children's literature scholar Jerry Griswold, who interviewed Sendak about Randall Jarrell, the accomplished poet for whom Sendak illustrated several books, including *The Bat-Poet* (1964) and *Fly by Night* (1976). This interview is the first of two included interviews (the other being Philip Nel's) to focus predominantly on Sendak as a collaborator with other children's authors. While Jarrell and Sendak were friends, their collaboration was not as close and intensive as his work with Ruth Krauss, providing illuminating insights into the work habits of these significant writers.

Glenn Edward Sadler's "A Conversation with Maurice Sendak and Dr. Seuss" offers Sendak fielding questions with perhaps his closest competition for most influential children's book author of the twentieth century, Dr. Seuss (Theodor Geisel). As Sadler recounts, Geisel was a private man, but welcomed the chance to meet and talk with Maurice Sendak in 1982. The resulting interview is alternately lively and perceptive, as the men joke around about their public lives as famous children's book writers as well as their respective artistic processes. By this point, Sendak appears to have settled into his life as a celebrity, and his playfulness in the interview underscores his growing frustration with certain lines of questioning and his skillful ability to navigate around them.

"Maurice Sendak Q & A," by Hank Nuwer, catches up with Sendak a few years after the publication of *Outside Over There*, the National Book Award–winning picture book that took Sendak years to write and illustrate. By this time, Sendak is at the height of his powers, and Nuwer explores not only how he perceives himself, but the author's thoughts on growing up and death. Indeed, death becomes a common theme in later Sendak interviews, one which he alternately treats with solemnity and sarcasm. Additionally, this particular interview includes details of Sendak's friendship with Modernist poet Marianne Moore and his fervent esteem for Herman Melville. Sendak would go on to illustrate Melville's *Pierre; or, The Ambiguities* (1995) and to create the cover art for both volumes of Hershel Parker's landmark biography of Melville (1996, 2002).

Steven Heller returns our attention to Maurice Sendak as an artist, specifically an illustrator. In addition to discussing Sendak's early training, Heller also focuses on the influences behind and preparation of Sendak's books, especially *Outside Over There* and *In the Night Kitchen*. A key aspect of the interview is Sendak's discussion of commerciality and the role it plays in his understanding of himself as an artist. Unlike other writers, Sendak saw himself as an artist first and foremost, and he closely guarded his creative property in order to prevent it from becoming overly commodified, like Walt Disney had. While Disney served as an early inspiration for Sendak, clearly Disney also became a model against which Sendak defined himself as an artist and, by necessity, a businessman.

In 2001, scholar Philip Nel interviewed Maurice Sendak in preparation for his biography of Crockett Johnson and Ruth Krauss. "'Don't assume anything': A Conversation with Maurice Sendak," published here for the first time, offers invaluable insight into the collaboration between Krauss and Sendak as well as the artist's life before stardom. Nel's interview also presents another side of Sendak rarely seen in the earlier interviews in this book—one in which Sendak is poignant and reflective, yet, at times, irreverent and acerbic. While popular impressions of Sendak seem to re-create him as a nurturing grandfather type, extended interviews such as Nel's and Spike Jonze and Lance Bangs's 2009 documentary *Tell Them Anything You Want: A Portrait of Maurice Sendak* reveal an edgier Sendak who prefers wicked humor and spirited banter over vapid platitudes and reassuring sentiment.

Once more the reader finds a reflective Sendak in an interview by Roger Sutton, editor of *The Horn Book*. While the men start off discussing the banality of reality television, the interview transitions to allow Sendak to survey his career over the previous fifty years. Again, he discusses his relationship with Ursula Nordstrom and the reception of his books, but also reveals the difficulties and failures behind his most well-known works. In particular, he explains how the 1932 kidnapping and subsequent murder of Charles Lindbergh Jr. (the "Lindbergh baby") haunted his childhood, leading to his revision of the events in *Outside Over There*, and his current efforts to confront the ghosts of the Holocaust by adapting *Brundibár* with Tony Kushner.

"Selected Sendak: Interviews by the Rosenbach" draws upon several extended interviews between 2007 and 2008 led by Patrick Rodgers, curator of the Sendak Collection at the Rosenbach Museum and Library, where Sendak placed over ten thousand items from his personal collections. An avid collector himself, Sendak found a kindred spirit in the Rosenbach, which houses collections of work by Herman Melville, George Cruikshank, and William Blake, all of whom were key influences on Sendak's work. Edited down from over 150 pages of transcripts, the resulting interview details Sendak's career in the theater and the opera, where, from the 1970s into the 2000s, he designed everything from sets and costumes to promotional materials. He reflects upon the relative success of *Brundibar* as well as his influences, including lengthy discussions of Melville, Dickinson, Blake, and Mozart. These interviews were also conducted around the time of the death of his partner, Eugene Glynn, and the public revelation of his sexual identity. In reading them, one picks up on a sense of Sendak's resulting melancholy, and his discussion of happiness underscores his sadness as well as his acceptance of its inevitability.

To end on Terry Gross's much-publicized 2011 interview with Sendak, of course, is bittersweet. At the time, the eight-three-year-old artist was publicizing the release of his latest book, *Bumble-Ardy*, yet what Gross found was a pensive, forthright Sendak, heartbreakingly honest about death yet reassuringly confident in the beauty of life. Like the most well-known of his books, the interview boldly presents emotions not often found in this genre. This expression—open, vulnerable, gut-wrenching—was classic Sendak, and it embodies what those who love Sendak love about his work. While the book ends there, I would encourage readers to seek out the two-part interview with Stephen Colbert as a worthy companion so that they may understand, as this book hopes to encourage, the richness and brilliance of Maurice Sendak: writer, illustrator, artist par excellence.

And now, let the wild rumpus start.

A project like this one is truly a labor of love. I must first thank my editor, Katie Keene, who believed in this project from our initial conversation through its publication. I am grateful to all of the rights holders, who believed in this project and graciously provided permission for the material to be reprinted. In particular, I must thank Patrick Rodgers of the Rosenbach Library, who alerted me at the outset to numerous interviews that might have otherwise escaped my attention, and Philip Nel of Kansas State University, whose collegiality, integrity, and patience were a model of academic professionalism. Their guidance proved invaluable to the formation of this book. Additional appreciation is due to Andrew Epstein, Glenn Edward Sadler, and Katie Bircher for their kind assistance in finding materials and permissions, and Philip Nel wishes to thank Stephen Barbara, David Austin, and Sara Austin. Finally, yet of no less importance, I am grateful to the librarians and support staff at the University of Albany, SUNY, where this project began, and the University of Texas at Austin, where it ended, for locating much of the content included here. The interviews and profile appear as they did in print, except when variations on spelling or mechanics were necessary for accuracy and clarity. Several worthwhile and important interviews were excluded because of length or cost. I have included a brief bibliography of interviews and profiles for further reading in the appendix.

PCK

The Estate of Maurice Sendak has not approved or endorsed the publication of this anthology, *Conversations with Maurice Sendak*.

Note

1. For more on the influence of Nordstrom and Krauss on contemporary children's literature, consult Leonard S. Marcus's *Dear Genius: The Letters of Ursula Nord-*

strom and Philip Nel's *Crockett Johnson and Ruth Krauss: How an Unlikely Couple Found Love, Dodged the FBI, and Transformed Children's Literature.*

References

Bodmer, George R. "Maurice Sendak: The Child as Artist." *PMLA* 129.1 (January 2014): 101–3.

Fox, Margalit. "Maurice Sendak, Author of Splendid Nightmares, Dies at 83." *New York Times.* 8 May 2012. Web. 15 March 2015.

Green, John (johngreen). "Maurice Sendak taught me and millions of others that it was no sin to be a child." 8 May 2012, 11:08 a.m. Tweet.

Marcus, Leonard S., ed. *Dear Genius: The Letters of Ursula Nordstrom.* New York: HarperCollins, 1998.

"Maurice Sendak Remembered." *Publishers Weekly.* 25 May 2012. Web. 1 April 2015.

"Maurice Sendak: *Where the Wild Things Are.*" *NOW.* PBS. 12 March 2004. Web. 18 March 2015.

Nel, Philip. *Crockett Johnson and Ruth Krauss: How an Unlikely Couple Found Love, Dodged the FBI, and Transformed Children's Literature.* Jackson: University Press of Mississippi, 2012.

Chronology

1928   Born in Brooklyn on June 10.

1932   Charles Lindbergh Jr.—the infant son of the famed aviator—is kidnapped and later found dead.

1947   Illustrates a textbook, *Atomics for the Millions*.

1951   Illustrates Marcel Aymé's *The Wonderful Farm* for editor Ursula Nordstrom.

1956   Jack Sendak's *The Happy Rain*, with illustrations by Maurice, published. Publishes *Kenny's Window*, the first book he wrote and illustrated.

1957   Jack's *Circus Girl*, with illustrations again (and for the last time) by Maurice, published. Meets his partner, Eugene Glynn.

1963   Publishes *Where the Wild Things Are*.

1964   Wins Caldecott Medal for *Where the Wild Things Are*.

1967   Suffers heart attack.

1968   Mother Sadie Sendak dies.

1970   Father Philip Sendak dies. Publishes *In the Night Kitchen*, which raises concerns over the protagonist's nudity. Becomes the first American to win the Hans Christian Andersen Medal.

1972   Moves to Connecticut.

1975   Produces *Really Rosie*, with music by Carole King, for television.

1979   Adapts *Where the Wild Things Are* for the stage.

1981   Publishes *Outside Over There*. Designs sets for *The Magic Flute* (Houston Grand Opera) and *The Cunning Little Vixen* (New York City Opera).

1982   Wins National Book Award for *Outside Over There*.

1983   Designs sets for *The Nutcracker* (Pacific Northwest Ballet). Wins Laura Ingalls Wilder Award.

1988   Publishes *Caldecott and Co.*, a collection of essays.

1990   Cofounds the Night Kitchen Theater Company.

1993   Publishes *We Are All in the Dumps with Jack and Guy*.

1995   Jack Sendak dies.

1996   Wins National Medal of Arts.

1997   Designs sets for *Hansel and Gretel* (Houston Grand Opera).

2003   Publishes (with Tony Kushner) *Brundibar*. Chicago Opera Theater stages the theatrical version. Wins Astrid Lindgren Memorial Award.

2004   Sister Natalie (Sendak) Lesselbaum dies.

2007   Eugene Glynn dies.

2009   Spike Jonze's live-action film adaptation of *Where the Wild Things Are* released.

2011   Publishes *Bumble-Ardy*.

2012   Dies at eighty-three.

2013   *My Brother's Book* published posthumously.

Conversations with Maurice Sendak

Among the Wild Things

Nat Hentoff / 1966

My son Nicholas, three and a half, was jumping up and down on his bed. "I want to wash your hands," my wife said.

"I don't care," Nicholas replied.

"Lunch is ready."

"I don't care."

"It will get cold."

"I don't care."

The leaping continued. Then my wife asked, "Who *are* you?"

"Pierre!" Nicholas announced.

The next jump was the most ambitious yet, and Nicholas fell off the bed. As he rubbed his knee, my wife asked, "Are you hurt?"

In a much softer voice, he replied, "Yes, Mother Bear."

Mother Bear is a large, comfortable source of reassurance in *Little Bear*, a series of four books written by Else Holmelund Minarik and illustrated by Maurice Sendak. The Pierre whom Nicholas had been emulating is the hero of a book called *Pierre*, which is part of the four-volume *Nutshell Library*, written and illustrated by Maurice Sendak; Pierre, even after he is swallowed by a famished lion, will say only "I don't care." On top of a chest of drawers next to Nicholas's bed is a large picture of a dancing creature with horns, sharp teeth, yellow eyes, and a scaly body. He is a wild thing—an inhabitant of *Where the Wild Things Are*, a book written and illustrated by Maurice Sendak. Some reviewers of children's books have asserted that the Wild Things are frightening, but Nicholas finds them quite funny.

My son's familiarity with Maurice Sendak's creations is shared by a sizable and constantly growing number of American children under eight. As a writer, as an illustrator, and as both, Sendak has been associated with a number of successful children's books of the past decade. In addition to the *Little Bear* series, the *Nutshell Library*, and *Where the Wild Things Are*, there have been *A Hole Is to Dig*, written by Ruth Krauss, *The Bat-Poet* and *The Animal Family*, both written by the late Randall Jarrell, *Lullabies and Night Songs*, with music by Alec Wilder, and *Hector Protector*. More than fifty other children's books contain illustrations by Sendak, and more than half a dozen have texts by him; many of them sell well enough to keep Sendak surprised by his affluence.

Sendak has trouble believing in his commercial success largely because his creations are so much at variance with the sort of thing that usually sells well in his field. Far too many contemporary picture books for the young are still populated by children who eat everything on their plates, go dutifully to bed at the proper hour, and learn all sorts of useful facts or moral lessons by the time the book comes to an end. The illustrations are usually decorative rather than imaginative, and any fantasy that may be encountered either corresponds to the fulfillment of adult wishes or is carefully curbed lest it frighten the child. Many of these books, homogenized and characterless, look and read as if they had been put together by a computer. Sendak's work, on the other hand, is unmistakably identifiable as his. He will not illustrate to order, increasingly depending on himself as the writer, and, when he illustrates the texts of others, choosing only those that seem real to him. "Maurice is not an artist who just does an occasional book for children because there's money in it or because it will give him an easy change of pace," Sendak's editor, Ursula Nordstrom, who is director of the children's book department of Harper & Row, has said. "Children's book are *all* he does and all he wants to do. His books are full of emotion, of vitality. When one of his lines for a drawing is blown up, you find that it's not a precise straight line. It's rough with ridges, because so much emotion has gone into it. Too many of us—and I mean editors along with illustrators and writers of children's books—are afraid of emotion. We keep forgetting that children are new and we are not. But somehow Maurice has retained a direct line of his own childhood." Sendak, moreover, does not subscribe to the credo that childhood is a time of innocence—a point of view that, as it is usually interpreted, results in tales and pictures soothing to parents but unreal to the children. The young in Sendak's books—particularly the books he writes himself—are sometimes troubled and lonely, they slip easily into and out of fantasies, and occasionally they are unruly and stubborn. Nor are they the bright, handsome boys and softly pretty little girls who are so numerous in so many picture books for children. The Sendak boys and girls tend to appear truncated, having oversized heads, short arms, and quite short legs.

In the past few years, I have become increasingly interested in Sendak's work, reading his books for my own pleasure as well as for the amusement of my children. His drawings, I have found, are oddly compelling. Intensely, almost palpably alive, they seem to move on the page and, later, in memory. This quality is pervasive in *Where the Wild Things Are*, the story of a boy named Max who assumes a demonic face and puts on a wolf suit one night and makes mischief. His mother calls him a "WILD THING!" and Max answers, "I'LL EAT YOU UP!" He is sent to bed without his supper. Standing in his room, Max watches a forest grow until it becomes the world. An ocean tumbles by with a boat in it for Max, and he sails to where the Wild Things are. The Wild Things—a colony of monsters—try to frighten Max, but, frowning fiercely, he commands them to be still. Cowed, they make Max King of the Wild Things. Then, at Max's order, a rumpus begins—six wordless pages of howling, dancing, tree-climbing, and parading by Max and the Wild Things. Max presently stops the revels, though, and sends the Wild Things to bed without *their* supper, and then, feeling lonely, gives up his crown. The Wild Things so hate to see Max leave that they try to scare him into staying, but he is not intimidated, and he sails back to his room, where he finds his supper waiting for him.

As I studied the pictures of Max and his companions, it seemed to me that I had never seen fantasy depicted in American children's books in illustrations that were so powerfully in motion. Brian O'Doherty, the former art critic of the *Times*, has written that Sendak is "a fantasist in the great tradition of Sir John Tenniel and Edward Lear," and I agree. O'Doherty has also described Sendak as "one of the most powerful men in the United States," in that he "has given shape to the fantasies of millions of children—an awful responsibility." I had known a few men who possessed power, but never this kind of power, so I made arrangements to meet the creator of the Wild Things.

Sendak, a bachelor, lives in a duplex on Ninth Street between Fifth and Sixth Avenues. On the street level he has a bedroom and a large living room with a piano and a profusion of bookcases, one of them reserved for first editions (he has close to two hundred) of works by Henry James. On the floor below are a spacious kitchen, a dining room with a brick fireplace, and a small studio, lit only by the lamp over Sendak's drawing board, which is to the left of the room's entrance. On the walls of the studio are paintings, photographs, and posters advertising art exhibits. A bookcase near the studio door contains an extensive collection of children's books, formed largely around Sendak's favorite illustrators: Randolph Caldecott and George Cruikshank, of nineteenth-century England; Ludwig Richter and Wilhelm Busch, of the same period in Germany; A. B. Frost and Edward Windsor Kemble, Americans who between them spanned the last half of the nineteenth century and the first three decades of this one; Ernst Kreidolf, a Swiss artist of those years; and, among contemporaries, the late Hans Fischer of Switzerland and André François of France. To the right of Sendak's drawing board is a worktable, and above this is a pegboard supporting a swarm of objects. Among them are talismans—a brontosaurus constructed for him by a nephew, for instance—and postcard reproductions of paintings by Watteau, Goya, William Blake, and Winslow Homer; there are also a number of toys that Sendak has brought back from Europe, where he goes about every other year. Across the room from the worktable, an imposing high-fidelity unit stands on top of another bookcase, this one containing a large record collection, in which works by Mahler, Mozart, Beethoven, Wolf, Wagner, and Verdi are heavily represented. What dominates the room, however, is a huge photograph. Taken at an orphanage in Sicily, it shows a ten-year-old girl standing sidewise in front of a whitewashed wall. She is wearing a ragged white dress, a fly has alighted on her back, and she looks out into the room with enormous black eyes. Her hand is on her hip—a pose that is frequently assumed by the children in Sendak's books.

The first day I visited his studio, Sendak, a short, shy man with dark-brown hair and green eyes, smiled after he saw me staring intently at the picture. "It's hard to get away from her, isn't it?" he said. "If you stay here long enough, you'll find that her eyes follow you around the room." He moved in front of the photograph. "Her face is unfinished—a round, beautiful child's face—but her eyes tell you she could be forty-five years old. Such knowledge and pain are already there. I couldn't do without her."

A Sealyham Terrier came in. This, I was told, was Jennie, who was twelve years old and had a tendency to brood. Jennie has appeared in most of Sendak's books, often looking more cheerful than she does in real life. Having sniffed at me briefly, Jennie left. Sendak lit a cigarette. As I looked at him, I found that he reminded me of the children in his books, and I told him so. "Yes, they're all a kind of caricature of me," he said. "They look as if they'd been hit on the head, and hit so hard they weren't going to grow anymore. When I first started showing my work to children's book editors, about seventeen years ago, they didn't encourage me, and a major reason was the kind of children I drew. One editor, I remember, told me they were too European. What she meant was that they seemed ugly to her. And even now I'll get a letter at least twice a year from a librarian who wants to know why my children are so drab. Well, they're not drab, but they're not innocent of experience, either. Too many parents and too many writers of children's books don't respect the fact that kids know a great deal and suffer a great deal. My children also show a great deal of pleasure, but often they look defenseless, too. Being defenseless is a primary element of childhood. It's not that I don't see the naturalistic beauty of a child. I'm very aware of that beauty, and I could draw it. I know the proportions of a child's body. But I am trying to draw the way children *feel*—or, rather, the way I imagine they feel. It's the way *I know* I felt as a child." Sendak leaned forward, and continued, "It may be that in projecting how I felt as a child onto the children I draw I'm being terribly biased and inaccurate. But all I have to go on is what I know—not only about my childhood then but about the child I was as he exists now."

I look puzzled, and Sendak smiled. "You see, I don't believe, in a way, that the kid I was grew up into me," he said. "He still exists somewhere, in the most graphic, plastic, physical way. It's as if he had moved somewhere. I have a tremendous concern for him and interest in him. I communicate with him—or try to—all the time. One of my worst fears is losing contact with him." Sendak frowned. "I don't want this to sound coy or schizophrenic, but at least once a day I feel I have to make contact," he went on. "The pleasures I get as an adult are heightened by the fact that I experience them as a child at the same time. Like, when autumn comes, as an adult I welcome the departure of the heat, and simultaneously, as a child would, I started anticipating the snow and the first day it will be possible to use a sled. This dual apperception does break down occasionally. That usually happens when my work is going badly. I get a sour feeling about books in general and my own in particular. The next stage is annoyance at my dependence on this dual apperception, and I reject it. Then I become depressed. When excitement about what I'm working on returns, so does the child. We're on happy terms again. Being in that kind of contact with my childhood is vital to me, but it doesn't make me perfectly certain. I know what I'm doing in my work. Especially in books for children under six. I don't think anyone really knows what kids that young like and what they don't like. They're formless, fluid creatures—like moving water. You can't stop one of them at any one point and know exactly what's going on. A child may react strongly to a book because it reaches him emotionally in some way the author intended. Then, again, it may be that he once saw a duck from a train window and never saw one again until he looked at the book, and though the book is rotten, he loves it because there's a duck in it. Once in a while I encounter reactions to one of my books that make me think I may be getting some idea of what happened. From letters and from talking to parents and librarians, I've found out that, of the four books in the *Nutshell Library, Pierre* is invariably the favorite with children. But here, too, I don't know what level the child is reacting on. On one level, *Pierre* is slapstick. Then, the text has a rhythmic quality—the repetition that kids like—and some children may be drawn mainly by that. On another level, Pierre is defiant—irrationally so, when it comes to the lion that finally eats him—and the child may enjoy a surface identification with the fun of rebellion. And, on a deeper level, Pierre is saying, "I'm *me*. I'll be what I am and I'll do what I want to do." The book that children have reacted to most strongly, though, is *Where the Wild Things Are.* They wear out copies at libraries and keep rereading it at home. Some have sent me drawings of their own Wild Things, and they make mine look like cuddly fuzzballs. My Wild Things have big teeth. Some of *their* Wild Things not only have big teeth but are chewing on children. I have yet to hear of a child who was frightened by the book. Adults who are troubled by it forget that Max is having a fine time. He's in control. And by getting his anger at his mother discharged against the Wild Things he's able to come back to the real world at peace with himself. I think Max is my truest creation. Like all kids, he believes in a world where a child can skip from fantasy to reality in the conviction that both exist. One seven-year-old wrote me a letter." Sendak rose, rummaged through a file folder in the bookcase, found the letter, and handed it to me. The boy had written, "How much does it cost to get to where the Wild Things are? If it is not too expensive my sister and I want to spend the summer there. Please answer soon."

Fantasy, I learned in subsequent visits to the studio, has been familiar terrain to Sendak from his earliest years. He was born in Brooklyn on June 10, 1928, the youngest of three children of Philip and Sarah Sendak. (His sister, Natalie, was eight when he was born, and his brother, Jack, was five.) Both parents had come to America before the First World War from Jewish *shtetls*, or small towns, outside Warsaw. The father, who worked in the garment district, told his children long stories based on tales he remembered from his childhood and alive with myth and fantasy. "He was a marvelous improviser, and he'd often extend a story for many nights," Sendak recalls. "One short one I've always wanted to make into a book was about a child taking a walk with his father and mother. He becomes separated from them. Snow begins to fall, and the child shivers in the cold. He huddles under a tree, sobbing in terror. An enormous figure hovers over him and says, as he draws the boy up, 'I'm Abraham, your father.' His fear gone, the child looks up and also sees Sarah. He is no longer lost. When his parents find him, the child is dead. Those stories had something of the character of William Blake's poems. The myths in them didn't seem at all factitious. And they fused Jewish lore with my father's particular way of shaping memory and desire. That one, for instance, was based on the power of Abraham in Jewish tradition as the father who was always there—a reassuring father even when he was Death. But the story was also about how tremendously my father missed his parents. Not all his tales were somber, though. My father could be very witty, even if the humor was always on the darker side of irony."

In addition to the tales his father told, and occasional stories told by his mother, books, to which Sendak early formed a passionate attachment, also stimulated his imagination. His sister gave him his first books—*The Prince and the Pauper* and *The Three Musketeers*. Besides being fascinated by the contents of the books, he was drawn to them as physical entities. "I can still remember the smell and feel of the bindings of those first two books," he says. "I didn't read them for a long time. It felt so good just having them. They seemed alive to me, and so did many other inanimate objects I was fond of. All children have these intense feelings about certain dolls or other toys. In my case, this kind of relationship, if you can call it that, was heightened because up to the age of six I spent a lot of time in bed with a series of illnesses. Being alone much of the time, I developed friendships with objects. To this day, in my parents' home there are certain toys that I played with as a child and when I visit my parents, I'm also visiting those toys."

In *Kenny's Window*, which was published in 1956, and was the first book that Sendak wrote as well as illustrated, he distilled much of his own childhood—the attachment to particular objects, the fantasy, the loneliness. Kenny wakes from a dream and remembers meeting in a garden a rooster, who gave him seven questions to answer. In the course of searching for the answers, he has serious conversations with several of his toys. Kenny is angered by a favorite Teddy bear, who reproaches him for having been left under the bed all night, but soon Kenny writes the bear a poem assuring him of his love, and that conflict is resolved. In fantasy, Kenny journeys to Switzerland and talks with a goat in order to find the answer to one of the rooster's questions: "What is an only goat?" An only goat, Kenny finally learns, is a lonely goat who is not allowed by an overprotective master to do what he most enjoys doing. There is also a meeting, on the roof of Kenny's house, with a talking, flying horse. Kenny resolves not to tell his parents about the horse and its ability to talk and to fly. ("They'd say it was a dream. They don't know how to listen in the night.") Another crisis occurs when one of Kenny's two favorite lead soldiers reminds the other of a promise Kenny has broken—to take care of them always. The first soldier is chipped in four different places. He complains to Kenny. Enraged at being made to feel guilty, Kenny exiles the chipped soldier to the outside ledge of his window in the cold, but then he brings the soldier in again and tells him he has not broken his promise. When the rooster later asks Kenny one of the seven questions again—"Can you fix a broken promise?"—Kenny answers, "Yes, if it only looks broken, but really isn't."

In his adult life, Sendak's rapport with particular inanimate objects has not been limited to the toys in Brooklyn. One afternoon, in his studio, he pointed out to me several pens on his drawing board, and said, "Some of these pens are with me, and some are against me. In a store, some look as if they want to be sold to me. Others will fight me to the end. I may antagonize some and not be able to win back their friendship, but others are less stubborn." He picked up a small, smooth rock. "This is a friend," he said. "I found him on a beach in Italy in 1953. He goes with me on all my trips." Sendak looked at me somewhat warily, and added, "I suppose that sounds strange." Since I have similar feelings about an old lighter and three pipes, I was able to tell him it didn't.

Sendak did have other friends besides objects as he grew up. He had a close relationship with his brother Jack. Both boys enjoyed drawing, and one of their amusements was making books. These combined cut-out newspaper photographs and comic strips with sketches of the Sendak family. The books were bound with tape, had elaborately illustrated covers, and contained a good deal of painstaking hand lettering.

"I was always conscious of usable material for books," Sendak recalls. "I remember examining my grandmother all the time and placing her in various fantasies. And I was so conscious of the streets on which I lived that I can remember them now in complete detail—how many houses there were, who lived in which house, what the people looked like. During my early teens, I spent a lot of time at the window, sketching the kids at play, and those sketchbooks are, in a sense, the foundation of much of my later work. Maybe that's another reason the children in my books are called European-looking. Many of them resemble the kids I knew growing up in Brooklyn. They were Jewish kids, and they may well look like little greenhorns just off the boat. They had—some of them, anyway—a kind of bowed look, as if the burdens of the world were on their shoulders."

The Sign on Rosie's Door, a Sendak book published in 1960, begins with the dedication:

> *Remembering Pearl Karchawer*
> *all the Rosies*
> *and Brooklyn.*

Rosie is a girl with an unusually lively imagination, and she gets her friends—who do indeed look like Jewish children on the streets of Brooklyn—to take part in her fantasies. At one point, Rosie, on a cellar door and covered from head to foot in a red blanket, identifies herself as "Alinda the lost girl." "Who lost you?" asks a neighborhood literalist. "I lost myself," Rosie answers. Like the fantasies in *Kenny's Window* and a number of Sendak's other stories, Rosie's often involve highly active play. She announces that her "Magic Man" is coming, and all the children close their eyes, because he will not appear otherwise. They hear her speak to him, and when they are allowed to open their eyes again, Rosie tells them that the Magic Man has informed her that they can all be firecrackers. Rosie and her friends proceed to leap and dance through several pages.

When the teen-age Sendak wasn't making books, he was reading other people's. Though some were stories for children, his reading was indiscriminate. His sister subscribed to the Book-of-the-Month Club, and he read many of the volumes she received. "Now I can't remember any children's books or artists that profoundly influenced me in those years except Walt Disney," he says. "I now say it to my shame, yet he did something tremendous for me. His pictures did move, and they often embodied lots of fantasy. With whatever money I had, I'd buy his coloring and cutout books, and I made animated sequences of my own based on his characters. And when I saw Disney's *Snow White and the Seven Dwarfs* at the Radio City Music Hall, I had an inkling of what it was I especially wanted to do. It was only later that I could see how Disney had despoiled beautiful stories and had abused the idea of animation. Kids don't always know about the vulgar and tasteless, and to me Disney was a god. I remember a Mickey Mouse mask that came on a big box of cornflakes. What a fantastic mask! Such a big, bright, vivid, gorgeous hunk of face! My ambition was to work for Disney."

Sendak graduated from Lafayette High School, in Brooklyn, in 1946. "I was an art major in high school, but we had no real instruction—I just sat and did what I wanted to," he says. After school and weekends, he had worked for All American Comics, his job being to adapt *Mutt and Jeff* strips for comic books, fitting them into the page, filling in backgrounds, and extending the story line when necessary. He enjoyed this work, but school, by contrast, was a place of acute discomfort. "Nearly every morning, in order to get there, I had to talk myself out of a state of panic," he says. "I couldn't stand being cloistered with other children, and I was usually so embarrassed that I stammered."

After graduation, he went to work full time at Timely Service, a window-display house in lower Manhattan, beginning in a warehouse, where he helped construct store-window models of such figures as Snow White and the Seven Dwarfs out of chicken wire, papier-mâché, spun glass, plaster, and paint. "It was one of the best times of my life," Sendak says. "I was in Manhattan, and, for the first time, I knew people who were artists, who considered their work for Timely Service just a job to enable them to do real painting at night in their cold-water flats. There were all kinds of people I'd never met in Brooklyn." When he had been at Timely Service for nearly two years, he was promoted to the department that conceived the window-display designs to be built in the warehouse. There he was unhappy. "The department consisted of another kind of artist—people in their fifties who had never got anywhere," he recalls. Sendak left the display house in the summer of 1948, and during the next two months, at home in Brooklyn, he and his brother constructed six intricate animated wooden toys, performing scenes from "Little Red Riding Hood," "Little Miss Muffet," "Hansel and Gretel," "Aladdin's Lamp," "Old Mother Hubbard," and "Pinocchio." The pieces, five of which Sendak now has in his studio, are in the tradition of eighteenth-century German lever-operated toys. When a lever on Little Red Riding Hood's basket is pulled, for instance, a ferocious wolf leaps out of bed and Little Red Riding Hood collapses. The Sendak brothers took their toys to FAO Schwarz. Their work was received with respect, but an official at the store pointed out that it would be too costly to reproduce the toys in large quantities. "Nor were we ready to compromise, if a compromise had been suggested," Sendak says. "We wanted a workshop of little old men creating the little wooden parts, and we would not have permitted any kind of plastic substitute." Ultimately, though, Richard Nell, Schwarz's window-display director, was sufficiently impressed by the way in which Maurice Sendak had painted the toys to hire him as an assistant in the construction of window displays. (His brother, meanwhile, although he went on to work in the electronics field, has also written several children's books, two of which Maurice has illustrated.)

Sendak worked at the toy store for three years, and attended evening classes at the Art Students League during most of that time. "It was the only kind of school I could endure, because it was freewheeling," he says. "What you learned depended on what you wanted to learn." Sendak took classes in life drawing, oil painting, and composition, and feels that he benefited particularly from the instruction in composition he was given by the illustrator John Groth. "He was important for me because he gave me a sense of the enormous potential for motion, for aliveness, in illustrations," Sendak recalls. "And he himself was so deeply committed to the field that he showed how much fun creating in it could be."

At FAO Schwarz, Frances Chrystie, the store's book buyer, who was a friend of Sendak's, knew that he was eager to try illustrating children's books, but when she suggested introducing him to Miss Nordstrom—partly because Harper's was the publisher whose children's book he most admired—he demurred, out of shyness. Miss Chrystie thereupon arranged for Miss Nordstrom to "happen by" one day, in the spring of 1950, when Sendak had tacked up a broad variety of his pictures on the walls of the store's studio. The next day, Miss Nordstrom called Sendak and offered him the opportunity to illustrate Marcel Aymé's *The Wonderful Farm*. He accepted, and the book was published in 1951. This was not the first time Sendak's work had been published; in 1946 he had done diagrams and spot drawings for *Atomics for the Millions*, written by Hyman Ruchlis, one of his high school teachers, and three years later he had illustrated a book about the Sabbath, *Good Shabbos, Everybody*, for the United Synagogue Commission on Jewish Education, but *The Wonderful Farm* was the first real children's book he had worked on. "It made me an official person," Sendak now says.

In 1952, Sendak became widely known in the children's book field as the illustrator of Ruth Krauss's *A Hole Is to Dig*. The book was quite unconventional for its time. It had no story. Instead, Miss Krauss, by talking with and listening to children, had assembled a series of children's definitions, among them "A face is so you can make faces," "Buttons are to keep people warm," "A whistle is to make people jump," and—a particularly favorite with the book's readers—"A tablespoon is to eat a table with." The general idea of *A Hole Is to Dig* has since been repeated many times, often coyly. But Sendak's small people, seen at play among themselves, sticking out their tongues, closing their eyes in anticipation of being kissed by their dogs' tongues, wiggling their toes, and sliding delightedly in the mud, never seem saccharine.

An established illustrator had originally been considered for the assignment, but when he was shown simply a collection of definitions, he felt that there was no book in them at all. From the start, however, Sendak was enthusiastic about the book's possibilities. "It was like being part of a revolution," he says. "This was the first time in modern children's book history that a book had come directly from kids. The notion was so startling to some academics, in fact, that the book was included in a course at Columbia on the uses of language. And, you know, some of those definitions *have* become part of the language. Working on that book, I learned something else, too. When it seemed to me to be all done, Ruth Krauss pointed out that I was giving the kids who would read the book middle-class attitudes toward their roles. I had the boys doing what boys were expected to do and girls doing what *they* were expected to do. God forbid a boy should be jumping rope! Of course, that isn't the way it is, and at the last minute I made some quick changes."

A Hole Is to Dig prepared the way for such later works by others as "A Friend Is Someone Who Likes You," "Love Is a Special Way of Feeling," and "Happiness Is a Warm Puppy," and it was influential in other ways, too. Its format was small, and its success brought back what Sendak identifies as "the little book," adding, "And, God help us, it hasn't stopped." The book was printed on brown-tinted paper, and for the illustrations Sendak had deliberately used his most "old-fashioned" style, his pen-and-ink drawings including a considerable amount of crosshatching, in the tradition of nineteenth-century German and British illustrators.

The success of *A Hole Is to Dig* was such that Sendak was able to leave FAO Schwarz, move to Manhattan, and become a freelance illustrator. Assignments poured in, from Miss Nordstrom and from editors at other publishing houses, and in the years that followed Sendak illustrated the work of various writers. There have been seven more books by Ruth Krauss, and seven books for older children by the Dutch-born writer Meindert DeJong, and Sendak has also had the privilege of collaborating posthumously with Tolstoy (*Nikolenka's Childhood*), the German Clemens Brentano (*The Tale of Gockel, Hinkel & Gackeliah*, and *Schoolmaster Whackwell's Wonderful Sons*), the German Wilhelm Hauff (*Dwarf Long-Nose*), and the American Frank Stockton (*The Bee-Man of Orn* and *The Griffin and the Minor Canon*). In a preface to *The Griffin and the Minor Canon*, Sendak describes his basic aim as an illustrator: "I wanted at all costs to avoid the serious pitfall of illustrating with pictures what the author had already . . . illustrated with words. I hoped, rather, to let the story speak for itself, with my pictures as a kind of background music—music in the right style and always in tune with the words."

Sendak elaborated on the degree to which he conceives his work musically in an article called "The Shape of Music," which appeared in the Sunday *Herald Tribune* late in 1964. "The spontaneous breaking into song and dance seems so natural and instinctive a part of childhood," he wrote. "It is perhaps the medium through which children best express the inexpressible; fantasy and feeling lie deeper than words—beyond the words yet available to a child—and both demand a more profound, more biological expression, the primitive expression of music." Sendak is convinced that children will respond most spontaneously to illustrations that, in his words, "have a sense of music and dance and are not something just glued onto the page."

In the work of the illustrators that Sendak most admires, he invariably finds a musical quality that he terms "authentic liveliness." He points to the linear arabesques in the lamb's dance of death in Boutet de Monvel's drawings for La Fontaine's *Fables Choisies pour les Enfants*, and to the same artist's "harmonic inventions" achieved by the subtle use of color and line. In the work of Randolph Caldecott, Sendak is fascinated not only by the abundance of actual dancing, singing, and playing of instruments but also by the many ways in which Caldecott used the theme-and-variations technique, combining simple themes into what Sendak describes as "a fantastically various interplay of images."

When Sendak is at work, he not only thinks in musical terms but often has music playing. He begins by trying to find the composer and the piece of music that fit the mood and tone of the story on his drawing board, and he may listen to many recordings before he hits on the right musical colors. "Books, too, can be evocative for me when I'm working on a series of illustrations," he says. "I often turn to James, Stendhal, D. H. Lawrence, and Melville—especially James, with his acute sensitivity to what happens inside someone growing. But it is music that does most to open me up. That's why I have all these records—and I go to quite a lot of concerts, too. The other night, for example, I was sitting here listening to *Die Meistersinger*, which I know by heart, and got excited about it all over again. What struck me this time was that Wagner, in some mysterious way, had made the atmosphere—the very night air—of Nuremberg into music. I could see the city and smell it. And that's the kind of thing I want to convey in my illustrations. The pictures should be so organically akin to the text, so reflective of its atmosphere, that they look as if they could have been done in no other way. They should help create the special world of the story. When this kind of drawing works, I feel like a magician, because I'm creating the air for a writer."

In illustrating stories of his own, Sendak sometimes encounters an odd difficulty in performing this magic. "I find myself writing things that I don't like to draw, as if I were two separate people," he explains. "As a writer, I may, for instance, ask the illustrator part of me to draw too many specific details of a room or of clothes. As an illustrator, I most enjoy interpreting emotions. In *Where the Wild Things Are*, those two selves fused, in that the illustrations were a complete imaginative backdrop to the feelings experienced in the course of fantasy. Being dreamlike and fluid, the scenes aren't hung up with the kind of particulars that are involved in aiming at literal verisimilitude."

Where the Wild Things Are, which was published in 1963, marked a key stage in development. In 1964, the book received the Caldecott Medal, awarded annually by the American Library Association for the most distinguished American picture book for children. Sendak went to St. Louis for the presentation, and in his acceptance speech he said, "With *Where the Wild Things Are*, I feel I am at the end of a long apprenticeship. By that I mean all my previous work now seems to have been an elaborate preparation for it." Miss Nordstrom says that *Where the Wild Things Are* is of singular historical importance because "it is the first American picture book to recognize that children have *powerful* emotions—anger and fear as well as the need Max had, after his anger was spent, to be 'where someone loved him best of all.'" She adds, "A lot of good picture books have had fine stories and lovely pictures, and some have touched beautifully on basic elements in a child's life—physical growth, coming to terms with a new sister or brother, and the like. But it seems to me that *Where the Wild Things Are* goes deeper than previous picture books have gone."

Miss Nordstrom was not surprised that the book met with some hostile reactions from critics and librarians. "The furor reminded me of the New York Public Library's refusal to give shelf room to E. B. White's *Stuart Little* for some months back in 1945, when it came out," she says. "The statement that Mrs. Little's second son was born looking very much like a mouse made one librarian there unable to sleep for three nights. Or so she told me. But the *children* who read and loved that book weren't thinking of any actual process of giving birth to a mouse—they thought it was nice to have a mouse in the family. There were even some negative reactions to *A Hole Is to Dig*. One librarian was appalled at the definition 'A face is to make faces with.' She said she didn't want *her* children making faces. And when *Where the Wild Things Are* came out, another librarian told me the book would frighten little children to death. 'But Max *conquers* those monsters,' I said. 'He becomes king of the Wild Things.' But she was obviously horrified, perhaps too horrified to imagine that children might react with pleasure to the book." A reviewer for the *Journal of Nursery Education* mused, "We should not like to have it left about where a sensitive child might find it to pore over in the twilight." *Publishers' Weekly*, after saying that "the plan and technique of the illustrations are superb," cautioned, "But they may well prove frightening, accompanied as they are by a pointless and confusing story." Among the adults who were not traumatized by Max's journey was a critic for the *Library Journal*, who wrote, "Each word has been carefully chose to express Max's mood precisely," and "The Wild Things who acclaim him their king are at once both ugly and humorous." The critic did, however, feel compelled to add, "This is the kind of story that many adults will question and for many reasons, but the child will accept it wisely and without inhibition, as he knows it is written for him." A reviewer for the Cleveland *Press* was also both appreciative of the book and apprehensive about possible adult storms, noting, "Boys and girls may have to shield their parents from this book. Parents are very easily scared."

Sendak had expected a certain amount of angry reaction to *Where the Wild Things Are*. In his speech accepting the Caldecott Medal, he referred with some acerbity to those noncontroversial children's books that offer "a gilded world unshadowed by the least suggestion of conflict or pain, a world manufactured by those who cannot—or don't care to—remember the truth of their own childhood." Of these he said, "Their expurgated vision has no relation to the way real children live. I suppose these books have some purpose—they don't frighten adults. . . . The popularity of such books is proof of endless pussyfooting about the grim aspects of child life, pussyfooting that attempts to justify itself by reminding us that we must not frighten our children. Of course, we must avoid frightening children, if by that we mean protecting them from experiences beyond their emotional capabilities; but I doubt that this is what most people mean when they say, 'We must not frighten our children.' The need for half-truth books is the most obvious indication of the common wish to protect children from their everyday fears and anxieties, a hopeless wish that denies the child's endless battle with disturbing emotions."

One afternoon, in his studio, Sendak told me more about his ideas on the proper use of fantasy in children's books. The light over his drawing board was out, and we sat in near darkness. Characteristically, Sendak spoke softly and rapidly. Occasionally, as he grew more intense, his words bumped against each other in a slight stammer. "There have to be elements of anxiety and mystery in truthful children's books, or, at least, there have to be in mind," he said. "What I don't like are formless, floating fantasies. Fantasy makes sense only if it's rooted ten feet deep in reality. In *Where the Wild Things Are*, the reality is Max's misbehavior, his punishment, and his anger at that punishment. That was why he didn't just have a cute little dream. He wasn't trying to deal with imperative, basic emotions."

Sendak leaned forward. "Then, the fantasy has to be resolved," he said. "If Max had stayed on the island with the Wild Things, a child reading the book might well have been frightened. Max, however, comes home. Mind you, he doesn't say, 'I'll never go there again.' He *will* fantasize again, but the hope is that, like other children, he'll keep coming back to his mother. So the book doesn't say that life is constant anxiety. It simply says that life has anxiety in it. Here, let me show you one of the ways Caldecott conveyed this."

From a bookshelf Sendak gently removed a first edition of *A Frog He Would A-Wooing Go* in the nineteenth-century British series Randolph Caldecott's Picture Books (which are, incidentally, still in print). He turned to a page showing the exterior of Mousey's Hall. Frog, accompanied by Mr. Rat, is paying court to Miss Mouse. Two small girls and their parents are watching a cat and her kittens approach the house. "Up to that point, Caldecott followed the usual plot," Sendak said. "He added this family to serve as an implied commentary on the action. The reader sees—but the family doesn't—the cat and her offspring devouring Miss Mouse and Mr. Rat. Nor does the family see Frog, while escaping, being gobbled up by a duck as he crossed the pond. But here—in the last picture of the book—the girls and the parents are looking at Frog's hat, lying on a stone in the pond. The children are holding tightly on to their parents. The look on their faces is as if they are saying, 'What a frightful thing must have happened! But we still have our parents to protect *us*.' Caldecott went one step beyond the nursery rhyme by relating it to life. Except for Caldecott, illustrators of this story have generally pictured it as a rollicking face—'Everybody gets eaten up. Ho-ho-ho!' But Caldecott, by bringing in that family, added an intimation of how grim reality can be. Even if the children didn't get the point explicitly from the drawings, the feeling was there. Caldecott did this sort of thing much better than I can. I don't have any evidence that he ever talked about what he was doing, but he often worked in this way. I grant that he himself may not have been all that conscious of expressing a touch of dread. Nor am I when I'm work."

Sendak lit a cigarette. "Recently, I gave a lecture at Pratt Institute, and a student asked me if I ever sit down with the intention of doing a children's book dealing with anxiety," he said. "Of course I don't, I told him. If I did, I'd hardly be any kind of creative artist. When I write and draw, I'm experiencing what the child in the book is going through. I was as relieved to get back from Max's journey as he was. Or, rather, I like to think I got back. It's only after the act of writing the book that, as an adult, I can see what has happened, and talk about fantasy as catharsis, about Max acting out his anger as he fights to grow."

The room was now quite dark, and Sendak put on the light. "For me, that book was a personal exorcism," he went on. "It went deeper into my own childhood than anything I've done before, and I must go even deeper in the ones to come."

I asked him if he would continue to concentrate on books for younger children.

"Yes," Sendak replied. "There'll be exceptions, I suppose, but for the most part I like to work for children no older than seven or eight. With them, you can be freer in the use of fantasy, and in various kinds of experimentation, because the picture itself still means a tremendous amount to them. There's no wall between them and the picture."

A few weeks after this particular talk, I moved my family to Fire Island for the summer. Sendak had taken a house there, too, and we often met on the beach, where he sat for hours, sketching. He and my son Nicholas came to know each other, but only slightly. Sendak does not extend himself to beguile children, but he is ready for conversation if they are. One afternoon, Nicholas made a futile attempt to play with a group of older children, who could run much faster than he could, and then trudged over to where Sendak and I were sitting. Seeing Nicholas sad, Sendak suggested that they dig a hole. When they had dug one, Nicholas jumped in and had himself covered with sand up to his shoulders. Then, observing that Sendak had been sketching, Nicholas asked, "Can you make me a ferryboat?" Sendak did, and then drew other pictures at Nicholas's direction, including some of seagulls—creatures that my son is very fond of. The next day, Sendak dropped in at our house with a watercolor scene that contained all the boats, birds, and fishes Nicholas had asked for the previous afternoon.

A few weeks later, the three of us were on the beach again. In the interval, Nicholas had largely ignored Sendak and had not referred at all to the watercolor, which his mother had hung above his bed. I walked down the beach for a few minutes to talk to a friend, and when I returned, Nicholas was chasing a sandpiper, and Sendak was looking pleased.

"We've been in contact again," Sendak again. "These last few weeks, I've been aware that he was conscious of me but also that he had no desire to continue what we had going that day. Maybe I projected it, but I seemed to get the message: 'Don't push it. Don't try to do it again just yet.' But right after you left, he pointed to himself, pointed to the sky, and said, 'Remember the seagull? Thank you for the picture.' There was a huge smile on his face for maybe half a second, and then he ran after the sandpiper. I was very much moved, very grateful that he did remember—and that he told me so in that way. It was as if he were saying, 'Don't be upset. I didn't forget. I still have the picture you brought me.'" Sendak laughed. "I did feel we had reached each other again."

On the way back from the beach, with Nicholas running down the road ahead of us, Sendak said, "I get a kick whenever I see a child react to something I've drawn or written. I like getting letters children write me, and I like having a chance to meet one who has enjoyed a book of mine. Not that I write basically for children. I really do these books for myself. It's something I have to do, and it's the only thing I want to do. Reaching the kids is important, but secondary. First, always, I have to reach and keep hold of the child in me."

Nicholas and I stopped at our gate, and Sendak walked on down the road alone. At the crossing, he turned around and waved. The wild thing trying to wrench the gate off its hinges paused to wave back.

Questions to an Artist Who Is Also an Author: A Conversation between Maurice Sendak and Virginia Haviland

Virginia Haviland / 1970

From the *Quarterly Journal of the Library of Congress*, 28.4, October 1971, pp. 262–80.

Maurice Sendak began his career as a professional illustrator while he was still a high school student in Brooklyn, N.Y., adapting *Mutt and Jeff* comic strips for publication in comic books. After completing high school he studied at the Art Students League and worked in the design and construction of window displays. His unusual talents soon came to the attention of Ursula Nordstrom, the children's book editor at Harper's, for whom he illustrated Marcel Aymé's *The Wonderful Farm* (1951). He has since illustrated over sixty books, including ten which he himself has written. His illustrations for Ruth Krauss's *A Hole Is to Dig* (1952) and Else Minarik's *Little Bear* (1959) drew widespread acclaim. As both writer and illustrator, he has produced a number of children's books which have already become classics, including *Kenny's Window* (1956), *Very Far Away* (1957), *The Sign on Rosie's Door* (1960), *The Nutshell Library* (1962), *Where the Wild Things Are* (1963), *Higglety Pigglety Pop!* (1967), and *In the Night Kitchen* (1970). Mr. Sendak was awarded the American Library Association's Randolph Caldecott Medal in 1964 for *Where the Wild Things Are*. In 1970 he became the first American to receive the coveted Illustrator's Medal of the Hans Christian Andersen Awards.

In a National Children's Book Week program sponsored by the Gertrude Clarke Whittall Poetry and Literature Fund, Mr. Sendak presented some of his ideas about children's literature in an informal question-and-answer session at the Library of Congress. The questions were addressed to Mr. Send-ak by Miss Virginia Haviland, head of the Library's Children's Book Section. The following article is based on a transcript of the discussion, which was held in the Coolidge Auditorium on November 16, 1970.

MISS HAVILAND: As a starter, let's ask: What did a book mean to you as a child? And what kinds of books did you have?

MR. SENDAK: I think I'll start with the kinds of books, because back in the thirties I didn't have any "official" children's books (I refer to the classics). The only thing I can remember is cheap paperbacks, comic books. That's principally where I started. My sister bought me my first book, *The Prince and the Pauper*. A ritual began with that book which I recall very clearly. The first thing was to set it up on the table and stare at it for a long time. Not because I was impressed with Mark Twain; it was just such a beautiful object. Then came the smelling of it. I think the smelling of books began with *The Prince and the Pauper*, because it was printed on particularly fine paper, unlike the Disney books I had gotten previous to that, which were printed on very poor paper and smelled poor. *The Prince and the Pauper* smelled good and it also had a shiny cover, a laminated cover. I flipped over that. And it was very solid. I mean, it was bound very tightly. I remember trying to bite into it, which I don't imagine is what my sister intended when she bought the book for me. But the last thing I did with the book was to read it. It was all right. But I think it started then, a passion for books and bookmaking. I wanted to be an illustrator very early in my life, to be involved in books in some way—to make books. And the making of books, and the touching of books—there's so much more to a book than just the reading; there is a sensuousness. I've seen children touch books, fondle books, smell books, and it's all the reason in the world why books should be beautifully produced.

MISS HAVILAND: Our questions to you, which are questions I think you have often answered for university and other groups, come as questions to you as an author and questions to you as an artist. Let's begin with the group of questions that have to do with you as an author. What part do you think fantasy should play in a child's life?

MR. SENDAK: Well, fantasy is so all-pervasive in a child's life: I believe there's no part of our lives, our adult as well as child life, when we're not fantasizing, but we prefer to relegate fantasy to children, as though it were some tomfoolery only fit for the immature minds of the young. Children do live in a fantasy *and* reality; they move back and forth very easily in a way that we no longer remember how to do. And in writing for children you just must assume they have this incredible flexibility, this cool sense of the logic of illogic, and that they can move with you very easily from one sphere to another without any problems. Fantasy is the core of all writing for children, as I think it is for the writing of any book, for any creative act, perhaps for the act of living. Certainly it is crucial to my work. There are many kinds of fantasy and levels of fantasy and subtleties of fantasy—but that would be another question. There is probably no such thing as creativity without fantasy. My books don't come about by "ideas" or by thinking of a particular subject and exclaiming "Gee, that's a terrific idea, I'll put it down!" They never quite come to me that way; they well up. In the way a dream comes to us at night, feelings come to me, and then I must rush to put them down. But these fantasies have to be given physical form, so you build a house around them, and the house is what you call a story, and the painting of the house is the bookmaking. But essentially it's a dream, or it's a fantasy.

MISS HAVILAND: Are you, yourself, remembering daydreams? And a belief in fantasy that came out of your own childhood?

MR. SENDAK: I can't recall my childhood any more than most of us can. There are sequences and scenes I remember much as we all do. But I do seem to have the knack of recalling the emotional quality of childhood, so that in *Wild Things*—I can remember the feeling, when I was a child (I don't remember who the people were, but there were people who had come to our house, relatives perhaps) and I remember they looked extremely ugly to me. I remember this quite clearly, and that when people came and, with endearments, they leaned over and said "Oh, I could eat you up!" I was very nervous because I really believed they probably could if they had a mind to. They had great big teeth, immense nostrils, and very sweaty foreheads. I often remember that vision and how it frightened me. There was one particular relative (I have some relatives in the audience, so I won't mention who it was) who did this to me, and it was really quite terrifying. Well, he is forever immortalized in *Wild Things*. *Wild Things* really is the anxiety and pleasure and immense problem of being a small child. And what do children do with themselves? They fantasize, they control fantasies or they don't control fantasies. It's not the recollection of my own particular childhood that I put down in books, but the feeling—like that particular feeling of fear of adults, who are totally unaware that what they say to children is sometimes taken quite literally. And that when they pinch your cheek out of affection, it hurts; and that, when they suggest they could "hug you to death," you back away—any number of such things.

MISS HAVILAND: It would be interesting to find out whether you can account for the fact that college students seem to enjoy *Where the Wild Things Are* and *Higglety Pigglety Pop!* as much as children do. The question is: who do you see as your audience?

MR. SENDAK: Well, I suppose primarily children, but not really. Because I don't write for children specifically. I certainly am not conscious of sitting down and writing a book for children. I think it would be fatal if one did. So I write *books*, and I hope that they are books anybody can read. I mean, there was a time in history when books like *Alice in Wonderland* and the fairy tales of George MacDonald were read by everybody. They were not segregated for children. So I'd like to think I have a large audience and if college students like my books, that's fine. I think young people tend to be freer about reading children's books. They don't think it's an odd thing to do particularly, if it's a good piece of fantasy, or even if it's just a good piece of fun. They aren't as hung up as perhaps we were about reading "children's" books. I know a lot of students think that I was "turned on" when I wrote some of my books. That is not just a guess, because I've had a lot of inquiries about what I smoked during certain chapters of certain books. And that may be partly the interest that they have in such things. Writing fantasies is really being quite sufficiently high (without anything more than an Empirin).

MISS HAVILAND: Some other college students have asked how you, as a writer in a post-Freudian era, can resolve the problem of not consciously manipulating the unconscious.

MR. SENDAK: [After a pause] Well, that's a problem. The Victorians were very fortunate. *Alice in Wonderland* is full of images and symbols, which are extremely beautiful and sometimes frightening. We know that Carroll had no Freud, and the book came pouring out of his unconscious, as happened with George MacDonald in *Princess and the Goblin*. These authors touched on some very primal images in quite a fascinating way. It is more difficult for us to do because we do know so much, we've read so much material. I do not analyze my work; if something strikes me and I get excited, then I want it to be a book. If it begins to die as I work, then of course it's not a book. But I think I do get away occasionally with walking that fine unconscious line. The things I've written in which there are conscious unconscious thing, are very—you can't put your finger on it, certainly children can put their fingers on it, but they are *the* most critical audience in the world, they smell a rat instantly. You cannot fool them, you really cannot fool them. They're tough to work for. And if they sense—and they know adults do these books—if they sense for one minute that I was faking this, I would know it. Now, *Wild Things* walked a very fine line in this particular sense. It was accepted by children largely, and that's the only proof I have that I've done it.

MISS HAVILAND: Another college student has asked about the recurring symbol of something eating something, ingesting something, and then giving it out again. For instance in *Pierre* the lion eats Pierre and then gives him out; and in *As I Went Over the Water* a sea monster ingests a boat, then gives it out; in *Higglety Pigglety Pop!* Jenny eats a mop and then gives it out; and *In the Night Kitchen* Mickey is engulfed in dough and then springs out. Would you comment on this?

MR. SENDAK: I don't know if it's safe to, but I began by telling you how much I liked to bite into my first books, and that is perhaps a clue to this subject. And, so far as I'm aware, I'm not an overeating person, but perhaps it is a hang-up from childhood. A pleasant one, I think. The business of eating is such an immensely important part of life for a child. Grimm's *Fairy Tales* is full of things being eaten and then disgorged. It's an image that constantly appeals to me; I love it. In *As I Went Over the Water*, the scene where the monster eats the boats and then regurgitates it is hilarious! I have the mind of a child, I think that's very funny. I will sit home and laugh myself sick over what I've done. Whether it appeals or makes sense to anyone else, I honestly don't know. It just seems right and occasionally children laugh too, so we laugh together.

MISS HAVILAND: Some readers have been intrigued by the relationship between your characters Kenny, Martin, Max, and Mickey. Would you say in what way these children may be the same child, or in what ways they are not?

MR. SENDAK: They are the same child, of course. Three of them have the initial "M." I don't think that's an accident, although I thought of that only while I was working on the last book. The first book was Kenny, and he was named after a specific person. But a thread of meaning connects all the children. I can do a very rough analysis, I suppose. Kenny is a frustrated and introverted child. And Martin is fussy and sulking and not very brave. Max is tremendously brave but in a rage. And Mickey is extremely brave and very happy. I can follow that—I don't know if you can—but in the characters there is a kind of progress from holding back to coming forth which I'd like to think is me, not so much as a child or pretending that I'm a child but as a creative artist who also gets freer and freer with each book and opens up more and more.

MISS HAVILAND: Many persons right now are asking what inspired you to produce this new book, *In the Night Kitchen*?

MR. SENDAK: Well, that is a difficult question. It comes out a lot of things, and they are very hard to describe, because they are not so clear to me. There are a few clues. When I was a child there was an advertisement which I remember very clearly. It was for the Sunshine Bakers. And the advertisement read "We Bake While You Sleep!" It seemed to me the most sadistic thing in the world, because all I wanted to do was stay up and watch. And it seemed so absurdly cruel and arbitrary for them to do it while I slept. And also for them to think I would think that was terrific stuff on their part, you know, and would eat their product on top of that. It bothered me a good deal, and I remember I used to save the coupons showing the three fat little Sunshine bakers going off to this magic place, wherever it was, at night to have their fun, while I had to go to bed. This book was a sort of vendetta book to get back at them and to say that I am now old enough to stay up at night and know what is happening in the Night Kitchen! The other clue is a rather odd fantasy of mine when I was a child. I lived in Brooklyn and to travel to Manhattan was a big deal, even though it was so close. I couldn't go by myself, and I counted a good deal on my elder sister. She took us—my brother and myself—to Radio City Music Hall, or the Roxy, or some such place. Now, the point of going to New York was that you *ate* in New York. Now we get back to eating again. Somehow to me New York represented eating. And eating in a very fashionable, elegant, superlatively mysterious place like Longchamps. You got dressed up, and you went uptown, and it was night when you got there, and there were lots of windows blinking, and you went straight to a place to eat. It was one of the most exciting things of my childhood, to do this. Cross the bridge, and see the city approaching, and get there, and have your dinner, and then go to a movie, and come home. So, again, *In the Night Kitchen* is a kind of homage to New York City, the city I loved so much and still love. It had a special quality for me as a child. It also is homage to the things that really affected me aesthetically. I did not get to museums, I did not see art books. I was really quite rough in the sense of what was going on artistically. *Fantasia* was perhaps the most esthetic experience of my childhood, and that's a very dubious experience. But mainly there were the comic books and there was Walt Disney, and, more than anything else, there were the movies and radio, especially the movies. The early films, such as the Gold Digger movies and *King Kong* and other monster films, were the stuff that my books are composed of now. I am now surprised, and this is really unconscious—I was looking at *Where the Wild Things Are* not too long ago with a friend, who had found something which amused her a good deal. She is a film collector, and she opened to one page of the book, where one of the Wild Things is leaning out of the cave. And then she held alongside it a still from *King Kong*, and it was, literally, a copy. But I had not seen the still, of course; I could not have remembered the sequence. Obviously, it had impressed itself on my brain, and there it was: I mean, exactly the proportions of cave to cliff, and proportions of monster coming out of cave. It was really quite extraordinary, the effect the films did have on me.

It was only much later, when I was a practicing illustrator and writer, that I got to know the classic children's books and read them. I did not know them as a child; I did know pictures or paintings or writing when I was growing up. Brooklyn was a more or less civilized place, let me assure you, but this particular thing didn't get to me until quite late. And I think it's reflected in my work. I am what is commonly referred to as a late bloomer. I am happy for that.

MISS HAVILAND: That brings us to the question of whom you believe to be some of the great writers for children? You have made some allusions already, but would you enlarge on that?

MR. SENDAK: George MacDonald I think of as probably the greatest of the Victorian writers for children. It's the combination of planes, levels, that he worked on. George MacDonald can tell a conventional fairy tale; it has all the form that a fairy tale must have. At the same time, he manages to inundate the story with a kind of dream-magic, or unconscious power. *The Princess and the Goblin*: Irene's travels through the cave with the goblins are so strange, they can only come out of the deepest dream stuff. The fact that he can weave both of these things together is exactly what I love so much in his work, and what I try to emulate. And he is a model; he is someone I try to copy in many ways. There are other writers, like Charles Dickens, who has precisely this quality of the urgency of childhood. The peculiar charm of being in a room in a Dickens novel, where the furniture is alive, the fire is alive, where saucepans are alive, where chairs move, where every inanimate object has a personality. That is that particularly vivid quality that children have, of endowing everything with life. And Dickens sees and hears as children do. He has a marvelous ear for what's going on socially and politically, and on one level he's telling you a straightforward story. But underneath there is the intensity of the little boy staring out at everything and looking, and examining, and watching, and feeling intensely, and suffering immensely, which is what I think makes Dickens a superb writer. The same is true of George MacDonald. Another favorite writer is Henry James. I first became enthusiastic over Henry James when I read some of the earlier novels about young children. His incredible power of putting himself in the position of young children, viewing the adult world; and his uncanny sense of how difficult and painful it is to be a child. And even harder to be an adolescent. Now, these are people who write from their child sources, their dream sources. They don't forget them. William Blake is my favorite—and, of course, *The Songs of Innocence* and *The Songs of Experience* tell you all about this: what it is to be a child—not childish, but a child inside your adult self—and how much better a person you are for being such. So that my favorite writers are never writers who have written books specifically for children. I don't believe in that kind of writing. I don't believe in people who consciously write for children. The great ones have always just written books. And there are many more, but I can't think of them now.

MISS HAVILAND: Now let's take a group of questions set to you as an artist. In a photo bulletin issued by our State Department, a comment is made that critics credit—and I'm quoting now—"a hidden little boy, Maurice, between four and eight, with the dreamlike quality of the pictures created by Sendak the man." And further in this piece, the journalist quoted you as saying that your new book, *In the Night Kitchen*, is your idea of what books looked like to you as a four year old. Would you elaborate on this question?
MR. SENDAK: Well, I think I did that already. I mean, the city as I felt it as a child. It also was an attempt to capture the look of the books that meant so much to me in the thirties and the early forties—they were not glamorous, "artistic" books; they were very cheap, full-color books that, up to a short time ago, I thought were contemptible. But for some odd reason, my old love for them has returned. My taste in English graphics and German fairy tales came much later, and it really is, I think, on my part at least an honest attempt to get back to those things that did mean an awful lot to me as a child. They weren't fancy, they were good, and *In the Night Kitchen* was an attempt to make a beautiful book that at the same time still suggested those early inexpensive books that were read by most children I knew.

MISS HAVILAND: One librarian recalls hearing you speak in the 1950s, a time between the publishing of your illustrations for *A Hole Is to Dig* and of those for *Little Bear*, when you said that your roots go back to Caldecott. And this past April, when you accepted the Hans Christian Andersen International Medal, you named another string of artists whom you credit with stimulating you. I remember you mentioned William Blake, whom you've already spoken of here, George Cruikshank and Boutet de Monvel, Wilhelm Busch, Heinrich Hoffmann.
MR. SENDAK: That's right.

MISS HAVILAND: Could you talk about the specific elements that you think you find there that are particularly relevant to the children's book illustrator?
MR. SENDAK: I hated school and my own particular way was to learn by myself. Many of the artists who influenced me were illustrators I accidentally came upon. I knew the Grimm's *Fairy Tales* illustrated by George Cruikshank, and I just went after everything I could put my hands on that was illustrated by Cruikshank and copied his style. Quite as simply as that. I wanted to crosshatch the way he did. Then I found Wilhelm Busch and I was off again. But happily Wilhelm Busch also crosshatched, so the Cruikshank crosshatching wasn't entirely wasted. And so an artist grows. I leaned very heavily on these people. I developed taste from these illustrators. Boutet de Monvel, the French illustrator, who is still not terribly well-known (which is a great surprise to me), illustrated in the twenties, or earlier perhaps—had the most glorious sense of design and refinement of style. His pictures are so beautifully felt, and they are supremely elegant as only French illustration can be. They are very clear, very transparent, extremely fine. At the same time, they can be very tragic. There are things in his drawings, which perhaps now would even seem too strong for children—although at one point, they did not. There is a perfect example of his method in one of his illustrations for the *Fables* of La Fontaine—"The Wolf and the Lamb." They are a series of drawings, very much like a comic strip. It's like a ballet. The little lamb moves toward the stream and begins to drink, and the ferocious wolf appears and says: "What are you doing here? This is my water!" Of course, he's rationalizing the whole thing, he's going to eat the lamb up anyway, but he's putting on this big act about it being his water. Now, the lamb knows that there's no chance for escape, and while the wolf is bristling—and in each drawing his chest gets puffier and his fangs get fangier, and his eyes are blazing, and he looks horrendous—now, in proportion to him, growing

larger on the page, the lamb dwindles. It has immediately accepted its fate, it can't outrun the wolf, it doesn't even listen to the words of the wolf, this is all beside the point: it is going to die, and it prepares itself for death. And while the wolf goes through this inane harangue, the lamb folds itself in preparation for its death. It leans down, it puts its head to one side, it curls up very gently, and its final gesture is to lay its head down on the ground. And at that moment the wolf pounces and destroys the lamb. It is one of the most beautiful sequences I've ever seen and one of the most honest in a children's book. There's no pretense of the lamb escaping, or of there being a happy ending—this is the way it is, it does happen this way sometimes, that's what de Monvel is saying. And this is what I believe children appreciate. People rage against the Grimm's fairy tales, forgetting that originally the brothers Grimm had—I'm going off the track a little bit—assembled the tales not for children but for historical and philological reasons. They were afraid their past was being lost in all the upheavals of that period, and the tales were put out as a scholarly edition of peasant tales not to be forgotten as part of the heritage of their homeland. Well, lo and behold, children began to read them. And the second edition was called *The Household Tales* because children were devouring the books—not literally—I'm going to be so conscious of that from here on. The whole point I'm making, although I have forgotten the point frankly, is that those illustrators and writers that attracted me were the ones who did not seem at all to be hung up by the fact that their audiences were small people. They were telling the truth, just the way it was. This could be done if it were aesthetically beautiful, if it were well-written—simply, if it were a work of art, then it was fine. Now *Der Struwwelpeter* was one of the books that I loved very much—graphically, it *is* one of the most beautiful books in the world. One might complain about the cutting off of fingers, and the choking to death, and being burned alive, and might well have a case there—but, aesthetically, for an artist growing up it was a good book to look at and a lot of my early books were affected strongly by the German illustrators. When I came to picture books, it was Randolph Caldecott who really did put me where I wanted to be. Caldecott is an illustrator, he is a songwriter, he is a choreographer, he is a stage manager, he is a decorator, he is a theater person; he's superb, simply. And he can take four lines of verse that have very little meaning in themselves and stretch them into a book that has tremendous meaning—not overloaded, no sentimentality in it. Everybody meets with a bad ending in *Froggie Went A-Courting*. Froggie gets eaten at the end by a duck, which is very sad, and the story usually ends on that note. But in Caldecott's version, he introduces, oddly enough, a human family. They observe the tragedy much as a Greek chorus might—one can almost hear their comments. In the last picture, we see Froggie's hat going downstream, all that remains of him. And standing on the bank are mother, father, and child—and it's startling for a moment until you realize what he's done: the little girl is clutching the mother's long Victorian skirt. And it's as though she's just been told the story, she's very upset, obviously. There are no words; I'm just inventing what I think this means—Froggie is dead, it alarms her, and for support she's hanging on to her mother's skirt. Her mother has a very quiet, resigned expression on her face. She's very gently pointing with her parasol toward the stream as the hat moves away, and the father is looking very sad. They're both expressing to the child, "Yes, it is very sad, but this does happen—that is the way the story ended, it can't be helped. But you have us. Hold on, everything is all right." And this is impressive in a simple rhyming book for children; it's extremely beautiful. It's full of fun, it's full of beautiful drawings, and it's full of truth. And I think Caldecott did it best, much better than anyone else who ever lived.

MISS HAVILAND: One critic, at the last Biennale of Illustration at Bratislava, said: "There is no fundamental difference between illustrations for children and those for adults." Would you comment on that?

MR. SENDAK: I don't agree at all, of course. I intensely do not believe in illustrations for adults. For preschool children who cannot read, pictures are extremely valuable. But even children who do read move in a very different world. As for adults, I personally find it offensive to read, I will *not* read, a novel that is illustrated. I always use this example, and many people here who know me have heard me carry on about this particular one, the case of *Anna Karenina*: the audacity of any illustrator who would draw Anna after Tolstoy had described her in the best way possible! Now, everyone who's read the book knows exactly what she looks like, or what he wants her to look like. Tolstoy is superb. And then to get an artist so asinine as to think he's going to draw Anna! Or Melville: it's incredible. People illustrate *Moby-Dick*. It's an insane thing to do, in my estimation. There is every difference in the world between illustrations for adults and illustrations for children. I don't know why there *are* illustrations for adults. They make no sense to me at all.

MISS HAVILAND: Out of that same Biennale of Illustration, where you represented the United States as our juror, there was considerable disagreement; I recall disagreement in theory, on the importance of kinds of art as illustrations. You were there, could you bring this into the picture?

MR. SENDAK: Well, I'm not sure I know exactly what you mean, but as I recall there was a European point of view as to what illustrations accomplish in a children's book, as opposed to what we believe is the function of illustration. I didn't know such a difference of opinion existed until we were in Czechoslovakia. And it was quite extraordinary. Partly, perhaps, because there is a dearth of original writing, they tend more often to reillustrate their classic and fairy tales, and the illustrations take on a dominance and importance which I, as an illustrator, do not approve of. The books often become showcases for artists. I mean, you turn pages and there are extremely beautiful illustrations, but so far as I can see they could be taken out of one book and put into another. Whereas here, we are very much involved in making the illustrations work in a very specific way inside a book. Now, a picture is there, not because there should be a picture there; there is a purpose for a picture—we are embellishing, or we are enlarging, or we are involving ourselves in some very deep way with the writer of the book, so that the book (when it is finally illustrated) means more than it did when it was just written. Which is not to say we are making the words more important; we are perhaps opening up the words in a way that children at first did not see was possible. In the United States we work to bring pictures and words together to achieve a wholeness in the book, which I was very surprised to find is not at all important in many European countries. It's not a matter of right or wrong, it's just that it is so different! There it was so much a matter of graphics, of beauty of picture; here graphic acrobatics are less important.

MISS HAVILAND: One critic has asked why you changed from the "fine engraved style" of *Higglety Pigglety Pop!* back to what this person calls the "fat style" of your earlier work?

MR. SENDAK: Umm, "fat style." Well, I think the only way to answer that is to discuss the business of style. Style, to me, is purely a means to an end, and the more styles you have, the better. One should be able to junk a style very quickly. I think one of the worst things that can happen in some of the training schools for young men and women who are going to be illustrators is the tremendous focusing on "style," on preparation for coming out into the world and meeting the great, horned monsters, book editors. And how to take them on. And style seems to be one of the things. It's a great mistake. To get trapped in a style is to lose all flexibility. And I have worked very hard not to get trapped in that way. Now, I think my work looks like me, generally speaking; over a series of books, you can tell I've done them (much as I may regret many of them). I worked up a very elaborate pen and ink style in *Higglety*, which is very finely crosshatched. But I can abandon that for a magic marker, as I did in *Night Kitchen*, and just go back to very simple, outlined, broad drawings with flat, or flatter, colors. Each book obviously demands an individual stylistic approach. If you have one style, then you're going to do the same book over and over, which is, of course, pretty dull. Lots of styles permit you to walk in and out of all kinds of books. It is a great bore worrying about style. So, my point is to have a fine style, a fat style, a fairly slim style, and an extremely stout style.

MISS HAVILAND: This question comes to you as both an artist and an author. Do you think of your books first in words or in pictures?

MR. SENDAK: In words. In fact, I don't think of the pictures at all. It's a very strange, schizophrenic sort of thing; I've thought of that very often. Sometimes after I've written something I find that there are things in my story that I don't draw well. And if it were any other person's book, I'd consider not doing it. But I've written it and I'm stuck with it, which is proof to me that I have not (at least consciously) been seduced by the tale's graphic potential. I don't think in terms of pictures at all; I find it's much more interesting and difficult to write, and illustration now becomes secondary in my life. So far as I'm aware, I think strictly in terms of words. And then when it's finished, it is almost a surprise as to "How'm I going to do *that*?" or "Why did I do that?" I'm stuck with an airplane, or I'm stuck with a building. If I'm stuck with an automobile, I'm ready to blow my brains out.

MISS HAVILAND: Some artists feel that creating a work is a very separate experience and vastly more satisfying than what happens when the work goes out in the world. How do you evaluate the private experience as compared with public experience?

MR. SENDAK: Well, there really is no comparison. The private experience is extraordinary because it's all yours, nobody knows about it, nobody's going to find out about it, and you have it all to yourself for as long as it takes you to finish the book. *In the Night Kitchen* took two years of concentrated work. *The Wild Things* took about the same length of time, maybe a little less. During that time you are completely absorbed in this dream, this fantasy, whatever it is. The pleasure you get is extraordinary. You live in a very strange world, really quite divorced from this dull, real world. When I'm working on a book, I see very few people, do very few things but think about my book, dream about my book, love it, hate it, pull hairs out of my head; and the only time I speak to people is when I want to complain about it. And then it's over, and then it's finished, and the great shock comes when it is printed! And that's much like giving birth, and always a difficult birth. A book being printed is a major topic in itself; it is a very difficult thing to see through. What was once very dreamlike and transparent and what you thought was a magic moment has now become a real thing in a printing press, and it's going through a big machine, and it looks lousy, and it has to be done all over again. And so gradually your particular transparent little dream is becoming more real, and more terrible every moment. And then finally it is a book. And you become extremely depressed, because you realize that what was so superb and different is really just another book! How strange. It looks like all the other things you've done. And then it goes out into the world, and your child, who was so private and who was living with you for two years, now is everybody's child. Some people know him on the head, some kick him in the rump, and others like him very much. It's a totally different experience. It takes me a long time to shift gears. I am now in the process. It's only a few weeks since the book came out, and I don't know quite yet how to adjust to the fact that people are looking at it, and criticizing it.

MISS HAVILAND: Looking at the publishing world, we can see a very big question: Do you think that children's book publishing is significantly different today than it was when you began in the early fifties? And, if you do, in what respect do you see this?

MR. SENDAK: Since I've generalized all this time, I could go a little further. There was a great moment in the middle fifties when, suddenly, the foreign books came to America. Books from Switzerland, the Hans Fischer books and the Carigiet books. We'd never seen them; it was a revolution in American bookmaking. We suddenly began to look very European. It was the best thing that could have happened to us, we *looked* terrific! But, of course, Europeans were then doing the most superb books. England invented the children's book as we know it. And now, in the sixties and seventies, certainly America is leading the world in the manufacture of children's books. It's disappointing, I find, going to Europe (with the exception of England and Switzerland) and finding so few contemporary children's books. I don't know if you found this to be true, but I did. In France there is *Babar* and the great old ones, but there are very few new ones. There *are* new ones, of course, but none that we get to see and none that seemingly even French people or Italians get to see—it seems they have dropped back considerably. I could be wrong. In my travels I've discussed this matter with illustrators and editors—and this is certainly the impression I've gotten.

MISS HAVILAND: Is there any point that you would like to make, aside from the questions that have been brought up to you before and which you've answered again tonight?

MR. SENDAK: I love my work very much, it means everything to me. I would like to see a time when children's books were not segregated from adult books; a time when people didn't think of children's books as a minor art form, a little Peterpanville, a cutesy-darling place where you could Have Fun, Laugh Your Head Off. I know so many adult writers whom I would happily chop into pieces who say, "Well, I think I'll take a moment and sit down and knock off a kiddy book! It looks like so much fun; it's obviously easy—." And, of course, they write a lousy book. You hope they will and they do! It would be so much better if everyone felt that children's books are for everybody, that we simply write books, that we are a community of writers and artists, that we are all seriously involved in the business of writing. And if everyone felt that writing for children is a serious business, perhaps even more serious than a lot of other forms of writing, and if, when such books are reviewed and discussed, they were discussed on this serious level, and that we would be taken seriously as artists. I would like to do away with the division into age categories of children over here and adults over there, which is confusing to me, and I think probably confusing to children. It's very confusing to many people who don't even know how to buy a children's book. I think if I have any particular hope it is this: that we all should simply be artists and just write books and stop pretending that there is such a thing as being able to sit down and write a book for a child: it is quite impossible. One simply writes a book.

Impressions of Sendak

Muriel Harris / 1970

Elementary English, vol. 48, no. 7. November 1971, pp. 825–32. Originally published by the National Council of Teachers of English.

His red front door was wide open, hailing the winter winds and rain. It was that way with Maurice Sendak, the man. He opened his heart like a wide swinging door, eagerly reviewing and revealing the elements of his life.

Outside, the streets teemed with the confrontations of living, 1970. Hippies and flower children gathered on street corners selling beads and belts; they sat on church steps clutching or rough housing with one another. Boys pedaled aluminum carts as their Gristede bundles bounced along. Junkies on trips tip-toed on tightropes or spread themselves out like giant crosses alongside the curbs. The honking horns of busses, cars, and motorcycles screeched at one another. Cats lurked behind vest pocket gardens of Village Brownstones . . . searching for what?

As I walked down the street to his home I couldn't help but wonder about the contrast; Victorian solidity solemnly displayed by the brownstones, their gas lamps, drooping ivy tendrils, their lace iron railings and balconies, mingled with the strength of steel skyscrapers piercing the skies. Luxuriating in their obvious affluence. When I walked into Sendak's home, all of this immediately faded . . . away like a 1940 movie fade-out . . . the Village and its clamor dissolved into nothingness.

I entered a corridor to another world; high vaulted ceilings, towering windows (sheer lace curtains wafting in the breeze), spacious rooms with breathing space, a voluptuous oversized baby grand, and bookcases, bookcases, bookcases. Books lining walls, books lining staircases, books comfortably lying on almost every step. This is the setting Sendak has chosen for himself—a fortress against any of today's distractions, a fortress for contemplation and immersion in one's work.

Downstairs was his sanctuary. A comfortable dining area and snug kitchen overlooked a raised stone garden (a garden that seemed to have been sitting there since Dickens's time).

Sendak (a bachelor of forty-two who looks like thirty-two), black-haired and porcelain-skinned, stood looking out on the garden as it rained. He mused, "I can still see Jennie sitting there. I can still see her." (Jennie, his fourteen-year-old Sealyham, died a short while ago.) Sendak was in England and had suffered a heart attack. A friend who was taking care of Jennie wired that she was seriously ill. Sendak, in spite of doctors' orders, flew to New York and Jennie. When he arrived home he also found that his mother was ill. As Sendak spoke, his face tensed, reflecting the anxiety of that time. His mother and Jennie died that year.

There was a relative of Jennie's leashed to the kitchen door. She was about a half foot high and seemed to have some terrier blood. I was about to scratch her neck and whisper dog nothings in her ear when I discovered she was inanimate. (Looking back upon it, why didn't I? There was something about Sendak and his house that made me feel that she was real and masquerading as a toy.)

The dining room led into a narrow, musty Victorian hallway that had the atmosphere of a time tunnel. At the end was a small, low-ceilinged, dark study cluttered with every imaginable kind of Mickey Mouse toy—books, records, paintings, prints, brushes, and bottles. And in all that darkness only one spot of light beamed . . . it was over his drawing board desk.

"Here's where I have all my 'chochkis,'" he laughed as he switched on the light. There Mickey Mouse on bikes, standing, dancing, sitting, and playing the piano. Puppets, marionettes, antique dolls, old tin trolley cars, Buster Brown images—all the toys that were the commercial art of the '30s.

I publicly proclaim disagreement with Sendak. That room was *not* full of "chochkis." I could feel, even see IDEAS buzzing and bumping into each other there. Wow! What a heyday his fantasy must have!

Sendak pointed to a huge tape recorder. "When I feel nothing coming on, an emptiness, then I turn to my music . . . the musical beat is my heartbeat. Nothing, no other form turns me on like music. When the music is on, the air changes, the mood changes, the room changes, I change. There's a chain reaction, and I am in communication with my childhood fantasies . . ."

I wondered, "Why the toys? Antique collector?"

Sendak grinned but was firm in his response. He wanted to get this clear. "I'm not an antique collector but do collect the symbols of my childhood, the culture I grew up in . . . in order to immerse myself in that period for a story. Before I write anything I seek out all tangible and intangible symbols linked with my work so that the essence of that period or time could filter through my story."

Everywhere I looked, there were sketches by friends and favorite artists (Tomi Ungerer) and originals by great children's illustrators (Cruikshank, Rowlandson, Busch). Paintings, lithographs, magnificent Renaissance prints, and art by his favorite American artist, Winslow Homer, sit on almost every shelf and every wall in his study. Art is in every corner seeping through every wall seam. There was a delightful painting over the fireplace (a fireplace whose hearth was filled . . . not with wood but with toys, tiles, books, and games of a bygone age.) Although it was a portrait of a young man, it was easy for me to see that Sendak had painted it.

"That's an old childhood friend . . . a very dear friend . . . as a matter of fact I still see him . . . but not as often as I'd like . . ."

I mentioned that he looked like a Talmudic student, and Sendak said he was. This Hebraic quality still exists and emanates from Sendak's children and Old World Talmudic *shtetl* child. His children are not the usual sugar-coated haloed ones we see in pretty books. They are droll, capricious, pugnacious, rebellious, gloating, loving, and REAL. They are Sendak, who is part Brooklyn-New York-America and part Jewish-Polish *shtetl*-Old World-Wonder. Sendak and his children are one and the same . . . inseparable, inviolate, and inevitable.

He fingered some of his books. "I collect first editions and rare children's books. I have Caldecott, Richter, Ernst Kreidolf, and Fischer. As a child I felt that books were holy objects to be caressed and sniffed and treasured. I remember my first readers in elementary school. The pages were a pale yellow or soft pastel green, and I can still feel my hand pressing over the page, feeling its smoothness . . . savoring its friendship. I used to love the stories . . . especially 'Chicken Little.' I hated school, but I loved reading my books. I was not interested in school . . . it frightened me. It turned me off."

This is a puzzling statement when one realizes that Sendak graduated from the schools he hated with honors. He still remembers P.S. 205, 177, Boody Jr. High, and Lafayette High in the Borough Park section of Brooklyn.

His parents, Sadie and Philip Sendak, were struggling immigrants and were unable to send their daughter Natalie and son Jack to college. So when Maurice, the baby came (June 10, 1928), they hoped that he would go further educationally. Philip Sendak was a tailor, and like all struggling Jewish immigrants, the scholar was his ideal. They wanted Maurice to go to college. But Maurice was turned off by school and only wanted to paint.

"My decision was hard on my parents, but they were very understanding. That's why I reached a compromise. I agreed to go to the Art Students League. From the time I was four, I knew what I wanted to be, an artist. My brother Jack and I used to make our own books. We'd draw, paint, print, paste up, bind . . . do the whole thing. Art was always part of me."

Sendak is a Man of the Renaissance—dedicated to his craft, involved with creating a more perfect whole by digging into the essence of his work, a man in love with his labor . . . perhaps even obsessed by it. His work occupies many roles on myriad levels . . . but there is no denying that Sendak reaps much from his art and writing. I even sense a reciprocation. His children, his animals, his creations all respond and return his love. Sendak appreciates and understands the past and carries it along within him into the present, inserting it, instilling it into his books.

His thoughts on education even reflect the pattern of the Renaissance. "I actually believe that education stifles and kills talent. School fundamentally destroys. Life, living, and working at your art are the only answer for artists. Teachers tend to crush delicate talents, originality, or inventiveness. Work! Work! WORK! Work at you art, and it will grow."

The Renaissance men felt the same way. They became apprentices at eleven or twelve and worked under an artist until their experience and production warranted moving to the stable of another artist.

At seventeen-and-a-half Maurice illustrated his first book, *Atomics for the Millions*, written by his high school science teacher, Dr. R. Hyman Ruchlis. At nineteen-and-a-half he illustrated *Good Shabbos, Everybody* for the United Synagogue Commission. He worked for display houses and did window display work for FAO Schwarz. He also did the backgrounds on *Mutt and Jeff* for American Comics. These were some of his happiest days. While working at Schwarz, the store's book buyer knew Ursula Nordstrom, Harper's editor, and invited her down to see Sendak's work. Miss Nordstrom was so impressed that she commissioned him to illustrate Marcel Aymé's *The Wonderful Farm*, his first important book. That was published in 1951. "That made me an official person," laughed Sendak.

Sendak waxed with enthusiasm when talking about his family. "My brother, Jack (five years older), is in the electronics industry but is essentially a writer and artist as he never stops. As a kid I used to watch him draw and wanted to be just like him. I copied all of Jack's pictures . . . even dared to put my name on a few of them. Little ones must feel like big ones. And I was the littlest in the family . . . that wasn't an easy role.

"My sister, Natalie (eight years older), was the most gorgeous female in Borough Park. My mother, father, brother, and I adored her. She was Miss

Gorge-e-ous-ity. Mom and Dad, like all Jewish parents, put their daughter on a pedestal. Naturally, Jack and I followed suit. My parents marked time in the universe this way: first was the coming of the ice age, then came Neolithic Man, and then came Natalie, my sister."

"Why do you write? Why do you draw?" "Why do you write children's stories? When did this all start?" Rather usual questions? Yes, but Sendak's responses weren't.

"You write or paint because you have to. THERE IS NO CHOICE. It's just there. I've always drawn. I can never remember a time as a child when I didn't. Remember when I mentioned drawing with Jack and copying his work?"

Sendak's voice slowed; he seemed to be conjuring up the past . . . summoning Maurice, the boy. "From the moment I drew my first drawing there was never any question, never any doubt in my young mind that I wanted to be an artist. Books were my life and still are. I drew for the school newspaper, did sets for school plays (*Macbeth*). I only wanted to create.

"NO, I do NOT write just for children. I write books, period! We live in a pigeonholing society. I don't believe in categorizing. Some books are directed more to children because they utilize children's images. I feel an impulse deriving from my childhood's emotional memory, and that is tempered by my experience and life in general. I get all my ideas from LIFE: the past plus the present. My books are for all ages."

There's always a rebellious child in Sendak's stories, and I wondered why.

"Children are extraordinarily vulnerable and have few defenses. Childhood suffering is intense. What I try to do is turn a vulnerability into a fantasy where the children can control their environment. And while my children are rebellious, they are always the winner. They slip into fantasy which they could control and happily return to reality completely satisfied. But remember, fantasy must be rooted in reality ten feet deep."

Sendak's children have always threatened parents, the Establishment, and have tamed the wildest, most ferocious of beasts with the greatest of ease. Sendak's children have stuck their tongues out at queens, leave home and go very far away, stand on their heads on chairs, threaten to eat tigers, rats, even robbers, squeeze cobras by the neck, or scream "No" and "I don't care," and put their heads in lions' mouths. They even threaten a herd of ugly, clawing, growling, bulbous-eyed creatures that they'll be sent to bed without supper. What immense bravery! What courage! What necessary fantasy!

Where the Wild Things Are won the coveted Caldecott Medal in 1964. A new era in children's literature had emerged. Up until now children behaved dutifully in literature, minded their p's and q's, bowed and curtsied, smiled and said "Thank you" to their elders . . . But along came the roaring and crescendo of *Wild Things* and the literary world literally somersaulted.

Sendak laughed, "I'm a late bloomer. I always was. I'm in no hurry to go anywhere special. I do what I want when I want. . . . I'm slow . . . at forty-two I'm just beginning to bloom. *Where the Wild Things Are* was always in my stories. There are elements of *Wild Things* in *Pierre* and *One Was Johnny!* It needed time to grow.

"Speaking of late blooming, my father had that rare gift of storytelling. He was always telling us little 'myselles' . . . He captivated my imagination with his magical gift in weaving mysterious and beautiful words. I was spellbound. Papa was quite ill this past year, and when he left the hospital he came home with me. He knew he was seriously ill. . . . What to do with him to refuel his spirit? I suddenly remembered his 'myselles' and suggested that he write them down and that I'd illustrate them. He became so alive, so excited, so involved with this project that I feel he finally fulfilled himself. Here he was a tailor all his life, and in his last year he became a writer. (*That's a late bloomer!*) I translated them, illustrated them, and his book will be published soon. I wish that he were here to see it. Speaking of Papa, when I was writing the dedication to my new book, *In the Night Kitchen*, I asked him if I could dedicate the book to him and Mom using just their given names."

"'What's the matter? You can't say *we're* your *parents*?' he asked. I told him that in using just their given names, I was not only paying tribute to them as parents, but that it was a very special ovation. They were individuals to me; each one wonderful and special in his own right . . . and that stating their names would give them individuality. Papa smiled and said that it was fine. A few days later he suddenly came up with 'Can't you say, "To my parents" next to our names?'

"I smiled and now you see what I've done." Sendak opened to the dedication page, and there in a little blurb spoken by the hero of the story was "Mama and Papa" alongside their given names.

Why do children like his books? A child spins concentric circles around himself. The nucleus never fails to be the "I." The "I" for identity and the "I" for "me." The ego is one big circus balloon swelling, soaring, ready to burst within the child. And when he opens a Sendak book he's peering into a mirror seeking, feeling, hearing, touching his own thoughts, his own actions. He sees Himself.

When I read *A Sign on Rosie's Door*, I immediately recalled my childhood games of fantasy. Gee, there was another girl just like ME. Rosie needs love. . . . Rosie needs an audience. Rosie needs approval. Rosie needs an outlet . . . she can't control her mother's directive, "No firecrackers." Rosie stomps out of the house and slips from reality into fantasy where she could solve her dilemma. The Magic Man visits her and informs her that she and her friends could become little firecrackers. Rosie announces the good news! "Boom! Crack-phizz-boom!" Everybody immediately vibrates and crackles with action, fizzing into firecrackers. Rosie, with a big red blanket around her, becomes the BIGGEST red firecracker in the world. And then she happily returns home to reality.

In *Pierre* we see a boy, Every boy, shouting to the Establishment. "I don't care! I don't care!" He pours syrup in his hair, stands on his head on a chair, and even tells a lion who threatens to eat him, "I don't care!"

What child hasn't felt this yearning? What adult hasn't felt this urge? Therein lies the secret of Maurice Sendak. . . . He gets down to the nitty gritty, to a universal concept . . . the need to vent one's emotion through fantasy. Sendak is talking about all human beings, not just children. I would even join Pierre—generation gap and all—in shouting, "I don't care!" when his lions eat him. Sendak's lion gives a roar, and Pierre falls out upon the floor, like Rosie eager to return to reality and home.

How delightful to shout "no" to a king and stick out your tongue to a queen and tame ferocious lions by bopping them over the head with a club! *Hector Protector* indulged in all this. As Shakespeare once said, "what stuff these dreams are made of."

In *One Was Johnny*, Johnny threatens to eat a blackbird, a turtle, a dog, a cat, a rat, a monkey, a tiger, and a robber. When he frightens them off with his fierce appetite and threats, he then happily resumes his reading all alone in his room.

The attitude of adults is clear in *Higglety Pigglety Pop!*, where a set of parents have moved and can't send for their offspring because they merely forgot the child's name and address. This book subtitled "There Must Be More to Life" is dedicated to Jennie and is all about her. There are many levels of interpretation. This, more than any of his other books, contains allegorical qualities. Jennie has everything—a round pillow, square pillow, comb, brush, two different bowls, pills, eyedrops, eardrops, a thermometer, a beautiful Renaissance painting (my favorite period), and for cold weather a red wool sweater. Now, did Jennie leave home because she thought there must be more to life than the material things she had, or did she leave because she went searching for Heaven? Why did the parents forget their baby's name?

Is that a comment on today's affluent mobile parents? What was the World Mother Goose Theater, Heaven, Fantasy, or anyone's Utopia? In order to get into the Mother Goose Theater you have to have experience. What is that experience analogous to—love, working at one's craft, or proving oneself in some fashion? Sendak says, "it's anyone's interpretation . . . whatever you see . . . that is what's there." Loneliness, cowardice, death, courage . . . all are here in *Higglety Pigglety Pop!* Jennie does pass through many trials, even putting her head into a lion's mouth, and is finally accepted into the Castle Yonder and is reborn as a great actress. The letter at the end is most touching. Jennie informs everyone that she gets to eat a mop at each daily performance and twice on Saturday. The mop is made of salami. What more could one ask? Actually, Jennie is still with us . . . she appears in all of Sendak's books. If only we could fare as well as Jennie did. Read his pictures; they tell all.

Where the Wild Things Are has Max who can't be anyone else but Maurice. There is a very strong resemblance between Sendak and his children, but a particularly strong one here. I can just hear Sadie Sendak calling to her youngest child, "You wild thing!" and Maurice stalking off and mumbling under his breath, "I'll eat you up!" Max, the protagonist in the story, is alive and vibrating. He puts on a Wolf suit and makes mischief of one kind or another. His mother sends him to bed without any supper. His mother calls him "wild thing" and Max, wearing a pugnacious and irascible face, threatens "I'll eat you up!" There in his room slowly and naturally the bedposts turn into trees, and a wild forest appears. An ocean tumbles by with a private boat for Max, and he sails off through night and day and in and out of weeks to where the Wild Things, a tribe of pre-historic bulbous-eyed beasts, are. But Max, looking like Svengali, hypnotizes them by staring into their yellow eyes without blinking once. These ferocious beasts submit immediately and call Max the most wild thing of all, making him king of all Wild Things. Then their orgy starts: six delicious pages of baying at the moon, hanging from trees, and dancing mysterious rituals in eerie night colors.

Sendak has captured the essence of what children would like to vent in his drawings. They are masterpieces of reverie (children's and adults' alike). Max stops everything and sends the Wild Things to bed without *their* supper. He feels lonely and wants to be where someone loves him best of all. So he sails back over the ocean into the night and into his room, where he finds his supper waiting for him, still hot.

No writer through his art or story line, up until now, had allowed fantasy, that has rooted in the real life of children, to take over. This is fantasy that is not conjured up through magic and witches spells like fairytales, but rather it is based upon the real fantasy life of children. This *is* what they think; therefore, it is real. Sendak created a revolution in children's literature with *Wild Things*. Previously, everything was written to conform to adults' perspectives (as they looked through rose-colored glasses). Sendak tells it like it is. Fantasy exists in our lives, and it is as real as reality. We need both.

In 1964, Sendak received the Caldecott Medal for *Wild Things*, which is awarded annually by the American Library Association for the most distinguished American picture book for children.

Miss Nordstrom, his editor and mentor, said of *Wild Things*, "it is the first American picture book for children to recognize that children have powerful emotions, anger and fear as well as the need Max had, after his anger was spent, to be 'where someone loved him best of all.'"

Wild Things did meet with some hostile reactions from critics and librarians because they thought it would frighten children to death. But Max conquers those monsters, even becomes king of the beasts, and turns down their invitation to stay longer because his preference was home where love was. A critic for the *Cleveland Press* stated, "Boys and girls may have to shield their parents from this book. Parents are very easily scared."

Sendak, in his acceptance speech for the Caldecott Medal stated that some books offer "a gilded world unshadowed by the least suggestion of conflict or pain, a world manufactured by those who cannot—or do not care to—remember the truth of their own childhood."

In the Night Kitchen, his newest book, is about Mickey (who resembles a miniature Rocky Marciano and Sendak), who can't fall asleep because of a racket downstairs. In his most vociferous and pugilistic voice he shouts, "Quiet down there," and as he does, he slips into a dream falling down, down into the night kitchen in which three Oliver Hardys reign as cooks. He falls into a gigantic bowl of bread dough and since dough rises, so does Mickey, soaring up into the sky wrapped in dough. He kneads it, punches it, pounds it, pulls it until he's formed a plane for himself and off he goes to the Milky Way for a cup of milk. What better way to obtain it than to drive right into a bottle of milk? (Why can't we all get milk that way? Cleopatra took milk baths.) Mickey does a jackknife in the milk bottle, sings, and even swims to the top, pouring milk from his cup into batter below while the Oliver Hardy bakers catch it in their pan. The bakers form a whimsical trio, singing, baking, and playing on their musical utensils on a two-page spread. We even see Mickey like a Renaissance cherub perched on the bottle top . . . feeling as pleased as a morning rooster and crowing like one. After proclaiming his heroics with a "cock-a-doodle-doo," Mickey slides down the side straight into bed into a calm and loving sleep.

Those worrisome critics who are overburdened with the false but damaging effects of seeing the body beautiful will tear their hair and gnash their teeth. But, isn't it easier to fall from sleep into a night kitchen without clothes . . . especially if one falls into a bowl of dough? How else would one dive into a bowl of milk? If I were diving into milk at this very moment, I would reach the same solution as Mickey.

This story is written and painted in a manner both new and unique to picture books. The illustrations have tremendous movement. The action depicted flows and drives forth with a vital energy. This is partially achieved by a cartoon strip effect. Instead of the usual one or two pictures on a page, Sendak has divided the pages into panel strips, whereby the eyes see the action occurring immediately. There's a continuity that speeds its way from one panel into the other. It is like watching an animated film.

The first four and last four pages comprise only two-thirds of the page thereby leaving a wide margin of white space around the film (oops, I mean illustrations). This bold block serves to emphasize the action on the page. The fact that the words are written above some pictures instead of under them also adds to the action.

In the Night Kitchen is a delightful romp into the life of any child when he can't fall asleep and tosses and turns until he falls headlong into a frolicking fantasy of a dream . . . which for me was a total recall of the thirties when Bond Bread Bakeries in Brooklyn dominated the local scene with its sight and smell, when children fantasized the wonders of what happened there in the mystery of black night when the rest of Brooklyn was silent in sleep.

And what better way to reach children than through fantasy (an area where most are fearful to tread), an area which is vital to their daily existence in coping with and accepting reality. Three cheers for Maurice Sendak and *In the Night Kitchen*.

There's an innocence, a sound of the piper's flute with a deep sense of understanding and sophistication in this work that children relate to and that is reminiscent of Blake. Therefore, it was not surprising to hear that Sendak's favorite writers are James, Melville, and Blake. He feels particularly close to Blake.

In talking of art 1970, Sendak said, "There is a pervasive commercialness of our society today that is reflected in all our culture. We are devoid of craftsmen. Look at pop art. Instead of creating the figure, plaster is poured over the form, and the mold that emerges is considered art. It *is* art . . . *our* art of the '70s. Old printers are dead or retired. It's difficult to find a craftsman at once able, knowledgeable, and devoted to his craft. We put the cork on wanting. We are a quickie hamburger society."

While Sendak represents Renaissance Man, he also represents the hippie culture of today in that he's rebelling against the saccharine content of most of American children's literature, eager to get down to the nitty gritty. Every one of his children rebels against the Establishment. Each one seeks his real identity through fantasy only to discover what the flower children profess, love is all, as he fights to grow through the elemental need of fantasy.

Freud once said in a letter to Wilhelm Fliess, "a man like me cannot live without a hobbyhorse, a consuming passion—in Schiller's word a tyrant. I have found my tyrant, and in his service I know no limits. My tyrant is psychology."

And so it is with Maurice Sendak. His consuming passion, his tyrant is his art, his books.

Epilogue

Maurice Sendak was presented with the Hans Christian Andersen Illustrator's Medal, the highest international honor to an illustrator of children's books. The award is given every two years. Mr. Sendak received it on April 4, 1970, in Bologna, Italy. He is the first American artist to be chosen by the International Board on Books for Young People (a board which represents over forty nations).

He also won the prestigious Caldecott Award, the highest American achievement for an illustrator of young children's books. He received the award in 1964 for *Where the Wild Things Are*. He was runner-up to the winner for five other works, and his books have been on the best illustrated lists fourteen times. Sendak has illustrated more than fifty-five books and has written and illustrated seven of them himself: *Kenny's Window, Very Far Away, The Sign on Rosie's Door, The Nutshell Library, Where the Wild Things Are, Higglety Pigglety Pop!,* and *In the Night Kitchen* (which appears to be slated for another award).

An Interview with Maurice Sendak

Walter Lorraine / 1977

From *Wilson Library Bulletin*, 52.2, October 1977, pp. 152–57. Used with permission of EBSCO Information Services, Ipswich, Massachusetts.

The picture book has been of overriding concern to Maurice Sendak since the early 1950s, when he began his career as an author/illustrator. Sendak was awarded the Caldecott Medal in 1964 (for *Where the Wild Things Are*) and the Hans Christian Andersen illustrator's award in 1970. This interview with Walter Lorraine, guest editor of *WLB*'s special issue on "The Art of the Picture Book," took place last June.

WL: How do you think an illustration functions in a book?
MS: It's either a mere decoration, or it's an expansion of the text. It's your version of the text as an illustrator; it's your interpretation. It's why you are an active partner in the book and not a mere echo of the author. To be an illustrator is to be a participant, someone who has something as equally important to say as the writer of the book—occasionally something more important, but certainly never the writer's echo.

WL: Do you feel there are different categories of illustration?
MS: I could make up categories, but I'll tell you only about the one I'm interested in and do well—interpretive illustration. It involves a kind of vigorous working with the writer. Sometimes you're the writer, too, so you're working with yourself; then the difficulty and strain and joy of that particular work is the balancing between text and pictures. You must not ever be doing the same thing, must not ever be illustrating exactly what you've written. You must leave a space in the text so the picture can do the work. Then you must come back with the word, and the word does it best and now the picture beats time.

It's a funny kind of juggling act. It takes a lot of technique, a lot of experience, to really keep the rhythm going between word and picture. It's a kind of muscular rhythm, though the reader isn't aware of it. You have worked out a text that is so supple it stops and goes and stops and goes, and the pictures are shrewdly interspersed. The pictures become so supple, too, that there's this interchangeableness between them and the words, and they're both telling two stories at the same time.

WL: How would you define a picture book?

MS: A picture book is not only what most people think it is—an easy thing to read to very small children with a lot of pictures in it. For me, it is a damned difficult thing to do, very much like a complicated poetic form. Some poets really like to get into difficult forms because they're the most challenging things in poetry. I think a picture book is one of those beautiful, challenging forms, which demands so much that you have to be on top of the situation all the time to finally achieve something that seems so simple and so put together—seamless if you will—that it looks like you knocked it off in no time.

It's like a good poem. You shouldn't be aware of the pastings together. You should only be aware of the work as a complete and total entity, and it should look as breezy as a moonlit night if that's what the poem's about. A picture book has to have that incredible seamless look to it when it's finished. One stitch showing and you've lost the game. I don't know of any other form of illustrating that is so interesting to me.

Grimm's fairytales are obviously not picture book material, but they do allow for interpretive illustration. The illustrations have as much to say as the text; the trick is to say the same thing, but in a different way. It's no good being an illustrator who is saying a lot that is on his or her mind if it has nothing to do with the text. But to say the same thing that the story is saying in your own *personal* way, so that you heighten the meaning of the original tale, contributes dimension to the story.

You're not out to do your own shtick—you're out merely to do your shtick within the confines of the story you're illustrating. Whatever the story happens to be—"Hansel and Gretel," "Snow White"—you have made it bigger than it was because you have had insight into the story as an artist. The illustrator is doing a tremendous job of expansion, of collaboration, of illumination. But he must be discreet. The artist must override the story, but he must also override his own ego for the sake of the story. It's more fun than any other kind of illustration.

WL: Is there a particular style of writing that encourages a good picture book?

MS: It can't be the pedantic form of writing where every nail is knocked in, every fact is obvious. For my taste, it has to be ambiguous—it has to allow for a number of meanings to shine through. It can't be a heavy-handed text that says little Johnny goes from the left to the right, because then the illustrator doesn't have any choice but to make little Johnny go from the left to the right. The text has to be less precise, less obvious. You can have facts, but the facts have to allow the artist to move the characters in any direction.

An example of what I mean is a nursery rhyme of Mother Goose, which might have meant something quite specific in an earlier century but means nothing now. One of my own books, *Hector Protector*, is a good instance. You can make up your own story.

> Hector Protector was dressed all in green,
> Hector Protector was sent to the Queen.
> The Queen did not like him, no more did the King.
> So Hector Protector was sent back again.

Now what the hell does that mean? Maybe a bit of a joke in Elizabeth the First's day. It means nothing to us now, but it's a super text. It's a very funny rhyme, the meter is lovely, and the language is peculiar. What is going on—well, that's the illustrator's game. You have a nice little piece of Mother Goose text that allows you to rearrange the characters in any way you like and make up a story, any story you want; it just has to spring from those words. Whatever imaginative tale you tell must begin with *Hector Protector* dressed all in green, but you can interpret that in new ways. He can be a boy in China, in Alaska, in Israel, but somehow or other he has to be dressed all in green. That's all you have to show. You can invent the rest. The whole book is your story as an illustrator.

WL: How important is technique to the illustrator?

MS: There is a need for only rudimentary grasp of drawing or graphic technique in my opinion. Edward Lear—not one of my favorite illustrators—is someone who had sufficient technique, incredibly sufficient technique, to convey concepts in a very few untrained lines. I think the better the illustrator is technically, the better off she or he will be—but it isn't essential. The peculiar gift in being an illustrator is that one has an odd affinity with words, that it's natural to interpret words, almost like a composer thinking music when reading poetry.

Arthur Hughes is one of my favorite illustrators, but he couldn't draw people in three-quarter view! He did beautiful paintings, he worked from models, and you wonder, why couldn't he draw people in three-quarter view? Well, he couldn't. You can see how wooden they look; you see how awful they look—like their noses have been chopped off. It doesn't take an inch away from *The Princess and the Goblin*—it doesn't take anything away at all. I notice it because I am a craftsman, but I wish I had his gift. It doesn't matter that he didn't have the prowess of a Norman Rockwell. (I don't mean to put Mr. Rockwell down, but that's not what Arthur Hughes is all about.)

Arthur Hughes was an interpretive illustrator. He used whatever technique and craft he had at hand. It's not necessary to do elaborate and refined drawings because elaborate and refined drawings with fantastic technique don't mean a hill of beans if you're not a good illustrator. Now, I suppose as Arthur Hughes got older, he learned to draw better. But alas, the last pictures he did look more graphically polished but have nothing of the magic and power of those earlier clumsy drawings.

I'm saying this clumsily, too, because it's so hard to put this into language. I've seen so many gifted people who were natural illustrators who didn't have technical facility, but to me they had a great treasure. They had what you can't learn. You can draw better by practicing, but you can never learn that other intuitive quality.

WL: What do you think of the quality of picture books today?
MS: Well, I'll have to make a very generalized statement because I don't see that many of them. Much of what I do see is bad, and I think the form of the picture book has been, in large part, debased. It is overused; it is overdressed; it is garish; it is vulgar; it is despoiled. Somehow we've forgotten along the way how difficult it is to make a good picture book. Why don't we look at the major works around? Why don't we look at the little books of William Nicholson, *The Pirate Twins* and *Clever Bill*, which are seemingly so simple they run through your fingers, you can't catch them fast enough. Most of the picture books I've seen are pedantic, obvious, and overcolored, overtechniqued, and overwritten. Very few have excited me. There are exceptions. Many of the young people I teach have a fresher, simpler approach to form. They give me hope for the future.

WL: Was there a time that you feel picture books were better than today?

MS: Yes. Of course there was Wanda Gág. There's always *Millions of Cats*. And we did have a very good period in the 1950s and '60s. I think we were influenced by the books that were coming from other countries. Remember the '50s when Hans Fischer's books were first published here, and *Finders Keepers* won the Caldecott Award? That book was so influenced by European illustration. I remember my excitement when I first saw it. It had an international flavor, which was something new in American children's books. The '50s was a very exciting time. Many of the books that were being done were influenced by what we were seeing from abroad. And there was Tomi Ungerer and a lot of us just beginning. We had about a decade's worth of terrific stuff, then we started getting very rich on it. We started shutting the door in the face of new talent—or so it seems to me.

WL: Do you think there is a lack of talent in the picture book area today?
MS: I did think that for a long time. I thought that historically and socially there was a wasteland, that the creative soil was infertile. But since I've been teaching I know that's not true. Believe me, I don't see many brilliant people, but I do see some very talented people. And I can say without any hesitation that a small number of my best students are quite ready to be published. They have an ethical approach toward the picture book, a vital and serious approach; and it has made me realize that my original view that talent wasn't there was probably false.

If talent is around but nobody is using it, what *is* wrong? It seems to me that the system is at fault. If you speak to publishers, every one of them will say, "We're always looking for new people." But I wonder why they aren't publishing them. I have, in all fairness, seen some books by new people, but there are far too few being published. I've had great difficulty in placing some of my gifted students. What's the risk? It seems to me that publishers are less ambitious than they used to be, in general less brave, less willing to go out on a limb. Now if you say this aloud, you get the response: "But we are publishing young people." Well, where are they?

My suspicion is that publishers are afraid to take risks. In the old days they did take chances. Nothing's happening now. I'm nearly fifty and when I turn around I see very few young people climbing up the mountain. When I was young, in the 1950s, we were given all the encouragement in the world.

WL: Do you think a new and truly innovative book by a new talent can reach an appropriate audience today?
MS: I don't know because I really have lost touch with how the books go out

and where they go to. I mean that. Now, my only feedback is the letters I get from children.

WL: Do you think there are others besides publishers who encourage this conservatism?
MS: I think there must be. I hear about this dearth of talent and the wailing about where is the talent coming from, which bewilders me—because I see some of it, and I say, it's over there and it doesn't get published. There's some jarring disharmony somewhere. It seems to me, to make a very general statement, that the way the industry is now, very few people would be willing to go out on a limb with a very different kind of book.

WL: Do you think that critical reaction today does encourage superior books?
MS: No. There are exceptional publishers, and there are a few exceptional critics—some very few exceptional critics—who take the trouble to evaluate a children's book in an intelligent way. They're not burdened with boring, tedious attitudes, such as whether a book is good for kiddies or not good for kiddies. They take an overall view of it aesthetically. Does it stand up as a work of art?

I think, from my own personal experience, I have not learned anything from reviews of my books. I've not seen reviews of other people's books that I ever thought did real justice to a book's special qualities. These statements are too general, because there are some few intelligent reviewers who do take their job very seriously—who are trying to encourage talent and can distinguish between the real and the phony. They take the larger view and escape the fatal "Kiddiebookland" disease that most reviewers suffer from. But they are exceptional, very exceptional. Too often, children's books are nailed down by whether they conform to the rules of the kindergarten, of what children ought or ought not to be reading. Hardly ever is the American children's book seriously or intelligently reviewed.

WL: What do you mean by Kiddiebookland?
MS: Kiddiebookland is where we live. Didn't you know? It's next to Neverneverville and Peterpanburg. It's that awful place that we've been squeezed into because we're children's book illustrators or children's book writers. Yes, we are! But isn't our work meant for everybody? How infuriating and insulting when a serious work is considered only a trifle for the nursery!

When you've worked a year on a book, when you've put your life into it, you expect the point of view of the professionals (editors, teachers, librarians) to be somewhat larger, more expansive. You expect the book to be read by people of all ages. When someone says, "Well, don't you like doing children's books?" I say, "Yes, apparently I do, I've been at it for a long time. But it also is a major part of my life, and I'm talking about all kinds of things in my work, which only happens to take the form of a picture book."

WL: Do you think critics should react differently to the illustrations in picture books?

MS: I think they should try to learn what picture books are all about. There is some fine mystery in this difficult form (I am aware of this and struggle with it), a mystery that is the artist's business. Any serious artist's work is never just one thing. What I'm objecting to is that picture books are judged from a particular, pedantic point of view vis à vis their relation to children—and I insist that any serious work of art is much more.

I think when people are reviewing our books, a collision inevitably occurs with preconceptions concerning children. There is a whole theory about childhood that everybody works from, and people look for whether a picture book has followed the "rules" about what is right for children, or what we *think* is right and healthy for children. This comes into conflict all the time with those things that are mysterious. Children don't need a pedantic approach to the book. Children are much more catholic in taste; will tolerate ambiguities, peculiarities, and things illogical; and will take them into their unconscious and deal with them as best they can.

The anxiety comes from the adults who feel that the book has to conform to some set ritual of ideas about childhood, and unless this conforming takes place they are ill at ease. A very important conflict occurs because the artist really doesn't go by any specified rules. The artist has to be a little bit bewildering and a little bit wild and a little bit disorderly. That's the art of being an artist. Artists run into difficulty because they're dealing with our most upright, uptight business, which is the industry called childhood.

Most people are out to protect children from what they think is dangerous. The genuine artists have the same concern. Their work, however, may not conform to what the specialists think is right or wrong for children. The artists are going to put elements into their work that come from their deepest selves. They draw on a peculiar vein of childhood that is always open and alive. That is their particular gift. They understand that children know a lot more than people give them credit for. Children are willing to deal with many dubious subjects that grownups think they shouldn't know about.

If a book doesn't follow the course of what a childhood specialist considers right, then it's a bad book for children. So picture book people are more easily condemned than almost any other artists in creation because we're dealing with such a volatile subject—children. We must protect the children, and yet children are unprotected in every other way. No one protects them from terrible television. No one protects them from life because you cannot protect them from life, and all we're trying to do in a serious work is to tell them about life. What's wrong with that? They know about it anyway.

WL: What elements make up a good children's book?

MS: The basic ground-floor element is honesty. Whatever you're doing—a realistic story or fantasy or far-out science fiction—must begin with a basis of honesty. You must tell the truth about the subject to the child as well as you are able without any mitigating of that truth. You must allow that children are small, courageous people who have to deal every day with a multitude of problems, just as we do, and that they are unprepared for most things, and what they most yearn for is a bit of truth somewhere.

Now if you honestly start with that, then you can proceed in whatever form you like, tell it whatever way you like. If it's a bitter pill that children don't want to swallow, give them the opportunity of saying no. Let there not be guards in front of children who decide what they should or shouldn't be reading. Why are children kept in ghettos, and why are there guards in front of the doors telling them what is right and what isn't right? We have the opportunity of choosing what we like to read. Why shouldn't culture have the same opportunity?

A woman once said to me: "I've read *Where the Wild Things Are* ten times to my little girl, and she screams every time." And I said, "Why are you reading it to her?" She said, "But it's a Caldecott book, she ought to like it." I said, "That's absurd. You're a sadist. If the kid doesn't like the book, throw it away." What's wrong here is that the mother insisted that the child should like the book. Why? Children don't give a damn about the Caldecott award. Why should they? We should let children choose their own books. What they don't like they will throw away. What disturbs them too much they will not look at. They're not going to fall apart if they look at the wrong book. It isn't going to do them that much damage. We treat children in a very peculiar way, I think. We don't treat them like the strong creatures they really are.

WL: What should we look for in a picture book?

MS: Originality of vision. Someone who has something to say that might be very commonplace, but who says it in a totally original and fresh way, who has a point of view, who has a genius for expressing the prosaic in a magical way. Do not look for pyrotechnics, for someone who can make a big slambang picture book out of very little, but look for the genuinely talented person who things originally.

WL: Can you define what a picture book is for you?
MS: Well, I think I have; it's everything. It's my battleground. It's where I express myself. It's where I consolidate my powers and put them together in what I hope is a legitimate, viable form that is meaningful to somebody else and not just to me. It's where I work. It's where I put down those fantasies that have been with me all my life, and where I give them a *form* that means something. I live inside the picture book; that's where I fight all my battles, and where hopefully I win my wars.

An Interview with Maurice Sendak

Jerry Griswold / 1978

From *Mother and Child in the Poetry and Children's Books of Randall Jarrell*, unpublished dissertation. © Jerry Griswold, 1979. Used with permission of Jerry Griswold.

Author and illustrator Maurice Sendak is well-known for his own work— *The Juniper Tree and Other Tales from Grimm, The Sign on Rosie's Door, In the Night Kitchen, Where the Wild Things Are*, and other books. Sendak also illustrated three of Jarrell's children's books (*The Bat-Poet, The Animal Family*, and *Fly by Night*) and provided a picture to accompany Jarrell's poem "Children Selecting Books in a Library" in the memorial volume *Randall Jarrell, 1914–1965*. He and Jarrell were also friends.

During the summer of 1978, I offered in San Diego a seminar on Jarrell's fantasies at the Children's Literature Institute sponsored by Point Loma College and San Diego State University. Sendak was in residence at the Institute and generously offered to come in and speak to the class about his work with Jarrell. The following is a transcript of the questions Sendak was asked and his replies.

QUESTION: How did you get to know Randall Jarrell?
SENDAK: We were introduced by the man who was his editor then at Macmillan. When the editor got a copy of *The Bat-Poet*, he wanted me to do it; [until then] I had never worked with the editor or Randall. They sent me a copy and, of course, I wanted to do it. An arrangement was made so that I could meet Jarrell. And that's how it began, on a very professional basis.

That often remains simply professional, or it turns into a friendship. In the case of Jarrell, it really did turn into a friendship, which included Mary, his wife. And it turned out that we were both opera addicts. So, he came to New York during the opera season, and we would go to the Metropolitan together and eat together and talk about books together. It gradually developed into a friendship.

And there was sort of an agreement that I would illustrate all his children's books, and if I didn't want to, I would at least have the first option, the first "no," if I didn't want to do it. But I would see it first, and that was promised me.

I had missed *The Gingerbread Rabbit*. I had regretted that but, at the same time, it wasn't the book for me to do anyway. Garth Williams is an old friend of mine and a terrific illustrator, and it seemed proper that he should do that book.

QUESTION: Did you talk over with Jarrell any of the work you did when illustrating *Fly by Night*?

SENDAK: No, we didn't discuss the book. I read the story. I thought it was the most difficult one of all. We had only a brief time together then because he was killed shortly after. He knew I felt ambivalent about it in many ways. But we never had a chance to talk about it. And then it was ten years from that time until it was published before I felt I could do it; I kept postponing it over and over again. Mary was very considerate because I knew she very much wanted to have his book published. But she understood that, one, I felt very complicated about the story and, two, I missed him so much I didn't want to do it. When a decade had passed I felt far enough away from his death to try again.

QUESTION: Which of the books do you like best?

SENDAK: Of the three, as a work, my personal favorite is *The Animal Family*. Of the three, I think the best constructed and artistically controlled is *The Bat-Poet*. And, in terms of my pictures, my favorite is *Fly by Night*. So, my likes really cover all three.

Fly by Night's pictures were really worth waiting ten years for. I couldn't do *Fly by Night* until I had done *The Juniper Tree*, the Grimm. That was the breakthrough for me in how to interpret Jarrell. I had to struggle so much with Grimm, and I felt I had succeeded. I felt brave enough to try *Fly by Night* then, and it sort of fell into place. And I know he would have liked what I'd done. Still, it was a consolation to hear from Mary after the book was published that "Randall would have loved this." I felt very good about that.

QUESTION: Is it *The Animal Family* that you said was so visual that you didn't want to illustrate it but only decorate it?

SENDAK: I didn't want to illustrate it at all. In fact, that was the only time

I got close to an argument with Jarrell because he was hurt; he thought I didn't like the book. I loved the book.

I felt he didn't need me. If you had drawn the mermaid dragging herself . . . it would have been so vulgar. Whereas, just the image of her is poetic. But you can't draw her. You couldn't draw the child. You couldn't draw the hunter. You could only draw the place where they lived. Little stage settings. I like what I did there, but the pictures are only theatrical stage settings for Randall. They're like little overtures for each chapter.

More than that, the shape and the design of the book is very square. I know how desperately Randall needed a family. That's the whole message of everything he wrote—this incredible *need* for a family—and so, I wanted to give him a fat, square, little book. And if you'll notice, the type is in the middle of the page with a great "island" of white space around it. That's for coziness and hugging. So, you have these little pieces of type, big margins, and thick boards—we got triple thick boards for the binding—so it's almost like a house, like opening a door instead of a book. You see, I wanted to illustrate it not just with those opening pictures, but with the whole shape, smell, and design of the book. It would look like his little family. It would be a gift for Randall—his home, finally, inside that book.

I love that book. In terms of illustrating a book without illustrating it, that's a very good example.

QUESTION: Was it very different illustrating *Fly by Night* because so much of it is about a dream?
SENDAK: That's the difference between *The Animal Family* where I felt I was intruding into Randall's private world and *Fly by Night* where I felt I shared that particular world. His particular longing in that book rang a bell in my own life; I had a similar longing. I was able to tie myself into that very easily. It has nothing to do with the names, to tell you the truth; it had to do with the deep level of fantasy in that book and what he was looking for. I happened to be looking for the same thing. And we meshed better on that book—after I knew what it was; it took me a long time to understand it. But *Fly by Night* is my book as much as it is Randall's, while *The Animal Family* is his book. That's how I feel.

QUESTION: Why do you feel that the pictures and the text worked so well together in *Fly by Night*?
SENDAK: When I discovered what it was that was so personal to me, I felt

I joined him almost in spirit in the book. What it was simply . . . what is *Fly by Night* all about? Randall—without going into the details, because I don't think I have a right to—had a very unhappy childhood, and what, perhaps, he missed most in the whole world was a mother. In most of the things, including *The Animal Family* and so much of the poetry, there is this painful longing for a mother. *Fly by Night* being, oddly, one of the last things he wrote, is like an open declaration of his need for a mother—the whole poem about the owl and the babies, David being alone and coming back to his mother in the end.

I had lost my mother a few years before the Jarrell book, and I had difficulties with my mother. This book was a way of resolving many personal issues via his issues. See what I mean? It was Mother that we were both talking about in that particular book. And I was able to talk about my mother through his mother; I was also able to substitute my mother for his mother. Pictorially in the book, my mother is there all the time. She is on the cover of the book; that's taken from a photograph of my mother in her wedding gown. In the double-page spread that's my mother on the far right as a young girl in Europe, a shepherdess. And in the middle of the book is my mother holding me under a tree; she's overweight having borne three children. On either side are two lambs; one is my brother and one is my sister.

The book was an *homage* to my mother. It was a farewell to my mother, just as it was for Jarrell. So, it was a farewell to Randall, a farewell to my mother, and a farewell to child dreams that don't come true.

QUESTION: Do you think that you might also have been attracted to the story because of a minor theme—the sister? In your interview with Jonathan Cott you speak of the first book you wrote about your sister, and Cott links it with the Grimms' "Brother and Sister." There is something like that in "The Owl's Bedtime Story" and in the mermaid.
SENDAK: The sister theme floods through a lot of my things. The sister theme became my book after *Fly by Night*; the picture book I am working on now is an exploration of the sister theme. The beauty of all this is that these pressing pains, needs, or whatever you call them, all find outlet graphically either in someone else's book like Jarrell's, or in my own books. And of course I'll talk about them endlessly until I die because these are the issues of your life and the resolutions you are trying to find to these things.

QUESTION: Can you tell me something about the picture you did for this book [*Randall Jarrell, 1914–1965*]?

SENDAK: After he died that book was published, and everyone who contributed to that book did so without payment. It was my present for him.

QUESTION: Is Jarrell the child in the picture?
SENDAK: No. That is specifically my brother. Somehow, my brother reminds me of Jarrell. There is a quality in the two men that is similar—which is why, perhaps, I was attracted to Jarrell. But when it came to doing that picture, instead of wanting a Jarrell photograph, I wanted a picture of my brother as a little boy.

QUESTION: Is there some symbolism in the owl?
SENDAK: There are many things in it, but I don't want to get into that. You can make it up yourself. Your interpretations are just as valid as mine.

QUESTION: But why the owl and the cat? Is that from *Fly by Night*?
SENDAK: Well, there's always owls and cats. Animals are threatening or loving or wise. You can decide which one is what for you.

QUESTION: It's just that the cat . . .
SENDAK: Oh, the cats were special to the Jarrells because they loved cats very much. Cats appeared often because he had one he was just nuts about. He wasn't a dog person. I'm a dog person, and he was a cat person.

QUESTION: I noticed a lot of pairing in the double-page picture in *Fly by Night*. Is that the desire for companionship?
SENDAK: It's actually a vision, that picture, which is both threatening and—the owl is a threatening bird but also a loving bird. And what I think I'm saying is that's what mothers are.

Because he didn't have a *pair* of parents, I gave Randall one in this vision.

QUESTION: Were you listening to any particular music when you did *Fly by Night*?
SENDAK: Probably Mozart. I really can't remember. But Mozart has been a kind of ambience or background for all the work I've been doing for about two years now. I don't listen to anyone else. No Wagner. I'll get back to those things, but during a time when I'm working on a specific theme and feeling I can't be interrupted with any other sound. Even composers I love. Even someone as close as Haydn is disruptive to me now. I don't mind living with Mozart. He's a great friend.

QUESTION: How do you answer people who ask why David is naked?
SENDAK: Because he is dreaming. Because between him and the dream there can be no clothing. It's the most personal thing that's happening to him. You don't want him dressed when something that personal is happening.

My conception of personal experience meaning exposure—of your soul but also literally of your body—really stems from my love for William Blake and the *Songs of Innocence and Experience* where people are naked. They're not naked to titillate people; they're naked because they are yielding up their most personal moment when they give themselves up to their dream or their fantasy or their wish. To have David in pj's or Fruit-of-the-Loom shorts while he's having this . . . it would have been horrible. He had to be only David.

A Conversation with Maurice Sendak and Dr. Seuss

Glenn Edward Sadler / 1982

From *Teaching Children's Literature: Issues, Pedagogy, Resources*, edited by Glenn Edward Sadler. 1992. Reprinted with permission of Glenn Edward Sadler. Copyright © Glenn Edward Sadler. All rights reserved.

"If a child doesn't like a book, throw it away. Children don't give a damn about awards; why should they? We should let children choose their own books. What they don't like, they will toss aside. What disturbs them too much, they will not look at; and if they look at the wrong book, it isn't going to do them that much damage. We treat children in a very peculiar way, I think; we don't treat them like the strong creatures they really are."
—Maurice Sendak

"Children are tough critics. You can't kid kids. They have a relentless sense of logic. If you create a character who is supposed to be stingy, say, and you suddenly make him do something that indicates some other dominant characteristic, jealousy perhaps, or a violent temper, the kids know instantly that you're violating the law of simplicity and consistency. They also know if you begin to condescend or write down to them. That's been the trouble with children's books and elementary textbooks for years—this 'now my little man' approach. The kids don't like it; why should they? The old tellers of fantastic fairy tales, Grimm and Andersen, never talked down to their audience."
—Dr. Seuss

Maurice Sendak and Dr. Seuss share a respect for the integrity of the child and the child reader. Of all the comments made at the public interview at the San Diego Museum of Art in Balboa Park in 1982, this was the most significant fact that repeatedly emerged. Although differing in style, Sendak and Geisel share more than talent. Each believes in the intelligence of children, that one cannot talk down to an audience. "Children are tough critics. You can't kid kids," Geisel affirms.

To hear these "two lions" (as one reviewer designated them) of children's literature together in a public interview is something I had long dreamed of happening. It all began with a visit to Sendak's art studio in New York City in 1970 (the year *In the Night Kitchen* was published). I recall dashing down with him to a local deli to get a sandwich as we exchanged quips on what some librarians would think when they saw the nudity of Mickey, whose name came from Mickey Mouse. I had come to talk with him about George MacDonald (the subject of my doctoral dissertation) and was fully prepared to flood him with questions: Why had MacDonald's stories had such an influence on him? And what was the connection between his great admiration for Mickey Mouse and MacDonald (a question to which I would still like to get an answer)? Through the years our friendship grew as we talked of the condescending attitude some academics and critics have toward writers for children.

It was while teaching at the University of California, San Diego, that I decided to try to get Sendak and Seuss together. I had suggested the meeting to Sendak, and he agreed. Getting to see Ted Geisel was another matter. For years he had remained a recluse in his La Jolla tower-parapet home overlooking the Pacific Ocean. The day I visited him he was doing a possible sequel to *The Cat in the Hat*, the publication of which, in 1957, was a turning point in his career as "Dr. Seuss." We talked about the neighbors who were building a structure that would obscure his view and how he was wishing for its demise. On a subsequent visit, after the interview took place, we talked of my plans possibly to leave San Diego and take a position in Bloomsburg. Geisel recalled visiting Wilkes-Barre many years ago, and we discussed how the town, whose name amused him, was founded. It was on my first visit in 1981, however, that I approached Geisel with the idea of meeting Sendak in a publish question-answer interview. To my delight and surprise, he agreed.

There were, of course, all the arrangements that followed: getting adequate funding and space for the interview and deciding when and how the event should take place. It was decided between the San Diego Museum of Art and the Programs for Extended Studies at the University of California, San Diego, that it should be a jointly sponsored event. The university would offer one unit credit and charge a fee, and the museum would have an exhibit of Sendak's art; Seuss's work would be on display in the library at the university.

It is difficult now to recall all the problems that kept jumping out of the hat, but I do remember the tremendous excitement and anticipation that mounted as the date for the event neared. Calls came from all the major newspapers, which gave the event front page coverage, and there was an endless stream of fans, all wanting a personal interview and their books autographed. (I did manage to arrange a private lunch for Sendak and Seuss.)

Finally, the evening of Wednesday, 8 December 1982, arrived. There was a sellout crowd of over five hundred at the Copley Auditorium of the San Diego Museum of Art. Sendak and Seuss, wired for sound, sat on the brightly lit stage. My decades-old dream of seeing these two men sitting together in a public exchange was to become a reality.

From the beginning, the interview was lighthearted, filled with laughter and repartees. The audience wrote questions that were given to two question-readers at either side of the auditorium. As coordinator, I repeated the questions asked alternately by the monitors. There were thirty-five selected questions in all.

Although the edited (by Sendak and Seuss) selection of questions here printed is representative, it is not inclusive. Many amusing comments are missing. One I recall—here omitted—was made by Sendak as he told of an autographing experience. Commenting on the parents' egocentricity in wanting to have their child's book autographed, Sendak noted that it is the parents' "presumption that children *like* to have their books autographed." Turning to Geisel, Sendak continued: "How many times has this happened to you, when you get a whole line of fatigued children who have been waiting for what? To come and see this nasty old man—what has he got to do with the pleasure they get out of books? The one extraordinary circumstance (I recall) was a little boy who had waited a very long time, was enraged, and here is his mother carrying on about this being the man that wrote your *favorite book*. He couldn't care less. He couldn't even make the association. The boy loved the book, but who was I? And then the book was handed to me. I began to autograph it. Suddenly the boy grabs the book, pulls it back, and screams: 'Don't crap up my book!' He probably had been taught at home never to write in a book, and here he is publicly taken to a place by his mother where a total stranger is trying to write in *his* book."

Dr. Seuss recalled, "The greatest autographing experience I ever had was in Detroit, in one of the Northlands, where one afternoon, two thousand mothers dragged two thousand children in for autographing. I got pretty conceited by the end of the day: I thought, look at all the people I'm dragging in. The next day I went to Boston, and only one child showed up, and he was looking for the toilet."

It was indeed an evening of jovial exchange. The audience applauded heartily as these men relived events from their own childhood and adolescence, which are celebrated in their books. Candidly, the unspoken laws of writing for children and young adults were expressed.

Law number 1: Try to find some way to outwit the adults in the story. For example, Max (*Where the Wild Things Are*) must go to bed without his supper and accept his punishment. But this does not mean that he cannot dream himself away from Adultland to the place where the wild things live: he can and does escape adult authority. Or take, for example, the young hero in Seuss's *I Am Not Going to Get Up Today!* who defies all the pleasurable incitements of the child and the adult world and who proves conclusively in the end that the child can win ("I guess he really means it").

Law number 2: Always keep the child reader guessing as to the outcome of the story. Finding the "hook" (Seuss's word) at the end of each page is, he claims, the secret. "Keep the child turning the pages," he explains. "The story has to develop clearly and logically with a valid problem and a valid solution. The characters, no matter how weird, have to be vivid and believable and consistent."

Law number 3: Never explain away the fantastic parts of the story. Perhaps Sendak's and Seuss's greatest legacy in literature for children—as indicated by the comments made during the interview—is their honest approach to what it means to be a child or an adolescent. One does not find in their stories and illustrations the modern trend toward "glitzy" (Sendak's work) illustrations that merely decorate the page. The fantastic in their stories remains the driving force that penetrates commonplace experiences. Commenting on his seventy-eighth Christmas, Dr. Seuss notes, with a chortle, "I hope Dick and Jane have a very sparse Christmas, and the Grinch steals all their toys." Seuss is proudest of the fact "that I had something to do with getting rid of Dick and Jane."

Of all the statements made during the interview, I think the most significant was Sendak's insistence on the influence of his own childhood on his work and, in contrast, Seuss's claim that his adolescence, not his childhood, affected him most. It is a difference of viewpoint that an adult senses when reading both writers' books. There is, especially in Sendak's illustrations, the subconscious feeling that the author is exploring, perhaps even at times exploiting, the dark fears and frustrations of childhood (the fear of the dark and nighttime is one of Sendak's favorites). As he often has remarked, Sendak *knows* what it is like to be a child because he has been one and has never forgotten the feelings of his own childhood. As in the work of Hans Christian Andersen, such an awareness of the dark side of childhood emotions is at the heart of Sendak's genius.

In sharp contrast is Ted Geisel's rejuvenating understanding of the adolescent mind. It is as if, in a Dr. Seuss story, the young adult or the child reader has just met a secret buddy with whom he or she can play. More than wacky characters, convoluted logic, or even silly vocabulary, for the teen reader there is the refuge of words in Seuss's books. One discovers the teenage game of developing an in-language that leaves the adults totally out of the picture. Such comradeship between reader and author through the security of words is Dr. Seuss's greatest achievement.

There probably never again will be two geniuses like Maurice Sendak and Dr. Seuss. Coming from different worlds and points in time (Sendak is now sixty-three and Seuss is eighty-one), they nevertheless share a high regard for readers of all ages, although their modes of writing are quite different. "None of my books," says Maurice Sendak, "come about through ideas or by thinking of a particular subject and claiming, 'Gee, that's terrific. I'll just put it down.' They never happen quite that way. They well up just as dreams come to us at night; feelings come to me, so I build a kind of house around them, the story; and the painting of the house is the picture making. Essentially, however, it's a dream or fantasy."

For Ted Geisel, creating a story is quite a different matter. "Now some writers, I am told," replies Seuss, "really do dream their stories. They just crawl into bed, they say, and along about four o'clock in the morning, a story idea comes floating into their heads. Then all they have to do when they wake up is write it down, but I never had any luck with my dreams."

Whether or not writing a children's story is a process of creative dreaming, Sendak and Seuss would agree that to enter the dream world of the child or young adult reader is essential. I recall vividly Sendak pointing this out to me after the interview, as we walked along the midnight crashing surf of Point Loma, San Diego, while the fairytale-like lights of La Jolla peninsula twinkled in the distance. We talked of many things. But I will never forget Sendak saying that writing or illustrating a children's book (or any book) is like giving the reader the present of, in Hans Christian Andersen's words, "the whole world—and a pair of skates." Maurice Sendak and Dr. Seuss have done just that.

Interviewer: How do you get your ideas for books?

Seuss: This is the most asked question of any successful author. Most authors will not disclose their source for fear that other, less successful authors will chisel in on their territory. However, I am willing to take a chance. I get all my ideas in Switzerland near the Furka Pass. There is a little town called Gletch, and two thousand feet up above Gletch there is a smaller hamlet called Uber Gletch. I go there on the fourth of August every summer to get my cuckoo clock repaired. While the cuckoo is in the hospital, I wander around and talk to the people in the streets. They are very strange people, and I get my ideas from them.

Interviewer: Mr. Sendak, I know a four year old who is afraid of your books. Should she be encouraged to work through those feelings and read the books aloud with us?

Sendak: I think you should leave her alone. I mean there's absolutely no reason why, if the child is frightened, that you would frighten the child still further by trying to make her read the book. Obviously this is a child with a problem. But taking that into consideration, I would not torment the child.

Interviewer: Mr. Sendak, were you Pierre as a child?

Sendak: No, I was never Pierre at any point in my life. Perhaps I harbored his thoughts, but I would not have dared speak to my parents in such a way. That's why I wrote the book.

Interviewer: Dr. Seuss, how do you handle the nonsense words in translation?

Seuss: The books have been translated into about fifteen foreign languages. I have no idea how they handled it in the Japanese. Oddly enough, the Germanic and Nordic languages—German, Norwegian, Swedish, Danish—are much more successful for translating the nonsense words than the Romance languages are. Why that is, I don't know. The Germans will take a name like Bartholomew Cubbins and turn it into Bartel Lugepros, which I think is a very beautiful approximation.

Interviewer: Mr. Sendak, when you illustrate books for other authors, do you become closely involved with them? Whom do you admire most, and how have they influenced your work?

Sendak: Well, I've worked with many, many writers. A good many of them don't want to be involved in the illustration process. They have written the book, the illustrator gets it, and that's the end of the relationship. That is, of course, the least interesting way to work. But I've had some half dozen or so writers—such as Randall Jarrell, Ruth Krauss, and Isaac Singer—who were intensely involved with the business of illustrating the book. The work is much better for that involvement. There's the joy of collaboration. One would assume that the writer would want to be involved because, after all, it is primarily his book. I'm just there to adorn and decorate.

Interviewer: How would you motivate the child who does not like to read?
Seuss: That is the job of the mother, I think. The motivation of the child is not Maurice's or my responsibility. It falls to the school and the parents. All we can do is create books and hope that someone steers them into children's hands.
Sendak: I think Ted is right. We're often confused with being sociologists and psychologists and teachers and parents. We're not. Primarily we are artists. We cannot urge children to read books. I don't know how one goes about doing that.

Interviewer: Mr. Sendak, do you ever draw for your own diversions? What do you like to draw?
Sendak: Occasionally portraits of friends, which I never show except to the people who posed. Mostly I draw to music as an imagination exercise. I put some favorite piece on the record player. I start with my hand at the top of the paper, and the whole point of the exercise is to finish that page by the end of the first movement. Needless to say, you get very few good drawings. It is a kind of pleasure drawing I do for myself for the most part.

Interviewer: Have the responses of critics made it easier or more difficult for you to accomplish the task of achieving your goals?
Sendak: It's made no difference whatsoever, alas. It just causes irritation and migraine. If one could learn something from criticism, it would be a marvelous thing. Reading criticism has been a grave disappointment in terms of what one doesn't learn. The process is hurtful for the most part, and in a sense the good reviews are no better than the bad because they don't tell you anything.
Seuss: I think about the only positive thing is that a good review sells more books than a bad review.
Sendak: It makes you more cheerful that morning.
Seuss: It wakes you up.

Sendak: Your friends who are waiting for you to get the bad review don't call you up to commiserate with you.

Seuss: And you always agree with the good reviews.

Sendak: You always agree with them. That person has hope for a long life.

Interviewer: Do you think there will still be a place for the traditional fairytale in twenty years?

Seuss: I would like to see it come back, but I don't think the average child is going to fall for it. No, I miss it, don't you?

Sendak: Well, there's almost not a place right now for the old-fashioned fairytale or fantasy. It's hard to imagine where children's literature is going; it's gotten so slippery and glitzy at this point. One almost feels that children's books are going to slide off the face of the earth. The old-fashioned fairytale at this point, I think, has already slid off. It is not considered seriously. It's already out of date, and most fairytales, when they are done, are watered down considerably. So we are not getting the real thing.

Interviewer: Do your characters live with you all the time?

Sendak: Well, I hope not. I think we would all be in the madhouse at this point. Is that true for you?

Seuss: Yes, that's so.

Sendak: We rid ourselves of these characters by writing them out of our lives.

Seuss: Yes, we expunge them.

Sendak: Then new horrors keep springing up all the time. If I ran into these people in my social life, I would flee. I think we are always being chased by these people, and we keep creating books to get rid of them.

Seuss: If I were invited to a dinner party with my characters, I wouldn't show up.

Interviewer: Would you comment on the effect of the media on children today?

Sendak: Well, it always aggravates me when people get colossally worked up about certain things in my books that supposedly will upset children or upset librarians or parents or teachers. But there seem to be no restrictions on what children can watch on television. Children see massacres continuously on the news—how do you control that? Books are quite controllable. The media is totally uncontrollable and vastly disgusting for the most part, and children are watching it all the time. I wonder how anybody's going to solve that problem. To make a great fuss over an odd word in a Dr. Seuss book or a naked child in a Sendak book seems so fatuously simple-minded in relation to television, where children are being poisoned.

Interviewer: Mr. Sendak, do you have a preference for writing or illustrating?

Sendak: I have a preference for writing. Writing is very difficult and gives me a great deal of pleasure, partly because it is so difficult. Illustrating is very automatic. I have a Polaroid kind of brain. I have to stem the tide of pictures. I don't get those writing images quickly; I have to struggle for them. So naturally I like writing better. When I do achieve something, it feels more victorious. I know I'm going to get illustrations if I just hang in long enough, and that's less challenging at this point in my life.

Interviewer: Dr. Seuss, was your first book, *And to Think That I Saw It on Mulberry Street*, rejected by many publishers before it was accepted?

Seuss: Twenty-seven and twenty-nine, I forget which. The excuse I got for all those rejections was that there was nothing on the market quite like it, so they didn't know whether it would sell.

Sendak: Publishers are always nervous about original work. They are worried about financial aspects, which corrupt their consideration of a new work. When *Wild Things* came out, there was a concern about the effects of this book on the public. It was a natural nervousness about publishing an odd book.

Interviewer: Would each of you comment on how much your own early childhood has influenced your work?

Seuss: Not to a very great extent. I think my aberrations started when I got out of early childhood. My father, however, in my early childhood, did, among other things, run a zoo, and I used to play with the baby lions and the antelope and a few other things of that sort. Generally speaking, I don't think my childhood influenced my work. But I know Maurice's did.

Sendak: I have profited mightily from my early childhood.

Seuss: I think I skipped my childhood.

Sendak: I skipped my adolescence. Total amnesia.

Seuss: Well, I used my adolescence.

Sendak: Isn't that interesting, because you get your inspiration from young manhood, and I go all the way back to the crib days for mine.

Interviewer: Mr. Sendak, how did you parents feel when you told them you wanted to be a book illustrator?

Sendak: They were relieved. They had no idea that I could do anything. I did so badly in school. I have a very brilliant sister who skipped grades. I hated her. I had a brother who was dutiful and serious, so I hated him, too. But I could draw, which seemed to be my salvation. In fact, when I could earn a living from that, my father was tearfully content.

Interviewer: Do your ideas for books spring forth from free drawing you might be doing, and do you have a direction for your books?

Sendak: There is a vague sense of a direction; there is no formulated plot. There are certain elements I want to get into the book, and I just dive off and don't know if there's any water in the pond. I find a kind of pleasure in that process. With perseverance I will gradually evolve a book. Creating is a kind of groping-in-the-dark procedure. Yet, when the book is finished, it should have all those elements that satisfy some part of me.

Seuss: Mine always start as a doodle. I may doodle a couple of animals. If they bite each other, it's going to be a good book. If you doodle enough, the characters begin to take over themselves—after a year and a half or so.

Sendak: Sometimes that happens quite accidentally. In 1969, I was doing a Mother Goose book, and I found that I was picking out poems that had to do with food, like bread and milk. It seemed a peculiar obsessive interest: "Little Jumping Joan, / She ate so much, / She went bananas." I finally decided that under the guise of preparing a Mother Goose, my own book was being written. It ended up being called *In the Night Kitchen*, and I even stole one of the verses. "I see the moon, and the moon sees me" became "I'm not the milk and the milk's not me." So my homage to the original project was in that book. But I had no knowledge that my book was sneaking in.

Seuss: Sometimes you have luck when you are doodling. I did one day when I was drawing some trees. Then I began drawing elephants. I had a window that was open, and the wind blew the elephant on top of a tree. I looked at it and said, "What do you suppose that elephant is doing there?" The answer was: "He is hatching an egg." Then all I had to do was write a book about it. I have left that window open ever since, but it's never happened again.

Interviewer: Dr. Seuss, I understand that much of your work contains actual figures from history and some political commentary. Could you identify these figures?

Seuss: Not in their actual form. Yertle the Turtle is Adolf Hitler. In *Yertle*, the turtle Mack was on the bottom of the pile until he solved the problem by burping. It makes me realize how much children's book publishing has changed to recall that they had a meeting at Random House to see whether I could use the word *burp*, and that was in the late 1950s. The other historical characters, I don't know about.

Interviewer: How do you shut out the reality of the world when you're creating your books? Do nuclear weapons, cancer, unemployment, and pollution affect you?

Sendak: Well, there is no way you can shut out those facts unless you're insane. Perhaps they permeate the work and color it in some particular way, but there is no magic way you can shut the door on all these things. We don't work in "airy fairy land" when we're doing books for children. We are dealing with real life, even though we're using forms that are nonsensical or funny or bizarre. In fact, real life should be in the book. It has to permeate the work. I live in this world.

Seuss: They're all there, but we look at them through the wrong end of the telescope. We change them in that way.

Interviewer: I encountered several discourses concerned with the underlying psychological meanings of your books, Mr. Sendak. How do you feel about that? It doesn't sound like you had those things in mind when you were writing your books.

Sendak: Well, I didn't. Of course, it's always fun to read about them. There are so many variations, some of them may be quite accurate; I don't know. As an artist you cannot consciously construct a book psychologically because it would not be a work of art. But such interpretations are fun to read.

Interviewer: As a closing note, I'd like to leave you with a little quote, something to take with you:

> Ninety-nine zillion,
> Nine trillion and two
> Creatures are sleeping!
> So . . .
> How about you?

Ted Geisel died 24 September 1991.

Maurice Sendak Q & A

Hank Nuwer / 1984

From the *South Carolina Review*, 16.2, 1984, pp. 81–97. Reprinted with permission.

Life's grim realities serve as creative fodder for Brooklyn-born Maurice Sendak, America's best-known writer/illustrator of children's books, who more recently has begun designing sets for England's Glyndebourne Opera House and the New York City Opera. The haunting worries of childhood become major themes in his best-known works, *Where the Wild Things Are*, *Outside Over There*, and *In the Night Kitchen*.

Sendak is interviewed on a muggy August afternoon at his rural Connecticut home, a substantial structure with black nineteenth-century wooden hearse shutters gracing the windows. The house is ornamented with vintage Mickey Mouse images, plush toy representations of characters from his own pages, and enough books to give a man not only solace, but comfort.

The artist seems irritable and phlegmatic at first meeting, no doubt a reaction to finding his workspace invaded by an interviewer. Later, hunched over a drawing board, however, he warms when conversation embraces literary and artistic concerns. He proves a more than cordial host ultimately; dispensing personal insights and philosophies the way others might serve refreshments.

NUWER: Now that you are a financial success, why do you still work?
SENDAK: I essentially work to please myself. What other reason can there be when there's nothing to prove anymore? But you also have to have high standards. Just to please yourself isn't sufficient.

NUWER: Are you careful to send out only your best work?
SENDAK: I'm very cautious. You have to be moral and ethical and worry about all that crap. If you're in vogue or the mode at a particular time, people will take anything of yours, unfortunately. You're the one who has to be

discreet and moral—and, as a matter of fact, I am. I don't want to sound like Pollyanna John Ethical, but I believe if you despoil yourself—if you use yourself for the wrong reason—then whatever's been working for you is going to go bad. Maybe it's a childish fantasy, maybe it's genuine, but I think there is some intricately balanced "something" within you that will only maintain itself if you keep yourself clean. I don't believe in giving in to bad things, and I'm as tempted by bad things as anybody.

NUWER: Is this a good time for you?
SENDAK: It's a good time; it's an astonishing good time.

NUWER: How do you control vipers encroaching upon your territory?
SENDAK: If you're in a strong position you can control it. I'm in a strong position right now. I suppose the minute I step down the rung I lose that power; that's how it goes. My artistry has given me this power personally, but in the world that power comes from success: how many books you sell, what your statistics are, your stature. There can be many vipers around, and there are; nevertheless, they will let me do what I want because I've proven myself. I will use my power to make everything better, because until you lose that power—which you will, eventually—that's all you can do with power. I don't know what else power means; tell me if you know. It means you can force the books to look better, force the printer, force the binder. Insist! Insist until they do it even if they hate your guts. "Ah, right," they'll say, "he's popular; he sells."

NUWER: Do you feel cynical?
SENDAK: I don't feel cynical, just practical. You can't expect people to know what you do or understand what you do. Most of them admire you because you've made it. You use that to further your own aesthetic principles. You hope that, given time, the book will mean more to them.

NUWER: Is writing more laborious than drawing?
SENDAK: Not more laborious, more difficult, and in a sense more interesting than drawing because it is more difficult. Drawing for me is automatic. I feel like a walking Polaroid camera. I take it so for granted that I underrate it.

NUWER: How do you conjure up ideas for your tales?
SENDAK: I don't get a great many ideas. I don't work in terms of plot like

other writers do. Something else must turn me on. Like I was listening to a tape of a never-before-translated play by Heinrich von Kleist broadcast on BBC that some friends from England sent me. That kind of thing stimulates me tremendously, tremendously, and I want to write. I want to write just like *he* wrote: in this case, where a dream has this incredible penetrating action, where a dream becomes insanity. It obviously touches something that is dormant in me that is totally unconscious. It's like throwing a picture up to the top of my brain where it triggers consciousness; then I begin to write.

NUWER: Could you talk about your friendship with poet Marianne Moore?
SENDAK: Marianne Moore was a friend in her last years. She lived on the same street that I lived in the Village [Greenwich], just two houses down. She was old then. I'd see her in grocery stores, and I'd go bonkers. There was that famous hat, the cape, *everything!* I didn't know what to do. I can't [sic] go up to her and say, "Oh you're Marianne Moore, right?" *Big deal!* But *then* I go this phone call from a woman and she said, "This is Marianne Moore." I didn't say anything, so she said, "Are you the man who wrote *Pierre*?" I said, "Yes," and she said, "I think that's *so* devilishly clever: Pierre, Pierre! I don't care. Ha, ha, ha, ha!"

NUWER: What was your reaction?
SENDAK: I was very cool because I did not, for one minute, believe this was Marianne Moore. I said some snotty thing like "Real cute, *whoever* you are!" I put it aside as one of my asinine friends doing this to me who knew I was dying to meet her. Finally, I went up to her after many months in the Jefferson Market. I said to her, "*You* are Marianne Moore." Then I said who I am and she answered, "Yes, you're that rude man on the telephone!" It *had* been her, and we became friends.

NUWER: What was your friendship like?
SENDAK: Shortly after I met her, she had the first of many strokes that finally killed her. I became the kind of friend who came up and read to her. From her I learned a lot about publishing, and the better things, too. We had a different relationship than if we had met sooner on a professional basis. I became a visiting pal who just sat and spent time with her. Amazingly few people did—only a few close friends—and I saw her right up to the time she died. I remember her apartment all a-clutter with this picture of Puss 'n' Boots, but she wanted him—oh, what's the word—"*tricky*." "Don't make him nice," she said. "Make him *tricky*." So I made her a *very* tricky Puss 'n' Boots

all dressed up in a sort of Dumas costume with a string of rats on his shoulder. She loved it and propped it up on the side of her bed. It was nice, but it was sad . . . sad. But she never complained. She was a tough woman—with a sour tongue, but funny, never bitchy, and always clever. I love gossip, but only a few people do it well. She was one of them.

NUWER: Did you like growing up?

SENDAK: No. I didn't like growing up. I mean the process. I hated school, hated the confinement of city street life. I remember nice things, but they mostly had to do with going to the movies.

Speaking for myself, I felt thirty very badly, and I felt forty very badly, but I was a very unhappy young man. My twenties were disastrous, my thirties were monotonous and unproductive to a large degree, and at thirty-nine I was really unhealthy and both my parents were dying. It was a time when all that stuff that has to happen to you happens to you finally. So I have very bad, negative feelings about that time of my life. To me, this is the best time. I've stopped counting years. I don't care anymore—I really don't—about how old I am.

Also I'm very lucky because I've been successful. I take for granted a certain amount of success that a lot of people in their fifties maybe don't have, and then they get paralyzed by that fact. I've contributed, I've done, and it's valuable. I know that must contribute to my own sense of well-being, at least mentally. But also I feel a kind of youthfulness, which I was incapable of feeling then, and maybe which no young person feels. Maybe it's all American bullshit which says you *have* to feel this way at twenty, this way at thirty, and so on. I see young people who are in a total state of misery about being young, while I really feel better than I've ever felt. Which doesn't mean I don't suffer from my depressions and my anxiety attacks. I do. For most of my life, I have been a notoriously unhappy man. And I'm not now.

NUWER: How do you feel about death?

SENDAK: I can look now at Erda's—my dog's—dying, and say, now that is something that is going to happen. They're all going to die; I'm going to die. I can't explain, but there's some kind of amalgamation that has occurred which didn't occur when I was young, but it's had its effect on me. Maybe it is a middle-aged man's thing—but its effect is to make me feel the youth now that I didn't feel then. I feel much more vigorous and curious and interested and even jovial about things than I ever before felt in my life. So what does that say about age? I don't know.

NUWER: You've built your own world here. You seem to have done everything worth doing. You're now designing opera sets.

SENDAK: Yep, it's done, and yet at the same time I have a sense that it can be *undone.* That I can give it up without that extraordinary fear of pain and loss that it would have once meant to me.

I've gone into another career in my early fifties. I'll go back to books, of course, but, in fact, I have started a new career. I didn't think, "Oh, major step, mid-life." I didn't think of all those words that annoy me so much. The urge to *do* comes not from a sense of maturity; it comes out of a sense of youthfulness. And why not? What am I saving it for? If you're going to try it, try it. You're not afraid of failing; you've failed before. You've gotten bad criticism that you hated, but you're not afraid of it. It's not mortal, fatal.

That's what it is. It's imagining what young people are supposed to feel that I'm only feeling now. It's almost a devil-may-care feeling. Despite what you see here, the load, this house and possessions and position and all that. There is that feeling, and I'm delighted with it. Really. Being Jewish, I used to dread having good feelings, because that's when Jehovah really gives it to you. I don't feel that, either, because I don't worry about Him anymore.

NUWER: Do you miss the human contact you had while teaching?

SENDAK: I taught for a long time in New York, and I love teaching. I love having young people around. I've never had children; I'm never going to have children. The students became my ersatz kids. Watching them, criticizing them, and loving them, they become my family. Some of them are enormously gifted, and I am devoted to doing whatever I can to further their careers—in the correct sense, not so that they clamber up the ladder to success, but that they cultivate what I hope they agree are the proper things in them that make them unique as artists so they don't get fucked up or corrupt or bored along the way. That's all.

NUWER: Do you ever see yourself retiring in this life?

SENDAK: Yeah. But I would like to retire in a very particular way. In the spring I was reading Proust's *Remembrance of Things Past.* I tried it before, and I couldn't make it. But with the new translation, I'm going to make it this time. But what really prompted me to read Proust was not Proust but Rousseau. I was reading his *Confessions.*

Certain books, I've always felt, were too hard to read—it's as though I'm always ten years old. There are certain grown-up books that I can't read no matter how old I get because I feel like I'm ten.

There's a wonderful chapter by Rousseau, which, by sheer coincidence, he wrote when he was fifty-three years old. He said he wants to retire, but [paraphrasing] let me explain to you what retirement is. I would like to retire by becoming a child but not in a sentimental sense. You start things and you do them for as long as they entertain you, and to be completed, and then you do something else: a sequence of interests, none of which have to be completed, to be published, to be announced, to be exhibited, to be performed, nothing. Just the pleasure of doing it. He equated it to the frenetic interest that a six year old has. It excited me. What a lovely concept of retirement. He saw himself as a child again in a vital way being free from the adult burdens of completing your work and getting it in on time. He said, your career, et cetera—fuck all that.

NUWER: People need titles—possessions and titles. And titles seem meaningless.

SENDAK: Titles are totally meaningless. But at the same time, sometimes you have to stick with something until finally . . . I mean, I can only reach the point where I could do a book like *Outside Over There* without having pedantically nailed in all the years previous to it. And I guess everybody's life is different. You may perfectly be able and best be able to express yourself by nailing in a lot of years doing a particular thing. There's no way I could. I had to be established to be free enough to say things I couldn't when I was young. It's interesting. Everybody's freedom is different.

My students got worried when they were in their twenties about what they should do with their careers. What Thoreau said was perfectly true: You have no right even thinking about what you should do until you're in your thirties. Only then are you reasonable enough to preserve your freedom; you're not reasonable in your twenties. His own measure of life was to do exactly what he pleased. I've never been able to live up to the things in him that I justly admire such as it is just as important to sit outside on your porch and stare as it is to read an important book or to write an important paper. I believe that, but I can't do it. That leisure, which I'm totally incapable of having, of allowing—just doing nothing—is sonorous with the universe. It's so compelling, useful, and healthy. I've tried, but my life has been so much the worker and that I find it very hard. I believe it, as I read these people, but I don't know how to do it.

NUWER: Do you think that children like to deal directly with the idea of dying and death?

SENDAK: I don't think they can *like* it. But I think if it's appropriate to whatever's out here—such as someone dying in your family—to me it's immeasurably more healthy to be direct and honest with them. Children are very pragmatic creatures. Some friends of mine are getting divorced, and they're upset about it. Long, good marriage. They are concerned about their child—how's he going to take it? And the father said the first thing that the child wanted to know is would he still be going to the ball game next week? And who would be giving him his allowance? They seem like unfeeling questions. But if you know children, you know that the effect of what's happening is sinking in deeply, but he's asking the prosaic things, because children have to take care of themselves. He has to know because he can't go by himself. And I think it's that quality that deceives people into thinking children don't comprehend these major things. An event such as this stuns the imagination, and the only things they can come up with quickly are the everyday things.

NUWER: Have you talked with children about any of the drawings in your last book, *Outside Over There*, for their reaction to the goblins?
SENDAK: No. I don't go out of my way to.

NUWER: What *is* a Maurice Sendak?
SENDAK: A determination, probably, in some way to uncover or find out as much of myself that is me and that has been me from childhood, and find out as much as possible before I die. To grow spiritually as a person, creatively as an artist, because spiritual and creative merge into one which is useful. I spend most of my time trying to figure myself out, though no longer for vainglorious reasons, but for aesthetic reasons. I just want to know.

Art is an exploration of yourself. If it's good art, then it's also an exploration for other people. If it's poor art, you're just playing, and you haven't added to that work that makes it meaningful for other people. Art becomes the expression, the metaphor for a lot of internal musings.

Outside Over There is a wonderful book, though it's vainglorious, maybe, to say that, but I know its intense, internal musings that have preoccupied me for years also affect other people. All that means is that what affects me affects everybody. We're all in the same boat. Artists somehow think more about the boat they're in and can express it better than most people can.

NUWER: Adults also react very strongly to your work, in an emotional sense, and in an intellectual sense.

SENDAK: I never consciously set out to do books just for children; I'm out to do books that express myself. I'm no longer a child, so I have to express things that belong to grown-up people. If you find it in there, it should be in there. There are books strictly for kids, such as how to make a paper airplane or how to dress a doll, but that's not my theme. My theme is living. I use a metaphor of children's imagery and the form of a children's book to express complicated, sophisticated adult feelings. I've never been able to demarcate that line which says here you're a kid and there you're a grown-up. When does that magic moment begin? I'm fifty-three and still coping with problems that were very real in my life when I was three.

There's a kind of emperor's new clothes to being a grown-up. I once dreamed that a grown-up knew everything and was smart. Well, you find out you don't know everything, and you're not smart. Only you have logic on your side, reason on your side, and experience on your side—three great aids you don't have as a child.

NUWER: Do you find the experiences of your middle years are adding to your art?
SENDAK: I'm a very late-blooming artist. Thank God. It's the one thing you hope for—that you don't dry up but rather you open up, however painfully, because there's a price you pay for opening up, no matter what the age, especially in middle age. But the achievement or the plus is that creatively you blossom. I'm reaching things that I have earned because I allowed myself the pain of looking at them. Internal things have now contributed to my store of themes and images as an artist. It was worth plunging in and taking a risk.

NUWER: Did you have a problem collaborating? Did you want to change some of those words?
SENDAK: Only when the book was poor, and when I found I was stuck with a piece of writing that was not for me, and then I had to do pictures to really almost overcome the weaknesses of the book. And that's really not the kind of work I like to do. I've been more fortunate in working with people who knew exactly what they were doing. Excellent, gifted writers. I love collaborating. I do less of it now, probably because I prefer working on my own things. And, too, there is a great dearth of original writing being done in America today. I see manuscripts all the time, but I don't see any that I want to illustrate. And I'm not going to illustrate anything at this point in my life that isn't worth doing; I don't have to. So if I do a book, it must be something that excites me and makes my life wonderful during the time I'm doing it.

And it will reflect in my work. Otherwise, it's just a book to make money, kill time.

NUWER: Does your life revolve around your art?

SENDAK: Yes. I'd say almost entirely. I was watching a television show about a monastery in Massachusetts—Trappist monks. They were talking about doubts—sometimes very startling doubts—about God, and giving rationalizations for being there, and describing the life they led, which I thought . . . somehow appealed—the simple life, the getting up, the singing, the chanting, the praying. It's not all that bad. I mean, they've given their lives to God or Jesus or whatever. But how are we so different? In the sense that we give our lives to art, which is what you have devoted yourself to. You lead the same, almost tedious and regular, life that they do. And you're just as much a monk—in a sense—as they are. But I was struck by the fact that I did, and that I was a devotional person. Whatever is religious in me I have turned to art, and this is the thing I believe in.

NUWER: May I ask what you're working on?

SENDAK: I'm working on sets and costumes for an opera, which is to be performed in Glyndebourne, which is a beautiful, gorgeous opera house in England, two hours south of London. I grew up with Glybdebourne recordings of the Mozart operas. For my generation, that was Mozart. Glyndebourne Mozart was Mozart as it should be done. And now in retrospect, even though the recordings are very dated, I'd say the performances are still some of the best the world has ever seen. So now, doing a Glyndebourne opera is very exciting. The opera I'm doing now . . . I'm sort of playing with it now, trying to make sense of it, trying to apply my illustrative brain to a libretto. Charming, but full of loopholes. Trying to build form and logic into a plot, which is rather formless and logic-less. I'm doing the storyboard here, trying to figure out the logistics on the panels and then have fun with it. But it must have form, roots—it's hard. I keep doing these drawings until I understand it and know what I want to do with it.

NUWER: So this is kind of an exercise to get to the next point?

SENDAK: Exactly. The next point is developing workable drawings, which these are not. They're just for me. But I can't do workable drawings until I have seen a sheet get to there, and move that to there, and how that works, and how that works. I've got to lay it all out. This is a very pedantic, detailed rendering of the entire actions of the opera. When I'm done with it, I'll feel secure enough to do drawings. Also, I really love doing it. I've been having fun with it. You want it to be very raunchy, because it is a raunchy opera, and I think people tend to—when they perform *Oranges*[1]—tend to move away from that. You know, sort of a puritanical attitude. A lot of the humor in the thing, a lot of the wit, depends upon one coming out and saying it's a sexy enterprise. Let's do it that way. Why should opera be so endlessly, tediously treated like some antiquated art that is totally sexless? I mean, you know, we have Tosca, and we know what Tosca does for a living. We want to have fun with this. But before we can have fun with it, we want to understand it.

NUWER: You also want to challenge audiences; it seems, in the books and with something such as this, even if they strike back.
SENDAK: But it shouldn't be done just to be bawdy.

NUWER: But that's part of the entertainment, just like in a Shakespearean play.
SENDAK: Exactly. You hear of Shakespeare, the Great Hallowed Name but, my God, how bawdy he is. How outrageous he is. He's more outrageous than we ever dared to get. And his suggestions, if you were really to examine and follow through with some of them, how just shocking! But that's Elizabethan.

NUWER: And yet today, if you go to a Shakespeare play . . .
SENDAK: That's right. And if it were suggested that that's what was meant, it would probably shock people. They would say you misinterpreted it. They refuse to admit that's what he meant.

NUWER: He was aiming for the groundlings.
SENDAK: Yes. He was a healthy man.
You always run the risk that your audience many not like what you are doing, but you don't want them to go to sleep. To me opera is one of the most beautiful forms ever invented. It's not a form to come to just because you have a subscription or because it's the thing to do. For lots of people opera is a snob form of art. For Mozart it was eighteenth-century vaudeville, it was show biz. To bring some of that element of liveliness back into the great classics not only would be a surprise, but would give pleasure to a lot of people who don't expect it to happen, on stage. A lot of people don't ever expect to enjoy themselves at the opera.

NUWER: Do you feel this outpouring of effort makes you feel healthier?
SENDAK: Yeah. If it's genuine. I'm a very scrupulous man. I'm always worried whether I'm diddling with an idea or genuinely expressing it. You can do all sorts of things if your intentions are well thought out. I worry a lot. I'm as capable of making an error as anybody else. There are works I've done that I would rather not have done. But you have to take that risk. You can't always be right.

NUWER: How did you find this place?
SENDAK: I literally stumbled onto it. I was looking for houses, and was very close to giving up. I loved this place on sight. I didn't get it very easily—I had to fight for it. It's late eighteenth century, a plain, simple soapbox, very small. I know none of the history of the people of that time. In the early twentieth century, a couple bought it. He worked for Mayor La Guardia and was a landscape artist. I was very lucky because he laid this whole thing out. It's beautifully laid out, professionally laid out. He and his sons built the pump house and did a lot of beautiful stuff. They lived here almost their entire lives. Their children grew up here and married, and he died here, and the old lady sold the house. Those people bought it in the late 1940s, early '50s. And they added onto it, some good things, some bad things.

The old lady came to see me. She drove up to the house in a long black car with a giant photograph book under her arm and just walked into the house. She hadn't come earlier because the *previous* owners had painted the shutters green and she said, "Anyone who painted shutters green is someone I don't know. But when I came by and saw the shutters were black, I decided that the old owners had moved, and I came by to show the new tenant these pictures."

NUWER: Do you take long walks around here?
SENDAK: Yep. Me and the dogs do about five miles a day. One of the reasons for buying this house is that at thirty-nine I had a coronary, and the doctor gave me then the typical coronary advice: Get out of New York. No one knows exactly what caused a coronary, so why *not* blame New York? I was ready to get out, anyway. So I moved to the country, exercised, and got into good physical shape; I'd been in poor physical shape previously. Now I cannot do without my calisthenics and my walk. And one of the sad things as my dogs grow older is that they can't keep up with me. I remember when I couldn't keep up with them. And I'm always aware of that change. I miss the energy coming out of them.

NUWER: Do you have a set time for working?

SENDAK: Yes. It's through the afternoon, anywhere from one until about four-thirty, and then I stop for another dog walk. I have a long dog walk in the morning. That's the big walk. The morning is just for exercising and walking. And then at four-thirty the brief walk with them, about a half hour. Then they get fed. Then I take a nap for about an hour. And I read for about an hour. Then I go back to work.

NUWER: Can you work in any sort of place?

SENDAK: No. I find I don't want to work in New York anymore. I can't or don't want to—I don't know which.

NUWER: Do you read critical appraisals of your work? Or are you immune to them now?

SENDAK: I read them, but I'm reasonably immune to them. I mean I hate a bad review, but I don't stay up all night thinking about it. I just condemn that person for being extraordinarily stupid and that's the end of it.

NUWER: Does your vintage Mickey Mouse collection trigger creative thoughts?

SENDAK: Yes. That's why I collect. I'm not a collector who collects just for collecting. Things have to refer back or give me some turn-on in my work. For instance, all the Mickey Mouse things started in the late '60s when I was doing *In the Night Kitchen*. I needed things from my childhood, and the Mickey Mouse things were my favorite. They helped me kind of taste that time and time again. The whole collection was really a means of turning me on to my book. All my collections, including my book collection, are always things that I can use in some way. They give me back something . . . like talismans. I don't collect them to invest or just collect. I have too much junk in my life anyway. Even the lucky things—that's all they are—wonderful junk.

NUWER: If I see any Mickey Mouses, I'll send you one.

SENDAK: They've got to be vintage. A woman I met at a party in Philadelphia said would I be interested in her Mickey Rocker. I thought I wouldn't, because she seemed too young to have a rocker that would have been of interest to me; she could only have been in her thirties. It turned out she was talking about a rocker that had been given to her aunt. Boy, did I get interested. She was talking vintage.

NUWER: Did you get it?
SENDAK: I'm working on it.

NUWER: Do your possessions take hold of you or hold you back?
SENDAK: I worry about them. You have to care for them. Yes, they do, indeed, take over more than you'd like them to. There would be something good in not having them, because you have to look after books, you have to look after paper. This is burdensome.

Things of mine, when I'm no longer in this world, I intend to leave in my will that they be auctioned off again. I don't want to leave them to anybody because I had so much fun getting them, I'd like them all dispersed. They don't "belong" to anybody; you don't "own" those things. You just have possession of them during that brief time you're here. In that sense you're taking care of them for anyone who is ever going to have them.

It's easy to understand how the Indians felt. I mean somebody comes up and says, "How many trees do you have?" In a sense you could almost think the trees are tolerating your presence. It's funny to think of owning trees, owning land. It's a funny idea. Somehow you think that if you said, "I own a tree," that the tree would never forgive you, and it would take vengeance every time you passed it for having the audacity to think you possessed it.

NUWER: Do you believe in heroes?
SENDAK: Yeah. Not many. The order of their priority is Mozart, Kleist, Melville. They're the core group.

Mozart and Kleist are both so diametrically opposed, and, yet, I know what links them together. Kleist stands for total destruction, this great big desperate need to find out why there's a reason for living, and then, NOT to find it. He collapsed under it. The work is all a hysterical plea. It's all so wonderful and touching, but he never succeeds. All of Kleist's work is there as imbalance in Nature, but in Mozart, there is the most quintessential perfect balance. There is suffering and everything you expect a grown man would have experienced in life, and, yet, in a way no other creature has done it. They are the pluses and minuses in my personal algebra.

NUWER: And Melville?
SENDAK: Melville is somehow more on the side of Kleist. He is a more comprehensible Kleist, a readable Kleist, a more lovable Kleist. In a way it's simplistic to say so, but Mozart and Kleist represent to sides of my own life. It's the Mozart that I want and lean towards. I want to believe in balance,

that you can put all these things into your life and subdue them in you work. But then there's another part that says any moment you may die. Any moment it may fall apart. Any moment this thing you have created is merely a surface image like a piece of glass that like a Kleist character, you will go crashing through. That's a part of how I feel, too. That's how quickly we can lose everything. Between listening to Mozart's *Jupiter Symphony* and reading a Kleist play is the wink of an eye.

NUWER: The quickness of an accident—you could lose your fingers.
SENDAK (nodding): Kleist's world is all about the gratuitousness of life. There's his wonderful short story called "The Earthquake in Chile." I don't have the whole plot, but very quickly: There is a man who is going to be hanged for a crime in prison. There's a woman who's going to be burned at the stake or something dreadful is going to be done to her because she's had a child out of wedlock. Both are going to happen at the same time. And the earthquake in Chile occurs—this famous earthquake. The whole town is destroyed, arbitrarily. And he gets out of prison, and she gets away from the people. They meet in the rubble. They escape. Marvelous scenes of the masses of people rushing through the destroyed city. The river is on fire. They get across in a boat. Then they go to a church at the end—I'm condensing it hopelessly. In the church they thank God for their safety. And in the church they are recognized by other people in the town as the infamous woman and the criminal. And they are horribly stoned to death. So they die anyway. And that to me is the quintessential Kleist—twist upon twist. It's something that—unfortunately—I savor in a story, because that's what I think life is really like.

I look to Mozart as God, as a teacher I want to save me from this perilous vision, and the result at my age is that both reside within me at equal times. I alternate between the two. I believe in the Mozart one because the Mozart incorporates the Kleist. That's what gives him the edge over Kleist. If Mozart had not seen the Kleist vision, he would have been less great, but he has, and within that he still got it all there. Kleist couldn't see the Mozart, just couldn't. Both personal visions are an amalgamation; I don't know if I can separate them.

There is a sense of perilousness in life—the way a house is robbed or the way an earthquake in Chile occurs or a flood in Louisiana or whatever you want. I love with a great sense of the gratuitousness that happens in life. Of nature's forces, of the lack of any ability we have to do anything about these things.

The great philosophers or religious people resigned themselves and said such is life; this, too, is the rhythm of life. It's not an exception. It's not an eccentric thing. You mustn't make more of it than it is. It's a procedure of life.

This view is an accruing of everything you were, always. I had an intensely sharp sense of death as a child, which came simply from the maladroitness of my parents in dealing with me when I was critically ill as a child. So I've always had this perilous sense of my own life, that my time would run out, that it could be snatched away from me when I was a child and helpless. Whatever is to protect you from that kind of attack? That is me more than anything else. Life is almost borrowed time (slight laugh), that when something is good it's almost a miracle. That it more normally is disastrous. I've tried very hard to reshape that thinking because it's unbearable to live with it. I've had to incorporate other modes of thinking to keep myself going.

NUWER: Do you owe much to any particular philosopher?

SENDAK: No, I can't take anything in a book that isn't by a fictional writer. If it's by a philosopher, I reject it outhand. If it's by Melville, I'll buy it. It's got to be that kind of artist who teaches me. I can't be taught by a Schopenhauer or a Kant. I can't. Don't ask me why. I just can't. I can't read things like that. But I trust artists. I don't trust philosophers. Of course, anyone could say, "But what a mistake you're making. They happen to be artists, too." Possibly. Maybe they're just too hard to read and boring.

NUWER: When did you start reading Melville?

SENDAK: In my twenties. I started with *Moby-Dick* for all the obvious reasons. I thought it was a great classic to read. And in fact it really hit an imaginary chord at that stage in my life. And when I fall in love with a writer, I have to read everything. And then I went through, for a long period of years, all of Melville. I've since gone through them again, and I love all of them. And the only one that has stumped me is *Mardi*. I just did volume one. And I did that one only about four years ago. I could not make myself go on to the next one. I couldn't stand it anymore.

NUWER: I couldn't stand *The Confidence Man*.

SENDAK: Oh, *The Confidence Man* was wonderful. I loved that!

NUWER: I read that at age twenty.

SENDAK: Too young. Too young. It's way too young.

NUWER: Do you remember, in *Moby-Dick*, the character Bulkington?
SENDAK: Oh, of course. Of course. Brave, good Bulkington.

NUWER: Do you think he was a mistake?
SENDAK: No—

NUWER:—I do. I think Melville might have gotten rid of him because Bulkington wouldn't have backed down the way Starbuck did.
SENDAK: He does get rid of him in a completely arbitrary way, doesn't he? "The Lee Shore." That's such a chapter, isn't it? Wow! "The Lee Shore."

NUWER: "O Bulkington! Bear thee grimly, demigod! Up from the spray of the ocean-perishing—straight up, leaps thy apotheosis!"
SENDAK: Yes. That's the end of him. Well, from a technical point of view, it's an error. But then there are no errors in that book. There just ain't none. I mean he [Bulkington] was just there for that. If only because he had to do "The Lee Shore," and that's all it was worth . . . listen, I'm too in love with that book to be critical. I can't worry about whether Bulkington made sense or not. I would have died without Bulkington. And Bulkington was one of his typical male fantasy heroes. Melville is full of men like Jack Chase—superman, heroes. He loved male imagery like that. It's very peculiar.

NUWER: That might account for Melville's falling out with Hawthorne.
SENDAK: Well, so much has been made of whether what we're talking about is repressed homosexuality that reappears over and over and over again in Melville. And maybe that's so. It really makes no difference particularly. I think it only makes a difference if we infer anything like that in the relationship with Hawthorne. And I don't think you can. The nineteenth century thing was so different from the twentieth century.

NUWER: Melville strikes me as a man's man. I think it was just pure friendship with Hawthorne.
SENDAK: It's really hard to know. Impossible to know. Do you remember that strange chapter in Melville of touching hands in the sperm? That is so *bizarre.*

NUWER: Touching in the ambergris, yes. Also there's the bed incident where the harpooner Queequeg drapes his leg over Ishmael as if they were married.

SENDAK: There is an awful lot of that. It's just that one is tempted not to think so because everyone so quickly does it.

But, you know, when you think of Melville's career—and Melville was an extremely successful writer, up until his masterpiece, *Moby-Dick*—it was not a successful book. But nevertheless, everything that made him a genius went into *Moby-Dick*. Everything. *Typee. Redburn. Omoo.* All of them are sketches for *Moby-Dick*. Then he does *Moby-Dick*, and you know that he achieved a kind of immense balance and comprehension that is awesome in that book. But then the thing that scares me is that Pierre, the book that came right after that, is—yes, it's a motion*less* book, but it's a great and ingenious work of art. But that's beside the point. I'm not sitting here as a critic of Melville . . . but he lost the balance. People say the book is a vindictive diatribe against all his critics. Bullshit! He might have been mad and hurt—he must have been mad and hurt. But he wouldn't have spent that much time on a book being *just* mad and hurt. He lost something vital. And *Pierre* is to me all about having lost. How did he lose it? That scares me.

NUWER: Right around that time he was looking to Hawthorne for inspiration. Hawthorne totally rejected his work. And I think that did have some awful effect on Melville.

SENDAK: Of course it had an effect. It's the reason I hate Hawthorne with all my heart. I'll never forgive Hawthorne for Herman. It's like . . . I'll take that up with him someday. I'll never forgive him for having so misunderstood. Mrs. Hawthorne understood better. Her journals have intuitive little things about what this poor man needed from her husband and how incapable her husband was of giving. I mean, you can't blame Hawthorne for being incapable. That's silly. But it's true. But I still can't believe that was enough to do it. That Herman Melville could have constructed everything—his whole balance of life—on this man. And that the withdrawal of that man, however cold and abrupt he was, could have meant this . . . maybe it did. Maybe I just am afraid to think it was that. I'm afraid. And why am I afraid? Because I identify. I go back to what I just said that between *Moby-Dick* and *Pierre* he lost everything. And that's how quickly we can all lose everything.

NUWER: Do you have any beliefs in otherworldly things—spirits around the house, etc.?

SENDAK: No.

NUWER: What are your beliefs in afterlife?

SENDAK: Death.

NUWER: Death? Blackness? Void?

SENDAK: Yes. It doesn't frighten me at all. I think if you're lucky enough to have lived long enough, and be old enough, it seems to me the gift of death is oblivion. It's weary to be alive. It's a chore. It's a happy chore, a good chore, but you have to be aware that it's an effort. To live any kind of reasonable, balanced life means you have to put a lot of energy into being reasonable and balanced. Right? It's not an automatic thing, because as human beings, we are neither reasonable nor balanced automatically. We have to learn to be that way. And I would think that when you're old, you must be weary of the effort. And you must wish to just not do anything. And, I mean, death is lovely for bringing oblivion. For being the wished-for peach that you've earned. It's terrible if it happens before you reach that stage. But the idea of another life—Mama mia!—once is enough. Unlike Jacqueline Susann.[2]

NUWER: Do you believe in taking your own life, if it's going badly?

SENDAK: Yes. But you've got to be sure it's going badly. For irreversible reasons. Yes, I do. I think that's the logical thing to do. I think you've got to be logical. But I don't know how many people can know for sure that it's irreversible. Terminally ill people do know and have every reason to take charge of their own fates. I worry more about states of depression, which would feel as bad as terminal illness. Taking your life at that point is very questionable.

NUWER: People change?

SENDAK: Yes. They get through it. But I know how hard it is. Many people have been through it. I have. Nowhere to the degree other people have, and I know people who have taken their lives in the midst of it and I understand.

NUWER: Do you seek out the company of other people, or do you find at this point you enjoy being alone?

SENDAK: I prefer being alone. I have good friends, but I prefer, in all truth, being alone. I like being alone with my books, with my music. It gets bad sometimes when I can't stand my own presence; I can't stand my own thinking of myself and my repetitive and tiresome thoughts. Then I have friends. They come up here; I go to them. I take breaks, which are normal and healthy. You get away from yourself. But in the end I'm always happier when I come back here again.

Notes

1. Editor's note: *The Love for Three Oranges*, an opera by Russian composer Sergei Prokofiev.

2. Editor's note: Jacqueline Susann, best-selling author of *Valley of the Dolls*, wrote another novel entitled *Once Is Not Enough*.

Maurice Sendak

Steven Heller / 1986

From *Innovators of American Illustration*, 1986, pp. 70–81. © Steven Heller. Reprinted with permission.

Maurice Sendak (born on June 10, 1928, in Brooklyn, New York) defined the look of modern children's book illustration. His drawing styles are derived from illustration and comics of the past, but his stories are psychologically rooted in the present. Although his illustrations appear in many story and picture books by other authors, his most significant books are those he's penned himself; *Where the Wild Things Are* and *In the Night Kitchen* are two of his most popular. In 1982, *Maurice Sendak*, a biography and retrospective, was published. Recently, Sendak's love of music, especially of Mozart, has become a professional passion: he now designs operas. Indeed, his own *Where the Wild Things* Are has been scored, choreographed, and performed, with his own unique sets.

MS: There was no conscious decision to become an artist. The first awareness of artists was my brother always drawing pictures, writing stories, pasting and stapling; that seemed the most natural thing to do. I did it, without considering if I could do it. And it has continued ever since.

SH: Did your brother continue?
MS: To the degree that he wrote at least a dozen books. I illustrated his first two.

SH: Were there any other artists in your family?
MS: It's hard to say. My father ran away to this country in 1903, from a *shtetl* outside of Warsaw. So I don't know his family at all. He had a huge family, but they were all incinerated during the war. On my mother's side, I've heard

stories about her father being an artist, but he died very young. And she so romanticized him that it's hard to know what's fact and what's fiction.

SH: What were your earliest pictures like?

MS: Cartoons, mostly based on Disney movies. People with huge, round shoes. Of course, the most available influence was Mickey Mouse, *Snow White,* and all the biggies that came out just when I was of age to go to the movies. So what Michelangelo was to a Renaissance child, Walt Disney was to a Brooklyn Jewish child.

SH: The comic strips as well?

MS: Comic strips and comic books, which we all read. Children's books were unavailable to a lower-class child in Brooklyn. My parents couldn't buy them. And library going didn't come until much later. I didn't read kiddie books, anyway; I only read older things. I wouldn't have been caught dead reading a book appropriate to my age, which I suspect is what children feel all the time. But comic books put you in connection with your peer group because you read them and traded them out in the street. And a lot of my books—up to *In the Night Kitchen*—were dramatically influenced by my early love of comic books, particularly panel movement. Animating the picture book has influenced me all my life.

SH: When you were doing these drawings, was there any idea of turning it into a profession?

MS: I was fourteen or fifteen when I illustrated my first book. It was *Peter and the Wolf.* Like so many children, it was also the first piece of music I got to know well. My inclination toward classical music started very early, again, probably influenced by my brother. I did a book, which was a very bad Disney version of *Peter and the Wolf.* But it had pictures and text, and the word *copyright* on the front. So, I was wired to be an illustrator. The second book was the libretto for *Louise,* by Gustave Charpentier, the French opera.

SH: Opera was an early influence, then?

MS: Very early. My first great experience was with Arturo Toscanini on the radio. . . . Everything was radio. I didn't go to concert halls and to museums. Nobody would take me, so it was a logistical and financial problem that could not be overcome. Toscanini did Beethoven's *Fidelio* over a two-Sunday program. I'll never forget it. It was like St. Paul on the road to Damascus.

But back to books. I did my favorite story when I was about seventeen. It was "The Luck of Roaring Camp" by Bret Harte. Which is interesting, because it's a theme that has run through all my adult work. It is the story of an abandoned baby in a miner's camp and of what happens to the baby. There may have been more books, but those are the ones I remember. I have never let them be published. I have never let them be seen. So, you see, it was there all the time; there was no choice but to become an illustrator.

SH: Why not music?

MS: I had no talent, but I wanted to play the piano. We moved every third year because my mother had an aversion to fresh paint. (It's true.) And in those days, they painted your apartment, whether you liked it or not, every third year. We lived all over Brooklyn, and I went to every school in the world, which made for a very dismal childhood. But that non sequitur had to do with the fact that one of these apartments we moved to had a piano that was too big to be taken out by the previous tenant. The terrible dilemma was, who was going to get lessons. And my brother got them because he was the elder. I'll never forget that because I wanted them so much. He never stayed with it; he became an accordion player and then a writer and illustrator. So there was no musical gift, or if there was, it was never cultivated. But I whistle on pitch, and I can whistle the entire repertoire of Mozart's operas and symphonies. I'm very good with Beethoven. When I'm home listening to recordings and working, I become part of the orchestra.

SH: Did you go to art school?

MS: Yes. To appease my father, basically. He was mortified that I was going to be a serious artist because I would make no money. It also mortified him because of something I didn't think he could admit to; it embarrassed him. He would much rather have had a son who was a doctor or a lawyer or a professional, like the typical Jewish fantasies. Instead I went to the Art Students League for a very short time. At the same time, when I was about nineteen or twenty, I was working at FAO Schwarz, the toy store, doing windows display. I went there because my brother and I made toys together. He's a genius with mechanical apparatuses; I simply painted what he told me to paint. We wanted to sell the toys, so we brought them to Schwarz. They told us they were beautiful but impractical, and instead I got a job. I stayed for three years, as an assistant to the display manager.

SH: Did you get anything from the Art Students League?

MS: Very little. The only teacher I ever had who was sympathetic to my peculiar nature and whom I could trust enough to learn from was John Groth. He had a course in illustration, which I took twice. He was the only generous teacher I ever had—the only one I could relax with and feel I could trust and who was really like me. He gave us wonderful exercises. We had to carry a sketch pad wherever we went, on the subway trains and in the parks. I got in the habit of drawing all the time. Alas, I don't do it anymore. But for years I drew on subway trains—where it was safe to look at people on subways. The other thing was to look at the work and study the compositions of Goya and Daumier. Daumier was his favorite artist. But in order to make us look, he would whet our appetites by saying, "Go home. And this week I want you to do the rape scene from *A Streetcar Named Desire*. I want Stanley screwing Vivien Leigh in the style of Goya or Daumier." Well, we could hardly wait to get home. He knew about young people, and what our energies and our drives were, and would try to tie that into educating us, without any pedantry.

SH: Did Groth encourage you to go into illustration?
MS: Oh, yes.

SH: Was it editorial illustration at this time?
MS: Whatever I could do. I mean, his encouragement was, "Go out and work. Don't stay in school." That's just what I've always told the students I've had at Parsons or Yale, that if you're really talented and really excited, why are you in school? You should be out there working. You should do-do-do-do, not study-study-study-study. Because the doing is the studying. The experience is the learning. And John was for not wasting time. He thought it was a kind of masturbatory act, to just sit around studying and looking at work and thinking about what you do. And the fortunate thing was, that in the early fifties in New York, you could go out and get work.

SH: Where did your first work come from?
MS: The first book I illustrated was back in high school, for my physics teacher. You can't really count it, but it was the first professional job. I was failing, as usual, in everything, especially in physics. He wrote a book which, I believe it's true to say, was the first book explaining the atomic bomb to a layman, called *Atomics for the Millions*. I also worked for All American Comics during the three years I was in high school, which undermined my grades, of course, but I did the backgrounds on *Mutt and Jeff, Tippy*, and

Captain Stubbs. So all the worst habits of comic-strip drawing were in my work.

After I had worked at Schwarz for quite some time and littered their windows with my pictures . . . it was like putting your fishing pole outside on Fifty-ninth Street and Fifth Avenue, waiting to hook an editor . . . a very well-known children's book illustrator named Leonard Weisgard came by. He was doing a book he didn't want to do for the Jewish Seminary, called *Good Shabbos Everybody.* So he got them to take me. My name is very small on the cover, and his name, as art consultant, is very big. I was happy to do it though. I had also been to publishing houses and been turned down, over and over again, because my pictures were considered old-fashioned.

SH: You mean you were too nineteenth century?

MS: The prevailing look was sort of vaguely thirties. Simple, flat color. The prevailing attitude was generally that kids liked simple shapes, simple colors, pretty people. There was nothing disturbing. There wasn't a ripple. And my work was cross-hatching, because I was copying from Cruikshank and other English illustrators. So it was very out of fashion. I kept a little notepad of criticism of editors, saying, "No, no, you can't look like that; go look at what's contemporary. . . ." So it was rough, until 1951 or 1952, when I met Ursula Nordstrom at Harper, who was a friend of the bookbuyer at FAO Schwarz, Frances Chrystie (whom I owe everything to).

Before I tell you about Ursula, I must say Frances ran the best children's book department in America. That's where you found the out-of-print books, the European books, the American books. It was fantastic. I got away with murder in Frances's department; she let me be there, reading books, studying, looking, copying. Then she introduced me to Ursula, who was the editor at Harper, and that was the beginning. I did my first book, which was a collection of French fairytales by Marcel Aymé called *A Wonderful Farm.* Again, the drawings are better than anything I previously did. But still, I had no training! I absorbed styles that were inappropriate. I think now they were inappropriate, but then I had no choice.

SH: You were wedding Disney to Tenniel?

MS: I was trying to. Although, it's funny, my earliest portfolios had indications of more complicated work that look more like me now. But those were the things that were rejected by the early editors; cross-hatched, peculiar images, which later became what I was well known for.

SH: Ursula Nordstrom had guts.

MS: Oh, yes, she had guts. Ursula's passion was for young people. If I can make a huge, generalized statement, and I shall, what's wrong with publishing today is that nobody has guts. I mean, they're all playing it safe, publishing safe, middle-aged people like me, who can sell books. The young people have a rough time coming in, because they can't guarantee sales. There's something wrong with the system when you can name only a few people. So you have to be very strong and gifted to break through that very commercial, immoral attitude. But Ursula was the opposite. I mean, a children's book department is something you made up, out of your head. So she made it up. Everybody was young. She went through the streets and swept them up like garbage. And we all worked; I had a job reading manuscripts.

The second book was *A Hole Is to Dig*, which put me on the map instantly. It was a *mad* success. That was by Ruth Krauss, who had written very inventive books, using children's language, children's gestalt, and children's attitudes toward life.

SH: And this book was something that just fit perfectly into your style?

MS: Well, Ursula is an amazing person, and so is Ruth, for taking a kid off the street and giving him an important book. Because I know for a fact there were at least two very famous illustrators at the time who had been approached with it and thought it was too bizarre. So they came to me. And after seeing my sketchbooks with big-headed little Jewish kids and ill-drawn caricatures but full of animation and life, they said, "Why don't you do it?"

SH: How did you approach that task?

MS: Every weekend I went to Rowayton, Connecticut, where Ruth lived, and we worked together on the book. Her husband, by the way, was Crockett Johnson, the great man himself. So I had the best of two worlds. And Ruth was way ahead of women's lib. She wouldn't let me get away with any myths about what little boys did and what little girls did. We did six books together, and that was my education in bookmaking, book layout, and typography.

SH: Were you surprised the book was a critical success?

MS: I was stunned. It was a tiny book with funny scratchy drawings and weird, crazy words. It's still in print. It was a bestseller for twenty years, and it is part of college curriculums. It's a very, very historically important book. And I was just lucky enough to be around to do it.

SH: Once that critical acceptance was achieved, was it easier for you to get projects?

MS: Oh, sure. But my projects were mostly through Ursula. She spoon-fed me. I had no taste. There was no way I could have had taste. You're not born with taste. If I wanted to do this, she'd say, "No, you do that." And so my entire early backlist is superb, from the variety of things she made me do. Books that I thought were inappropriate for me she said were appropriate. Drawings for books that forced me to do homework on Dutch landscape and costume. So she taught me how to be an illustrator. I learned how to be a chameleon and change my style and change my look and change my emotional everything to suit the book I'm illustrating. That was a million-buck education.

SH: It's interesting, because in the fifties, when an illustrator picked a style, that was it virtually for life.

MS: That's what doomed a lot of the illustrators working then. And that was the one thing Ursula was absolutely not going to let happen to me. I was going to have catholic taste, and I was going to learn how to draw in a variety of styles. I think my books are identifiable, but they all look different because illustrators are secondary to the text. If you insist on being primary to the text, then you're a bad illustrator. Which is why I list Arthur Rackham as one of the worst illustrators that ever lived—one of the best draftsmen—but he's one of the worst illustrators.

SH: At that time, was the book the only form you wanted to deal with?

MS: No. Because it was very little money. The fees were small; the advances were small. I didn't get royalties in the early days. Life, happily, was cheap enough so that I could leave Brooklyn and live on my own in Manhattan. It was an enviable time, socially and historically, but there wasn't enough to really make out. Besides, one wanted to be commercial, to be in the magazines.

SH: "Commercial" meaning advertising or editorial?

MS: Editorial and advertising, yes. The sad thing for me was that however gifted I was, I wasn't gifted in that direction. I required the density of a book. I'm a very slow and ponderous artist. It takes forever. The book was wonderfully my medium in that it allowed me to stew and steep, and each picture built and built and built, until at the end it all flowered into a kind of conglomeration that was suitable. Whereas a specific magazine picture had to be quick. I did drawings for *Esquire*, and they are terrible! My best friend in the mid-fifties and sixties was Tomi Ungerer. Tomi had the ability to round out, steep, and thicken in a book, and with the other to *blast off* in a given image. And I was jealous of that. But I was also aware of the uncanny quality of his talent. He could make an enormous success out of being a commercial, literature, and poster artist. I couldn't. I've learned, though, how to do my book jackets better.

SH: Did you want to make statements, political, social, or otherwise?
MS: Not really. The most political I made was in my high school yearbook. I grew up during the war and lived off the business of dead Jews. So, Holocaust drawings and that kind of thing was an obsession with me. An obsession I rejected with violence as I grew older, because I felt like I couldn't get out of it. I couldn't be happy. I couldn't live in the world. But outside of that, politics was not my forte. Instinctively, I didn't want to do what didn't come naturally to me. I never have.

SH: When did you start making decisions about your own subject matter?
MS: I thought of writing from the beginning, but it was the wrong time. I had to keep illustrating, just to keep books going, to make some money.

SH: Could you write?
MS: Yeah. I wrote for my own pleasure, but I had no confidence in what I was writing. Again, it was because of Ursula. The first book was *Kenny's Window*, which is still one of my favorite books. But it was done mostly with her propping me up and convincing me I could write. It was completely idiosyncratic writing and idiosyncratic subject matter. *Kenny's Window* was a story of a little boy who has contradictory attitudes toward life, and toward his toys and toward his parents. His parents never appear, and the whole thing is a series of dialogues. It's seven chapters; a series of seven fantasies acted out by himself or with toys, in which he is battling out forces within himself—it sounds grandiose, but I am not able to describe it better now. He has a dream at the beginning, and the book is an effort to fulfill it. The ending is an irresolution. He cannot fulfill his dream. Which is anti-American. Some of the reviews said, "What a terrifying book. We're led to believe he's going to get it, and then he doesn't get it." But it was mostly him acting out sometimes irrational rages toward his toy soldiers and then trying to compromise emotionally and get some understanding for those actions, because the assumption was there was no discussing this with your parents.

He comes to a resignation, which is, "I've got to figure it out myself; and I guess I've gotta wait; and I guess I'm going to be alone."

SH: Was this true for you?

MS: Yes. Except, in a sense, it was idealized in the book because my rages and my quandaries were severe, and there literally was no one except my brother, and my older sister later, to work them out with. *Kenny* was a very forthright book. It's overwritten. It's not well illustrated. But it's still one of my favorite books, for its bravery. People liked it, but it never sold. It won critical praise, and it even won an illustrator's award, which it didn't deserve. I'm not being modest. I *wrote* better and stronger than I was able to illustrate.

SH: Did Ursula encourage you to get in touch with yourself for new material?

MS: Oh, yes. The miracle was that she was encouraging me to write very uncommercial books. She wanted me to be me—to become the artist she smelled in me. She was Mama.

SH: That kind of person is a rarity.

MS: She did that with everybody. We were known as the Ursula kids. None of us was jealous of the other. We all thought we had our distinct place in her heart and that each of our gifts was different from the other. She was cultivating the best in us.

The second book I wrote was *Very Far Away* in 1958, which I am now considering reillustrating. I will not touch a word of that text; I love it so much. But the pictures are not good enough.

SH: What is this book about?

MS: It's almost a rough study for *Outside Over There*. It's about a little boy who so bitterly resents his mother coming home with a new baby, that he leaves. He puts on a costume so he won't be recognized, and he goes very far away. He meets a horse, a sparrow, and a cat; and they go live somewhere else, where you don't have to put up with parents who come home with gratuitous unwanted children. And he finds, living with them, the vanity of these creatures. The stupidity and irrationality of all creatures is so wearying and tiring, that they have a terrible fight, and he goes home. And the going-home has to be rationalized because basically he's going home because who else is going to feed him? He can't take care of himself. So it's, "Well, maybe I'll get used to the kid." But you don't know that he does.

SH: Your books seem to subvert commonly believed myths.

MS: I sometimes think it's amazing I've had success because they are so idiosyncratic and personal and run against the American grain that says if you persevere, you'll get what you want. What I'm saying is: you may persevere, but you may not and often probably won't get what you want because, one, you don't deserve it; two, you're too young to have it; and, three, that's the way life is.

SH: I think the American grain is actually a veneer, and underneath there's the hardwood that is difficult to penetrate.

MS: Yes, my books were vulgar, pushing and striving for inner things rather than outer things.

SH: I noticed you have the *Journal of the American Psychoanalytic Institute* in your home. Was psychoanalysis something that became an interest at the time of *Kenny*?

MS: Those aren't my books. But yes, I was in psychoanalysis at a very early age. Maybe that, too, was fashionable in New York in the fifties. Maybe not. But I was in need of it. I was also entranced with the subject from a very early time. And *Kenny* is all about the *outrageous* rage that you inflict on inanimate objects because you don't dare inflict them on your parents or your siblings. So *Kenny* is all about how to deal with rage. Even Martin, the hero of *Very Far Away*, is dealing with that issue.

The third book was *The Sign on Rosie's Door*, which is the most cheerful of my books, and I love it. It is also the first book where the pictures melded with the text. After that came *Where the Wild Things Are* in 1962. *Wild Things* was an amalgamation of everything that had gone before. Max was one burly little boy, a terrific, strenuous, volcanic embodiment of all the things that were unnerving Rosie, Martin, and Kenny. But the people who at that point said, "What a novel thing," "What a weird thing," "What a disgusting thing," "What a strange thing," hadn't read my earlier books.

SH: Were the early books an attempt, consciously or subconsciously, to say to kids, "It's okay to have all these feelings"?

MS: No. To say it to myself. I wasn't interested in other kids. I was not a humanitarian or a social worker. Or even someone who understood children. I don't have children. So I cannot pretend that I set out to help other children. Primarily, my work was an act of exorcism, an act of finding solutions so that I could have peace of mind and be an artist and function in the world as a human being and a man. My mind doesn't stray beyond my own need to survive.

SH: To share that need to survive is not so bad.
MS: Yes. If you can touch other people, as I apparently have, that's fine. I'm very proud of that. But those things are inadvertent.

SH: Well, *Where the Wild Things Are* was really an explosion.
MS: Yeah, it was an explosion. But it was an explosion that only meant to me that I could render more concisely and precisely the theme that I had overwritten in the earlier books. I had also fallen in love with the picture book; because just previous to *Wild Things*, Ursula had given me my first picture books to illustrate—*The Moon Jumpers; The Giant Story* by Beatrice [Schneck] de Regniers; *Mr. Rabbit and the Lovely Present*. And the form entranced me.

SH: What is the difference between a picture book and a storybook?
MS: There are many pictures with little words, but combustible little words are really like time bombs. And the pictures are the explosion. What I could do with a picture book was to condense language into metaphor and symbol. The pictures are like the operatic stage, and the words are the orchestral accompaniment.

You couldn't, in fact, do without one or the other. So I abandoned the storybook completely. In *Where the Wild Things Are* I finally came to grips with what my theme was and found the form most suitable to me as a writer and an illustrator.

SH: Where did it derive stylistically?
MS: From everything I had done previously. People think it looks different, but it doesn't! The drawing is better, but I was growing better. As I should have. God forbid I was going the other way. Curiously, by the time *Wild Things* came around, people thought I was out of the head of Zeus. I had been around for a decade, working very hard, having illustrated over two dozen books. It wasn't spontaneous combustion. And I was annoyed, frank-

ly, that suddenly I was a star on the firmament, as though I hadn't been around all this time.

SH: As the star, what was happening?

MS: I won the Caldecott Award and began to make money. But by then, I was sufficiently knowledgeable and savvy about life and people so that I was not impressed, nor have I ever been impressed, with being a star. Don't forget, I was thirty-three when the book came out.

So I proceeded on my way. I illustrated books for other publishing houses, which bothered Ursula a lot. But I had a very strong feeling that Harper books, at their very best, looked like Harper books, the way Viking books look like Viking books and Random House like Random House, et cetera. What I was afraid of was I'd start looking like a Harper illustrator; that all my books would have the cast. And my sense of self-preservation was strong. So I began illustrating other books. My ethical code was that I would only write books for Ursula, but I insisted on my freedom. My instinct was right. I learned to look different.

SH: What was the next book that you wrote?

MS: After *Wild Things* was *Higglety Pigglety Pop! Or, There Must Be More to Life*. I wrote it in 1956; it was published in 1967, the year of my coronary. I almost didn't get to see that book. But I'm very proud of it because it's the only funny book I ever wrote. I'm not a funny writer. That's another weakness. I have a good sense of humor, but I'm serious when I work. And *Higglety* is full of laughs. It's a sad book, though, being about death. I was then enamored of the English Romantic woodcut artists; they were called "Artists of the Sixties," such as John Everett Millais and Arthur Hughes, and the pre-Raphaelite brotherhood. Where *Wild Things* is big and noisy, *Higglety* is all chamber music. I didn't write many books after that. In 1970, I did *In the Night Kitchen*, which again is very different and offended people in a very different way.

SH: Was *In the Night Kitchen* influenced by Winsor McCay?

MS: Absolutely. That's when I got into collecting Mickey Mouse nostalgia stuff and learning all about Winsor McCay. *In the Night Kitchen* is in homage to him. When I steal, I go all the way. But *Night Kitchen*, however much Winsor McCay it is, is mostly me. I just took from him what suited me, as I have taken from other people. That book occurred when my mother was dead, my father was dying, and I had a heart attack—rough years. And so, it was in homage to everything I loved: New York, immigrants, Jews, Laurel and Hardy, Mickey Mouse, King Kong, movies. I just jammed them into one cuckoo book. After *Night Kitchen*, I didn't write anything for almost ten years because the very next book was *Outside Over There*.

SH: And you worked on that for a very long time.
MS: I worked on that for five to seven years. I began it in 1972, and it was published in 1980.

SH: What was so difficult about doing that book?
MS: It was the pursuit of the theme I had been tracking since *Kenny's Window*, but now I had it trapped in a corner. I was really like Sherlock Holmes, sniffing it out in myself. I'm not saying it was a religious experience, although in fact it was. And did it change my life? In fact, it did.

SH: How?
MS: In terms of my attitude toward my work and my attitude toward myself. The most significant thing that happened was, immediately after finishing that book, I did an opera.

SH: You also said that it would be the last book you'd ever do.
MS: Yes, I said that. But I meant that in a metaphoric sense, in that it probably is unlikely I will do another picture book. I want to write books, but I don't know what kind. It was definitely the end of a certain kind of book that I would do. Maybe I will never write again. I haven't got a clue. But it freed me. I became another man. I became an opera designer. I began not only whistling, but attending rehearsals of, Mozart operas. Since 1980, when that book was published, I've had five years of not publishing, except books that were related to theatrical works, like *The Leopard* and *The Love of Three Oranges*. *Outside Over There* allowed me to be the person I wanted to be. And that, I assume, is what the work of art is supposed to do for the artist. I don't know what it does for the people who read books. But I can't worry about that.

SH: It must have really scared you while you were doing it.
MS: Yeah. It gave me a mini-nervous breakdown. It was unquestionably the hardest book I ever worked on. It caused me the most pain. Psychically and physically the pictures drove me crazy because they were so difficult and so

slow that I had callouses all over my fingers. But the end result was that I knew it was my masterpiece. That's what I planned all along that it would be. Commercially it's been zappo, but that was never my concern. It's a disappointment, not because of the money, but because I think it should be read. By its noncommercialness, I know kids are not reading it. But that's secondary to what I set out to accomplish.

SH: How did the opera work come about?
MS: I was working on *Outside Over There*, and Frank Corsaro, a great opera director—the greatest, I think, in America—called and said he admired my work. He's one of the few artists from another profession who crosses over. (Who else does that? God forbid we should ever meet, like a Stendhalzian salon, and discuss things.) Well, here is Frank looking me up and telling me, "Hey, I'm crazy about your books. Have you ever thought about opera? Do you like opera? How about *Magic Flute*?" I was nearly having my second coronary on the phone while he was talking to me. I agreed to do the sets for *The Magic Flute*, and right in the middle of *Outside Over There*, everything turned Mozart. Mozart became the godhead.

SH: Somebody said to me after looking at these drawings, "For some reason, this line feels like Mozart."
MS: Oh, that's the nicest thing anybody could say. If anybody could prove to me that Mozart was God, I would believe in God forever. But I do believe in Mozart as though he were God. If God is someone that's supposed to give you comfort, I think of him and I listen to him when I'm in trouble. When my dog died last summer and I couldn't bear it, it was only *The Marriage of Figaro* that got me through the last two weeks of August. Because there is a truth, a revelation, spirituality, humor, and earthiness. What a break, to do *The Magic Flute*. And that began an opera career and a ballet career, which hasn't ceased. Now, I'm just about to illustrate a Grimm's fairy tale. It will be literally my first proper illustrated book since *Outside Over There*. So it's going to be almost five-and-a-half years since I've illustrated a book that way, and I'm looking forward to it.

SH: How do you prepare for that book?
MS: You don't. There's no way you can prepare. The manuscript has just been recently discovered. So I'll be the first illustrator for this story, and it will be its first publication. It's a fabulous, fearfully sad little story. I know just what I'm going to do, emotionally. But technically, I haven't a clue. And

what it looks like, I don't know. I never think about what it looks like. I just know that at the end of February I'm going to sit down on my backside, in front of my drawing table, and begin Grimm. And that's how I do it. Because I have total and complete faith in the fact that I've already done it, in my head. For however long, a year and a half now, I've been thinking about it. I was in England working, and I was in Los Angeles at the Huntington Library. Whenever I go and look at pictures, I'm looking at something. I say, "What am I looking for? Oh, I know. Cottages. Trees. German settings." I'm doing homework all the time. Even when I'm sleeping, I think I'm doing homework. So although I'm going to be scared and go through the same "I can't draw," "What does it look like?," "How do I compose it?"—the nightmare of beginning a book—the truer thing is that it has always been conceived and envisioned. The trick now is to calm down and schlep those visions up.

"Don't assume anything": A Conversation with Maurice Sendak

Philip Nel / 2001

From interviewer's private collection, 28 June 2001. Maurice Sendak/Philip Nel interview © 2015 The Maurice Sendak Foundation and Philip Nel. Published for the first time by permission of The Maurice Sendak Foundation and Philip Nel.

In June 2001, I went to hear Maurice Sendak speak at Yale University. A couple of years earlier, I'd started working on a biography of Crockett Johnson (whose real name was Dave, as you'll see below)—which became a double biography of Johnson and his wife, Ruth Krauss, the children's author and poet. I knew Sendak was close to both of them and had written him to see if he would be willing to chat. Unfortunately, the previous April, he had declined via a letter from his assistant. But, to write this biography, I *needed* to talk to Sendak. Since I was doing research in the area, I decided to go to his talk at Yale and then ask him during the Question-and-Answer period. I was very nervous. But I plucked up my courage and asked.

Sendak looked me in the eyes, and after the briefest pause, said, "Yes." I should talk to him after the Question-and-Answer. I did. He wrote his home number down in my notebook and told me to call. At 9 p.m. on June 28, I phoned his Ridgefield, Connecticut, home from my mother's house in Hamden, Connecticut. Sendak and I talked for the next two hours.

Philip Nel: Let's hope the tape works.
Maurice Sendak: Oh, you're taping it?

PN: Yes, if that's all right with you.
MS: Yes, that's fine. You're going to hear an odd sound now and then, which is my putting a colored pencil into my sharpener 'cause I'm going to try and draw as we speak.

PN: OK.

MS: I have to finish a page a day, a layout a day, for the book I'm doing.

PN: What are you doing?

MS: Well, it's a book based on an opera, an opera that I'm going to produce. I have a little children's theatre which I'm getting rid of, but this is our last thing to do. It's an opera that was performed in a concentration camp in Prague; there's a very famous concentration camp called Theresienstadt. It was actually Emperor Tiresias's army encampment right outside the city. During the war, it became a camp, and it was known as Hitler's favorite camp. There was a movie made to impress the Red Cross and diplomats coming that all that they were hearing about dead Jews, dead gypsies, dead gays was all a lie. And a film was made showing volleyball and chess and children, part of a children's opera, some brief moments. And the true fact is that there was an opera composed in the camp. A young composer named Hans Krása and his librettist wrote an opera for the children in the camp. And the opera is called *Brundibár*, and it's one of the only things we have of Mr. Krása except for a trio and some songs because he was incinerated when he was about thirty-five along with the librettist *and* all the children who performed the opera.

PN: Wow.

MS: We now have the rights to the opera—took us a long time to get it—and Tony Kushner, the playwright—

PN: Yes, *Angels in America.*

MS: Yes . . . is one of my very most wonderful friends. I begged him to take the job of translation because the original English translation is horrible. The Czech is beautiful, but it's got to be sung in English; so we translated it, and we got people interested in doing it, staging it. It has been done, but in schools, in community centers. It's never had a real production. And so in order to raise the money for it, we agreed we would do a picture book. So, Tony extrapolated from the libretto into a very gorgeous complex story—the first time he's ever done anything like this. He's amazing. He just adapted it, without any fuss or feathers. Gorgeous, gorgeous funny language. And I'm doing the picture book because we need the money for the stage production. Hyperion will pay for a good part of the stage production, and the trade is they get the picture book. And I was very sick for a year and a quarter, and of course I'm terribly late. I'm trying so hard to catch up.

PN: Wow.

MS: And, it's beautiful, beautiful work—it's a perfect way for me to wind up, actually. So that is it.

PN: Wow. I'll be fascinated to see that—the book—when it comes out.

MS: Yes, the book is evolving because Tony keeps rewriting and I keep re-thinking, and we swore we would not make it too dark. It would be the sweet, little Czech peasant opera.

PN: Well, good luck.

MS: It's hopeless already. I have Hitler in it, I have Eva Braun in it, I mean I'm just uncontrollable.

PN: It would be difficult to avoid the darkness.

MS: Impossible. But, really, seriously [you] must to an extent in order to not obscure what these people set out to do, which was to write a charming piece to amuse the children. It's just that history beclouds it so much. It is difficult to do. It is difficult. But it's also great fun. I'm having a wonderful time.

PN: I'm fascinated. I'll be interested when it comes out to show it to my class.

MS: Now, what is your class?

PN: I teach Introduction to Children's Literature.

MS: Where?

PN: This is at Kansas State University.

MS: Oh, right. Of course you do. From Kansas.

PN: Well, that's where I live. I'm from here [Connecticut], but I live in Kansas.

MS: I see. Does Kansas have a good children's collection?

PN: It's OK. It's not one of the big collections in the country, but they're working on it.

MS: Is it a good place to be? Is it a good school to teach at?

PN: It's the best one I've had so far. I have a 2–3 teaching load, which—in case that's an obscure phrase—means that I teach two courses one semester and three another, which is much better than what I had before; and it's a tenure-track position; and they may hire my wife into the tenure-track as well. That's what brought us there, was the prospect of two tenure-track jobs. But, I have colleagues who teach children's literature, which is great because I learn a lot from them. And I don't teach composition anymore, so that feels like deliverance for me.

MS: I always wonder how one teaches children's literature.

PN: Well, I could send you a syllabus.

MS: Yes, why don't you?

PN: OK. I will.

MS: To me, it's really a great mystery.

PN: Well, I'm new to teaching it. I've taught it only for a year. So, I'm pretty close to that sense of mystery.

MS: Well, once the mystery settles deep on you, then you'll know how complex this thing is. It's always been considered low man on the totem pole, one page in the *New York Times*, and it's all treated like Peter Pan–ville.

PN: Right.

MS: It's very tiresome. It used to irritate me profoundly when I was young, and now I just can't afford the energy that goes to being irritated.

PN: Yeah. Well, I don't know. I mean, the reviewers they pick aren't great, but at least the *Book Review*—four times a year or so—does devote some time to children's books. Although—

MS: Yes, but it's really asinine.

PN: Well, they don't pick experts. They pick celebrities. Or sometimes they do.

MS: Well, also, critics have never been people you honestly can take very seriously. And certainly people who write reviews of children's books often horribly always start with their own children: "I read little Myra . . ."

PN: Right!

MS: Well, who cares about little Myra?

PN: Right! [*Laughs.*]
MS: I wish her ill!

PN: [*Laughs.*] Well, you know, that's actually one of the reasons I decided to write this little pamphlet [*J.K. Rowling's Harry Potter Novels: A Reader's Guide*], if you will, on the *Harry Potter* books to get people to think about it as literature. I felt that the hype had kind of obscured it—and the marketing and the movie and all that. And its best-seller status. But I think they're actually good books, and I wanted to make people actually see her wide reading and what goes into them, what's behind them—the E. Nesbit, Jane Austen, Lewis Carroll, all the stuff that she's read.
MS: Yes, I read the first one. I didn't care for it.

PN: Oh, really?
MS: No.

PN: I think they get more interesting, but—.
MS: I don't like books for young people. They aren't what I want to read. And, two, I've never been turned on by *The Hobbit* or the *Ring* or mythology. It's just not to my taste. But I was really kind of interested in how well she stole and who she did it from. And I approve of that. That's all I do. But she does it very well. And I was very admiring of her ability to get all these guys and gals in English literature. But I wasn't interested enough to go on to the second.

PN: Oh, well.
MS: I thought I'd done enough for the first.

PN: Well, they get more interesting, and they get darker as they go on. But if it's not your taste, it's not your taste, so—.
MS: Well, and there's so little time to read all the things you want to read. You have to be very—I have to be very—critical of what it is I'm about to take up. Spend a lot of time worrying about what I'm going to read next.

PN: Right, right.
MS: OK.

PN: So.
MS: So.

PN: Shall we switch over to—
MS: Yes.

PN: Dave and Ruth?
MS: Yes.

PN: Do you want me to ask you questions, or would you prefer just to free-associate and—
MS: Well, whatever suits you better.

PN: Well, I can start with a question. Describe that first meeting. Did [legendary editor and director of Harper's Books for Boys and Girls] Ursula Nordstrom introduce you? What was it like to meet these two for the first time?
MS: What had happened was I had been peddling my work unsuccessfully, my portfolio. And part of my portfolio were little black bound sketchbooks, where I put little fantasy drawings. And then I had the appropriate portfolio of scenes from Andersen, scenes from Grimm, and that kind of thing. And I had no success whatsoever because my work was very early eighteenth [century] European and out of fashion. And that I cross-hatched and looked so much like [George] Cruikshank—and I was in love with Cruikshank—and using pen. But back—when was I looking?—this was in the very late '40s or early '50s, really. And I kept notes on what publishers said about my work; and they always advised me to look at children's books; and it was the time of flat colors; and the idea was that children really preferred flat colors, that squiggly lines just confused them. It's as idiotic a theory as whatever the theory is today. I don't even know, don't even care.

And so I was discouraged. I had a job at FAO Schwarz where I was a window display artist, and people saw my work in the window—it's the greatest way to have a portfolio. And Ursula was best friends with the book buyer Frances Chrystie, who was the most remarkable woman. I mean, FAO Schwarz was *the* best bookstore for children in America.

PN: Really?
MS: Yes. Well, now the store is a super-supermarket of nothing. But in those days, the book department was completely under Frances's control; and it was the first department anywhere that imported foreign children's books, where you saw it was like a renaissance going on in Switzerland and in Germany; and we got to see it first. And I spent lots of time in the book

department, looking at everything. So, I knew Ruth Krauss's books. And my portfolio was at Harper's. I had already done one book [Marcel Aymé's *The Wonderful Farm*] for Ursula. And I had left my portfolio and sketchbooks with her. And I had no idea that Ruth was looking for an artist to do *A Hole Is to Dig*. And a number of famous illustrators had been approached, and—I want to be clear in my memory here—I don't know how many, but the ones that were approached did not care for the book. And they did not see why it was a book. They just couldn't figure out what was this all about.

And Ruth was very good friends with Ursula, although it was a very touchy relationship, a very stormy relationship between these two women. It was extremely volatile. And Ruth had been sitting in Ursula's office, going through my sketch pads, and she said she wanted me. The little fantasy sketches especially. Tiny figures. And that was it.

And I was asked to come up and to meet Ruth, and I was very uptight. And I adored her. She had this little girl's laugh, this uncontrollable giggle. She was voluptuous; she was a very sexy woman. Very warm, very original. I never met, and I haven't since met, anyone like that. And she was charming. And she told me how that's what she wanted the book to look like with the tiny little figures, and she said we would work together, which thrilled me.

She also insisted that I share royalties with her, half and half. You know, you would maybe be given—you would be given an advance. Someone like me would have been given $200 or at most $500, but I doubt it was as much as $500. And she told Ursula that the royalty had to be split fifty-fifty, which is unheard of. I would have done it for free. And it turned out that *A Hole Is to Dig* was a runaway bestseller. And it allowed me to quit my job at FAO and freelance. If Ruth had not done that—it was amazing generosity.

She loved young people. She loved helping young people. She loved taking on young people. I was perfect. I was about twenty-two or -three. She was about, maybe ten years older than me, maybe less. She seemed very much older than me at the time. She seemed very, very mature. And she immediately invited me to spend time with her and Dave in Rowayton. And I was a Brooklyn boy and not very happy with my parents, nor were they happy with me especially. So, here I was, free invitation to work with the famous Ruth Krauss, married to the famous Crockett Johnson, in Rowayton in an old-fashioned white house with a porch, with the water there. And Dave had a sailboat, and, well, you can imagine how I felt. Like the luckiest kid on the block.

And we worked. But she was tough. Once you got working, she had such a particularity and was so determined to make such a point, and her drawing—my drawings were thorough. She really could be rough. And she found all these clichés in my work—what little girls do, what little boys do.

PN: Right. I remember that from your *Horn Book* article ["Ruth Krauss and Me: A Very Special Partnership," May-June 1994].

MS: Yes, well, it was really true. She really taught me. [Imitating Ruth:] "No, don't let the girl do that. Let the boy do that. Let the girl do this." And threw me into turmoil and wore me out. Really wore me out because she had this explosion of energy and laughter or rage, whatever it was. Her hair piled on her head. She had the most wonderful hair, lustrous; and there was, as I recollect, it piled on top of her head like a turban. And on the very top was like a bun, but not on the back of her neck, but right on the top of her head. And she had hair on her forehead and strands, long strands, falling down the sides of her face. And she had a very mobile face. She had a broad nose and a very large, voluptuous mouth. And she threw her head back when she laughed, and her eyes closed. That's when she was in a good mood. When she was in a bad mood, she was a banshee!

I never heard her fight with Dave. I never understood the marriage. But, you know, now I'm a much older man, I still don't understand. I don't understand anybody's marriage. [*Laughs.*] You know, you're never going to "understand" anybody's marriage if you're lucky enough to understand your own. It was a kind of—I don't know what it was. They were very different people. He was as quiet as she was noisy. He was as calm as she was like a hurricane. And yet it seemed to work. She would go up after a session and have a headache, and I would just sit and tremble from everything I'd just been through. Afraid she'd throw me out of the project. And then I'd have a little time with Dave, who was shy. He had this great big bald head, and this big burly body—he'd been a football player. And he wore t-shirts, and you could see the big chest and the big arms, which at that point were sort of going too soft a little bit. He looked just like everything he drew. The face was Barnaby. And yet it was a beautiful face. It was—he was not a beautiful man, but it was a beautiful face. And then he would just sit and talk to me by the fireplace, in short spurts, and I just was so amazed that he took the time with me, that he thought me worth his time.

PN: What did you talk about?

MS: We talked about reading. And he was disappointed in how little I had read of great literature. I told him high school was a nightmare, and I loved to read. My hero at that time was Tolstoy. I had read everything by Tolstoy and wanted to become a Tolstoyan but for the beginning of Gandhiism. The war was on, the idea of Gandhi's theory of nonviolence. But he thought I should go beyond that. And he pushed me to Dostoyevsky, and he pushed me to Chekhov. And he would do reading lists which he would like me to follow. And there was no test. He didn't check up on whether I'd read it or do anything like that.

And in large measure he was a referee between me and Ruth. There were many times when we got into fights where I was near tears. I just—I was disappointing her. And I remember—I don't remember the spread—but I do remember him coming in while we were pasting, constant gluing and pasting and cutting up little figures and all those things. And she'd put it here, and I'd suggest there. And she'd put it there, and she would say "no"; and she would rip it off the page and glue, glue, glue! Such a part of our relationship: paste! Gee whiz. And Dave would come in. And he'd hear us yelling, and he would just help us with the composition of the page—very quietly, make a suggestion that was not always accepted by Ruth. But he was fond of me. I was very touched that he cared for me. And I know that she cared for me. And part of her fury was educating me, the dumb Brooklyn kid, into a more interesting human being. She was determined that I have more insight, that I think higher. And so it went from book to book to book. My life in Rowayton was my precious life.

But she was unforgiving. I remember one very unhappy occasion where I went up, and I had my room upstairs, and you could see the water from my room. And she was waiting for me to come down to work, and I had not brought my work with me. It was one of those Freudian moments where clearly I just wanted to be with them. And I went down shaking, and I said, "Ruth, I forgot it." She just went berserk, like "What the hell are you here for? What do you think this is, a hotel, for Chrissake?" You know, and he didn't let her do that. He said, "Maury"—as they called me—"Maury can come when he likes. And I think I'm going to take him for a sailboat ride." And I was just so embarrassed and hurt and despising myself that I gave myself away, meaning I just wanted to be with them. I didn't care if we worked. He was willing to accept it that way, she—she was too, but she wasn't going to let me know that. Her training was more terse and thorough.

PN: So, you just told them you really just wanted to be there, to be with them.

MS: He knew that.

PN: He knew that.

MS: He knew that without making me say it or him say it. He never spoke directly, like she did. Everything was oblique. It was not said. He showed sympathy by saying, "Let's go for a sail." Of course, I was phobic about water, but I didn't dare tell him that. I thought, "If I drown, at least I'm drowning with Crockett Johnson."

PN: [*Laughs.*]

MS: And I think the big year was '63. It was a very difficult year for me because I was working on *Wild Things* and having a very, very difficult time with it and with Ursula. And he was working on *Harold* [*Harold's ABC*] that same year, and I was staying at some place in the country—I don't remember where, up in New York State. And I was going half out of my mind with two lines in the book that were bad and that I couldn't get right, and whatever I did Ursula didn't like. And on just impulse, I went to their house. At this point, by '63, I had already had—you know, I had done the *Nutshell Library*. I had done *Little Bear*—I had a successful career.

PN: Oh, yeah. I mean, you'd done all eight of Ruth's books that you would do by that point, too.

MS: Oh, yes. In fact, I wasn't doing any book by Ruth at that point. I think the five that we did were done almost in a row. I could be wrong about that.

PN: I thought your last one was *Open House for Butterflies.*

MS: Yes, and that was a good time after *Charlotte* and *I'll Be You and You Be Me* and all the other ones which came really in a row. And the relationship had changed very seriously because she—how do I put this?—she was less inclined towards me just because I was becoming successful on my own. I don't mean that she was jealous. She wasn't jealous. She was very happy for me, but she felt there was less to do for and with me. And she began to seek other young people to work with. It made me wretched. I was very jealous. I was very, very jealous of anybody working with Ruth. It was unbearable. She did a book with Remy Charlip, and I was very angry. And yet it was inevitable that she would want to work with Remy or somebody like that who, again, was beginning like I was. I'd been launched, and once I'd been launched, not only was our collaboration ceased but even the friendship did. And Dave was not one to salvage something like that. That would have been totally unlike him to have called and said, "Gee, we miss you" or "Why don't you come anyway?" No, because I don't think—something collapsed, and I just didn't see them. And I saw Ruth on occasion, and he would send me a new book with an autograph in it. I would send him my book with an autograph in it, but that wonderful nest which lasted almost ten years was just gone. There was no discussion.

Attempts at discussions with Ruth later always ended in arguments. She never would see me as grown-up. She didn't want me to be grown-up. She didn't want me to be independent. She never said anything about my books. She never said, "I like them" or "I didn't like them." That was a topic that was avoided, so I assumed she didn't like them.

PN: She did. She saved all the cards that you sent.
MS: She did?

PN: They're there in her papers.
MS: Really?

PN: Yeah.
MS: I'm very touched to hear that. I didn't know how she felt about me. I really thought she had grown a little bit to dislike me.

PN: I don't think so.
MS: Nothing happened. And I was too young. If I were older I would have forced her to reconcile and to talk about whatever this difficulty was. But I was too young, and I didn't think I had the right to do that.

PN: Yes. But, you started to say that in '63, you were working on *Wild Things* and Dave was working on *Harold.* . . .
MS: And I would come to him with *Wild Things* problems, and we would talk about the nature of the book. And I thought it was poetry. I still think it's poetry. And getting the lines just right and just thin enough so that the picture would thicken the language. It was very experimental work for me, and I then had become—I'd really lost interest in picture books. I'd had great luck working with Else Minarik and *Little Bear.* Else is still alive, and we work together and see each other. We talk endlessly. She's very old and ill, and I will lose her soon. But she's the only part of my past that is still there. Everyone else is gone. And so, Else never knew Ruth, so I didn't—no reunion, no way of talking about all that, actually, except you right now.

PN: Right. Right. Well, you know, Nina [Stagakis] went through something sort of similar, in a way. She felt that Ruth was upset with her because she didn't come see Dave when he was sick. But Ruth saved everything that she sent her. I mean, she saved the letters from her and from her husband. I think Ruth thought about Nina a great deal. So, I don't think she said it, but I think she felt it.

MS: No, I don't think she did. If she had, maybe Nina wouldn't have felt so bad.

PN: Yes.

MS: But, as open as Ruth was and as wild as she was, there was a certain uptightness about personal relationships and how one verbalizes one's feelings. It was partly a generational thing. Nobody talked like we talk now. Everybody talks too much!

PN: Right.

MS: You know, in a minute, you know what their psychological and bowel problems are! That was not necessarily the way things are done. I knew Nina but slightly. She was a lovely blonde-haired girl. And I can't remember her father's name, Phyllis's husband.

PN: Well, there was Sid Landau who was her stepfather, and her natural father was, um . . . [Gene] Wallace. His first name has left my brain, but I have it written down.

MS: I remember he was a very good-looking man.

PN: Right.

MS: I don't know what happened to him. Did he die?

PN: He died [in September 1954].

MS: He did die.

PN: Yes.

MS: I remember I was struck by his good looks. And Phyllis [Rowand] was a very—oh, God, let me render her correctly. I liked her very much. She had long hair. She was thin. She was devoted to Ruth, and Ruth to her, or it seemed so to me. And Phyllis was very generous about my entering the picture. She liked my work; she liked me. There was no, like, I was trampling on her ground. And they had just done *Bears* together, and I know I told you that I'll be doing *Bears* for Harper's.

PN: Yeah. [Note: Krauss's *Bears*, with new art by Sendak, was published in 2005.]

Maurice and I spoke of Phyllis Rowand (Nina's mother), who also died young—at the age of forty-seven from a brain aneurysm, when Nina was eighteen. He was very sympathetic, remarking that "it was very hard on Nina. She lost her father, and she lost her mother." Maurice acknowledged that he and Phyllis "were not really personal friends," but he remembered her fondly because she "came to visit when I came to stay in Rowayton." At this point, side A of my tape ran out, and as I flipped it over, he apologized for giving such detailed, "fat answers" to my questions.

PN: No, fat answers are good. In fact, you paused at a perfect time. I just had to change the tape. Well, some details in what you said: you spent weekends, you had a room you stayed in there.
MS: I had a room, a guest room. It was a very large, rather Victorian house. Big clunky house with a rickety porch. I sort of recall as you came into the front room, there was a big fireplace—a big, big space when you came in. Work table, fireplace, porch, right near the water.

PN: And so this was every weekend you would spend there?
MS: No.

PN: Or how many weekends?
MS: Well, during the working I would maybe spend one or two weekends a month working there. I was mostly inspired by what happened on the weekends so I could get through the rest of the week. I also had to hold on to my job. So, I worked at Schwarz, and I found a nasty little room to live in. And, I did *A Hole Is to Dig* in that little room. I also was invited to go on a skiing trip with some friends in Canada—and I remember that so specifically only because I got there and I hated skiing. I thought I was going to break every fucking finger I had. So, while they did the slopes, I did *A Hole Is to Dig*. A lot of it was illustrated in Canada, strangely. And I could carry it around—it was a little book, and it was easy to do it anywhere. And then I'd bring a whole sheath of little drawings of little people over the weekend, and we'd decide, Ruth and I, which ones where good enough to use in the book. It's a very happy memory. I mean, when I discuss the troubles, that too is a happy memory.

PN: Well, it's all of a piece.

MS: The collaboration was so rich and real. You know, I realized her whole life was invested in this.

PN: Oh, yeah. And, of the papers that you see, she had a lot connected to *A Hole Is to Dig*. She has the notebooks from the Bank Street School; she has notebooks of her own, what she recorded of what children said, several dummies. There's a lot connected to it in there.

MS: I have some things from *A Hole Is to Dig*, too. It was a turning point in my life: one, to work with her; two, that book is so totally original. Neither of us knew what a clamor would occur when it was published. It was immediately a book that was taken up in colleges, in the interest in how children spoke, in pragmatism in children and seeing the world just for their needs. "A rug is to stand on," everything is—from that view of little children as these little hard-assed creatures—so much truer than what, starting with Hans Christian Andersen, who I have still a very lively dislike for . . . to Ruth Krauss people, who are my kind of people. You know, I just fell in. These are the kids I knew. We did—I think my favorites were *A Hole Is to Dig* and *A Very Special House*. That was—

PN: I was just looking at her—

MS: That was just a great, great book. And we had then tuned in on each other. There was much less her having to schlep me up intellectually. I was ready for her on that one. And I believe that that's probably my favorite.

PN: *A Very Special House.*

MS: Yes. *I'll Be You and You Be Me* was great fun because every page was an experiment, every page we changed our minds. And yet the book hangs together in a way that's fascinating because it's the two of us. And it's almost like a love book. *Charlotte and the White Horse* was my first attempt to unite poetry with William Blake, the little picture, the little box underneath. I love Blake; I have all my life. Although *Charlotte* was the wrong book for Blake, it nevertheless ended up being a very pretty book and very simple book. The only book we did that I really didn't like was *Open House for Butterflies*.

PN: Really?

MS: No, I don't like it. I think Ursula was intent on getting us to do another *A Hole Is to Dig*, and I felt that. And I didn't feel easy about the project because it just seemed to be a non-spontaneous version of *A Hole Is to Dig*.

And my drawing of little people by then had hardened. They had none of the evanescence and silliness and clumsiness of the drawings in *A Hole Is to Dig*. I had worked it out technically, and thus, I kind of deadened the children. I don't know how Ruth felt about that book, but I was never happy with it.

PN: That's funny. I always liked it, so I'm surprised to hear you say that.
MS: Well, you're the one who's supposed to like it. [*Laughs.*]

PN: [*Laughs.*] Well, good.
MS: You're the reader.

PN: Yeah.
MS: I don't have to like it. You know, it's not that I didn't like it, I just felt we'd gone a long distance since *A Hole Is to Dig*.

PN: Well, you felt like you'd been there before.
MS: Yes, I felt that exactly. And I felt like this was *A Hole Is to Dig II*. And I don't remember how Ruth felt about that one. I have no idea.

PN: I can't answer that one either.
MS: Even, I don't even remember how it all happened, which tells you how I kind of dumped it out of my memory. There are no associations with that book at all now. I just cannot remember. OK.

PN: OK, so I started to ask that other question just to figure out how often you were there, and you were there when you were working on the books on the weekends. And you worked on all eight of the books you did with Ruth like that?
MS: Yes.

PN: Staying there on the weekends?
MS: Yes.

PN: OK.
MS: I suppose we did a lot of work, too, in Ursula's office. We could not have worked in my apartment because I didn't have one.

PN: But then you first met in Ursula's office, right?
MS: We first met in Ursula's office. Ursula's office was like our studio. And

there was this extremely explosive relationship between the women, which scared the shit out of me.

PN: You can see it in the correspondence, too.

MS: God, I mean, "love-hate" is like Hallmark card compared to what this was like. It was love—I mean, Ursula knew she had a genius by the tail. But that genius wasn't going to be manipulated. And, when we had that awful meeting where Ruth demanded that since our books had been so successful that we should be getting more money. A conversation that I would have rather committed hari-kari than had with Ursula. Anything relating to money with Ursula was a nightmare. She became the House of Harper, suddenly. And all her freedom and expressiveness, suddenly she had all the chains of the bank. And Ruth had the gall to bring this up, and I remember this one experience where I was sitting with Ruth and I was cowering. I didn't care if we got more money or not. I just wanted this to be over. And yet I knew Ruth was right. I knew we were being underpaid. I knew it. And we knew that the books were very successful for Harper's.

And Ruth was brave. She just simply brought up the matter, and Ursula began to holler, right away—instantly, like somebody'd stabbed her. And she always used "ingratitude." If you wanted more money, you were not grateful. "I did this for you. I let you do that book. And you chose this artist, and he had no experience, and who else in the whole world would do that?" And Ruth would say, "OK, it happened already. And we've done it, and we're a successful team," and she would insist. And I remember Ruth just—rather, Ursula—and I don't remember how many conversations, but it's all condensed in memory into one—where she cleared the desk with her hands.

PN: Ruth did?

MS: No, Ursula did.

PN: Ursula did.

MS: And some of it fell on to Ruth and on to me. And we both pushed our chairs back hastily. Ursula was berserk and screaming at us and told us to "Get out!" And everybody could hear it 'cause her office was right in the middle on 33rd Street. And we left like the Angel of Death sending us out of Eden, hustled out of the room. And we went to the elevator, and my heart stopped because I thought, "Jesus Christ, this is the end." I was only through at twenty-seven. Why had Ruth blown it just for money?

PN: And what had you just done at that point? *A Hole Is to Dig* and . . .

MS: No, no, no, no. We would have done two or three books by then. She wouldn't have done that after *A Hole Is to Dig*. *A Hole Is to Dig* was a surprise success.

PN: Then, when the others were successful, too, then—

MS: The others were never as successful. Never. There was a novelty to *A Hole Is to Dig*. And there was a kind of eccentricity to the other books. This isn't my thinking, but that is sort of the popular thinking about those books. We both knew—or I did—that *A Special House* was even better. Much better, much more reaching and fun than *A Hole Is to Dig*. And we didn't have to compare them. But it must have been by the third book that the scene occurred, and Ruth thought that we deserved that. I agreed with her, but I was a coward. Also, she had the authority, and she had the—she had the power to make such a demand.

Anyway, we went out of the building with Ruth trying to console me that it's not the end of the world. I thought it really was the end of the world.

PN: Understandably.

MS: And, but we got to the bottom of the floor, the elevator opened on the ground floor. Ursula was there. She had run all down the flights. She wasn't finished screaming at us. It was like one of these horror movies.

PN: Wow. [*Laughs.*] That's amazing.

MS: [*Laughs. Then, imitating Ursula's voice:*] "I never want to see you again, and get the hell out of my sight, you bastards!" Jesus Christ, I just was so frightened.

PN: Wow. So what happened?

MS: Well, we got more money. [Note: Krauss and Sendak *each* received a $1000 advance for *I Want to Paint My Bathroom Blue*—twice as much as the advance for each previous collaboration.]

PN: [*Laughs.*] So, so, did she call you up and say, "I'm sorry" or . . .

MS: I don't remember, honestly.

PN: Maybe you just never spoke of that conversation again.

MS: I mean, Ruth had every right to win and she won. But I don't remember. I just know that suddenly there was a little bit more money. [*Laughs.*]

PN: [*Laughs.*] Wow.

MS: And, yes, it was not easy. These were two hair-raising women. It was Medea and . . . think of another nightmare woman. But otherwise I remember seeing Ruth at occasional parties. And, when I did finally get an apartment in Greenwich Village, I remember Ruth—not often—came. He never did; he never did. As far as I know, he didn't go to parties. He may have gone to parties in Connecticut. But he had his buddies, like Ad Reinhardt, and I don't remember him as being sociable, social.

PN: Well, you said before he was kind of quiet. There was a shyness to Dave.

MS: Intensely quiet. And he puzzled people. They didn't know what to do with him. I remember the only time he ever shocked me was: there was a young woman working at Harper's who still is in the business, and she was one of what we called "Ursula's girls." She had many young women—they were all ladies, literally, in waiting to become the next editor-in-chief—and they were marvelously—. I mean one was extraordinary: Susan Hirschman was a fantastic young woman, and she's now just retiring. There's a retiring party next weekend, I think. But, in any case, what is my point here?

PN: You said Dave shocked you.

MS: Yes, he shocked me because he noticed this other young woman, and he said to me, that is—it never made much sense, but coming out of his mouth—he said, "What a fantastic ass she has."

PN: [*Laughs.*]

MS: [*Laughs.*] He said, "It looks at me. It's like a bagel at one point." I mean, coming out of his mouth, I was stunned. I didn't even know he knew the word "ass."

PN: Well, yes, he seemed so gentle and so circumspect, he wouldn't say something like that.

MS: It was a glimpse into—wow, this is a hot patootie, this guy. [*Laughs.*] And that was the only mad expression I ever heard coming out of Dave Johnson. And he was right—she had a great ass.

PN: [*Laughs.*] Oh, that's funny; that's funny. Well, I have an odd collection of questions, so maybe I'll just ask the odd ones. Well, let's see, we're still on creative stuff: I've often wondered if Ruth's creative methods influenced you at all. There's an improvisational quality to her work which to me suggests that there's a lot of improvising, a lot of letting the ideas come, and then editing and figuring out which ones work. I've often wondered if that influenced you at all.

MS: You know, I don't know. But I'm thinking: sure. I think the influence I'm most aware of is not being nervous about experimentation, or not being fussy about the muse or the construction of the picture book in the traditional—she hated the traditional, which is what I learned to do naturally, too, was to hate it. When I did the *Little Bear* books with Else Minarik, one great thing about Ursula is that she was such a great teacher. She would have me do Ruth Krauss books and then books by Meindert DeJong, who was a fabulous writer. He's gone now, and he's long out of fashion. But then I had to draw little Dutch vignette scenes in wash and pens. Of course, I went straight to Rembrandt, studied all his etchings and his drawings, and I made these cozy little tight Dutch pictures for Meindert, who became a wonderful friend of mine. A deep, deep emotional tie between Ursula and him. And then the *Little Bear* books, there's another thing to work with—with Else. And Ruth chose for me, like a great teacher—I mean, Ursula did. I had to keep changing styles, and this is something Ruth did too. Beating me over the back not to become a stylist.

PN: Don't fall into a rut.

MS: Yes. Don't get a style where you're always recognizable. Change and change and change it, change the form, change the form, beat the material until you make it scream but give to you what it's all about. Don't assume anything. And I think, yes, there's a rich learning heritage from both these women. I was very lucky. I had both of these women caring about me. I wasn't the only one: Tomi Ungerer came into the picture, and Ezra [Jack] Keats came into the picture, and Arnold Lobel came into the picture. But, well, like the family I knew, I was the one she loved best. And I can honestly say that was breaking and disorganizing the work in such a way that it revealed its true material to you. You didn't block it in ice quickly. I've never done a book that was premeditated. Never, never, never—except if I'm illustrating somebody else's book, and I have no choice. And most of my income came from illustrating other people's books. You didn't get to do a picture book quickly simply because you had to prove you could earn your way. A picture book then was a very costly thing—color separation was laborious, and you had to learn how to do it *right*. Dave was a very good teacher about color separations because all his books were, obviously, separated.

PN: I was going to ask you what his influence would be, if any.

MS: His would have been technical. Brushes, pencils, watercolor, paper. I was very careless with materials 'cause I didn't know materials. So, unfortunately, a lot of my early work is jaundiced, yellow, and brittle, and breaks when you touch it. The *Wild Things* illustrations are all but gone at this point. Just lack of knowledge—nobody teaches you not to work on paper that is full of acid, and so we all did. So, I think his was of a literary kind. I always associate books with Dave.

PN: He was a big reader.

MS: He was a big reader. And I am a big reader. I really think that's maybe more important than anything else I do is reading. And that reading drips down and begins to, in embryonic—everything I do comes from reading. Everything I write comes from reading and from music. Now, classical music did not come from Ruth and Dave—I don't remember their musical tastes at this point, I really cannot recollect—but from my brother, who was also my teacher. He was five years older than me, and it is through him—who I adored, he was a fantastic artist, engineer of toys, he was an intuitive artist. He wrote any number of books. I illustrated his first two books, and then I stopped because it just wasn't good. The Sendak Brothers were hard for him. He never complained, but my parents always complained that I had done his reputation ill by simply being more popular. That was not an easy time. I didn't mean to go off on that track.

PN: No, no—that's all right.

MS: To answer your question: yes, but it was not very obvious what the influence was, except my first book, *Kenny's Window*, which has purple prose in it but I still like it. It's a very disorganized book that is organically organized. And I'm very proud of that first book. It isn't at all like somebody's first book. But I was working with real intellects, with people who saw this form—the picture book form and the children's book form—and they took it very seriously, like you would poetic forms. And they weren't typical. I mean Ruth worked so hard at the little nonsense things. Perfect sense and perfect order, however casually they may have been put down on the page. So, it was respect, it was love, and I had my own innate passion for books. I was illustrating books when I was a little boy. I was illustrating Oscar Wilde's fairytales, operas, . . .

PN: That love of books in themselves is something that Dave had very much—he was interested in typography and layout. I mean, he knew all that stuff; he knew how books were made.

MS: Yes, well look at your little dummies. [Note: I had sent Sendak a photocopy of Johnson's dummies for *Magic Beach*.] It's so casual and repetitive, . . . but it's not. It's amazing how little he moves from page to page.

PN: And that's the thing that people miss about *Harold* is that it's deceptively simple. It's not simple at all.

MS: No, it isn't.

Maurice and I then spoke of Crockett Johnson's *Magic Beach*, originally published as *Castles in the Sand* (1965) with illustrations by Betty Fraser, an artist whose style was at odds with Johnson's concept. Maurice stresses that, in his criticisms of the art, he is not making fun of the artist: "I'm really not so much laughing at her as laughing at the period."

MS: Look what she learned: how to disguise the words of the writer. If the story was a bit strange—and it is totally original and open—then her job was to obscure it and make it look as banal as possible. That's what she was taught to do.

PN: And she did.

MS: And she did. And that's what art school teaches you. And if you don't have the instinct or the intuition, because you should be the guardian of the text, and you should be the backseat driver, you have no business intruding on the text—none. And if you don't know that, you don't know anything. And I've never felt myself to be equal to the writing. I was always there to enhance the language, bring out what was invisible and make it visible, or add to it, give it another meaning, which is just as interesting, perhaps, and as important as its original meaning. And that was the lesson I took over when I quit books and—around 1980, because I was just fed up with this stupid publishing world. I hadn't realized that it was really going to get a whole lot worse. And I went into opera, and then I was designing Mozart and the rest and the same—your job was to make the music clearer. Everything you did was to enhance the work of the composer. I learned that so profoundly.

PN: Well, it's a collaboration. It's not you versus someone else.

MS: I love working with others—what's happening now with me and Tony, it's like fine-tuning instruments. It's really, you know, screw your ego, this is something—I don't have to tell you that. It's a very important thing, and I look at this girl's [Betty Fraser's] work and I think so many art students look like that. And it's pathetic. Who knows whether she's really good? Who knows who she is? There's no knowing from looking at these pictures.

PN: No, there really isn't.
MS: And, of all things, to stick her with a Crockett Johnson.

PN: Well, she was herself perplexed by the pairing. I mean, Dave did his own illustrations; why would they want her to do it? She was young, a new illustrator.
MS: You mean he chose her?

PN: No, no, he didn't. The publisher chose her.
MS: And he didn't object.

PN: I don't know. This was published by—not by Harper. And I haven't seen the correspondence with this company.
MS: I think it was with Macmillan or Norton or one of those.

PN: I think it's Macmillan. I think it's—it's Holt, Rinehart, and Winston, I think. [Note: It is.]
MS: Oh, that's right. It's here. I can turn around and look at it.

PN: That's right. I need to see their correspondence to figure out why. According to her, the publisher felt that his illustrations weren't right for it—which may be their way of saying the book was too odd and, as you suggest, that she could make it more conventional.
MS: Yes, and he would just make it odder by allowing it to be odd. Those kids in his drawings have no intention of clarifying anything. Far from it. Far from it.

PN: Now, this is kind of a strange segue, but it's vaguely related to the influence and the collaboration and so on. But, after Ruth passed on, you had just—your book *We Are All in the Dumps with Jack and Guy* was out, and you did that [27 September 1993] *New Yorker* cover in which you have the children reading Ruth's books. Did you know that she left most of her estate to homeless children?
MS: To who?

PN: To homeless children.
MS: No!

PN: Yes, it's in her will.
MS: [*Gasps*] Jesus. No.

PN: Seriously. I wondered if you knew that and—
MS: No.

PN:—there was—
MS: No, I knew nothing about that. I—my hair is standing on end. Her spirit was so with me in that book. It was going back to the *A Hole Is to Dig* kids. And I was so unnerved by that subject when I heard about it—Venezuela, South America, children being killed on the street by police like rats and vermin. That brought me back to the happy little ragamuffins in the Krauss books. That was a very serious book for me, *Jack and Guy*. It was much maligned; it is much maligned.

PN: Really?
MS: Oh, yes.

PN: I like it.
MS: Well, you have good taste, what can I tell you?

PN: I see it as part of the group that includes *Wild Things* and *In the Night Kitchen* and *Outside Over There*. I see it as a logical progression from there.
MS: Well, those are the most important books I've done. I mean *Wild Things*, unlike Herman Melville who bitterly complained that he would always be remembered for *Typee* and the Cannibal writer that he was—the *New York Times* never mentioned *Moby-Dick*. I don't have that complaint. I will only be known for *Wild Things*. Just because people are too dense to think—who cares? That little bugger has kept me in prosperity so I could do my own weird books. And if that's the way it is, that's the way it is. But the books coming after *Wild Things*—*Wild Things* was important because it was my breakthrough book, because it was my first picture book by me. And I could be myself. And Max has his roots in Ruth Krauss. You know, her phrase that children were allowed to be as cruel and maniacal as she knew they were. Studying them at Bank Street, she knew what monstrosities children are.

PN: Do you know if she ever met Margaret Wise Brown at Bank Street? Did they know each other?

MS: I don't know. I don't know. I have a suspicion they had to have met because they were both at Bank Street as young women, but I don't know.

PN: It would be a great story if they did and if anyone knew, but I don't know.

MS: No, I don't either, and according to the [Leonard] Marcus book [*Margaret Wise Brown: Awakened by the Moon*], I don't recollect him ever mentioning Ruth.

PN: No, I asked him, too, and he said he's not sure if they knew each other. He's sure they knew each other's work, but he doesn't know if they knew each other.

MS: I really think they must have. It was a tiny world. I mean, wouldn't they have *wanted* to know each other?

PN: I came across a letter from him [Leonard Marcus] to Ruth asking about Bank Street—today, when I was going through her papers. I don't know if she answered it. I'll have to ask him, but it was interesting to see.

MS: Well, she was a great Bank Street-er. But I have a feeling, too, there was a—as Bank Street froze (as all these things freeze) into rules and regulations and meetings and stuff, I think she sort of wasn't interested in . . . . She was interested in childhood and had an intensity of interest in the behavior of children. It was the beginning of all that in the '50s: what children said, why they said it, the Freudian things, the child as—the interest in the infant and the child growing were fantastic news back in the '50s. And that was Ruth. She was a social worker, basically.

PN: Yeah, well she had a background in anthropology before—.

MS: And she was very proud of it and her mind was wide open to the idea of the cannibalistic, egomaniacalness of children and their need to be so to survive. They were the first such children in children's literature.

PN: Yeah. I'm just going to switch tapes here. . . . Do you know why they [Ruth and Dave] decided not to have children? Does anybody know?

MS: No. How could I possibly know that?

PN: Well, I don't know. I just always ask, because—

MS: It was the most reasonable and sane thing that they didn't have children. And I say that not out of criticism. I think most people I know—all my life—shouldn't have had children. But working artists who are so imbedded in their work make the worst parents imaginable.

PN: Well, that makes sense. That makes sense with what other people have told me.

MS: And also Ruth was smart enough to probably know that. She was very interested in sex. She loved things of the body. She was very unusual in that department, too, in her ability to talk about such things. I was stunned. I lived in Brooklyn. I didn't know women knew what happened to them until it happened because that was what my mother always said—that men were plunderers and pigs, and one had to endure it. That was part of what the marriage thing was all about—a woman's endurance. God forbid she should enjoy it. And then to meet Ruth Krauss who boasted of her sexuality. It was always strange because she was so richly sensuous, and not so much in front of Dave—it's funny, that memory just came back to me. A little less boisterous in front him. So, what their sexual lives were like, what their amorousness—.

PN: Well, that's not really part of this, so—.

MS: No, it isn't, but it's interesting to me because I've long pondered what it was between them.

PN: Well, Nina said they had separate beds.

MS: Well, that answers something. They did not seem to be a married couple. They seemed to be partners who had been through a war, and it made sense to stay together. I never felt, I never could imagine him embracing her or her embracing him, or any kind of touchy-feely thing between them. I never saw it.

PN: I think that was very private for them. Nina saw that, but I don't think a lot of people did.

MS: Well, I'm glad to hear it.

PN: I think they were private about that.

MS: It's like all kids cannot imagine that their parents have sex.

PN: Right, right.

MS: Like that's so boringly traditional. They all go to their therapists and carrying on, pouting about how their parents haven't been put together and that's why all their lives are fucked up. And then they find out when they're fifty that their parents fucked endlessly. And they're so ashamed that you could *think* that was possible.

PN: Right, right. Yeah, no, you're right. It's interesting what you say about them. That makes me think of their—they both were married before and those marriages didn't work out.
MS: She was a woman that it was hard to imagine her being married, even to Dave.

PN: Well, it's interesting: it took me a while to figure out when, exactly, they were married because the published sources differ. One says '39, one says '40, one says '41. I finally found on Dave's will that they were married in June of '43, although they lived together before that.
MS: June of '43.

PN: They met in '39 and they were living together by 1940. But that date was interestingly elusive, in that regard.
MS: That was two years before the end of the war.

PN: Yep. They would have been living in Darien then.
MS: By then?

PN: By then, yes.
MS: She was from Baltimore.

We spoke of Ruth's family. I had just spoken with Betty Hahn, who was married to Dr. Richard Hahn, Ruth's cousin. Both Hahns were very close to Ruth. As I told Maurice, Betty told me quite a bit that I didn't know, including that Ruth had studied anthropology under Margaret Mead.

MS: Yep, I knew that.

PN: Did you? You see, I didn't know that. Which explains a lot about her willingness to talk openly about sex.
MS: Oh, yes. Goodness. I think it made her crazy that people didn't. It's as though everybody was pretending. Now, of course, it's just the opposite. I wish that they'd shut the hell up.

PN: [*Laughs*] Let's go back in the other direction.
MS: Yes, but they're not any more honestly talking about it than they were about not talking about it. That's the interesting thing. Now, they heave it out, but it's not—it doesn't ring true.

PN: Yeah, well, on TV, it's all, it's all entertainment. It's not to learn something; it's just to be explicit for its own sake.
MS: Just turn on the customer and titillate them, like going to the whorehouse. I mean, that's what television is: it's a form of whorehousing, and a very bad form of whorehousing, as far as I'm concerned. There's *nothing* titillating about it. It's revolting. But Ruth—to me, timid Brooklyn boy— her ability to talk about the body and the orifi was an amazing adventure. I was both shocked and so elated that my thoughts were not sick and putrid, as I thought they were, as I suspect most young people of that generation thought that what they were thinking was sick. Because how could you know? No one else talked about it. No one would confirm your fantasies or answer your questions.

PN: She wrote an interesting prospectus for a book (which was never published) on gender, on gender roles and how people learn them—these behaviors—and how it's different across cultures. Which I keep coming across references to, which I thought was pretty interesting, in light of her sociology work.
MS: I think it was necessary for her to live that way.

PN: To live what way?
MS: To live with the body, from being an anthropologist and having seen primitive people who don't know what it's like to be ashamed, and our shame is so disgusting—it comes from religious sources, and it's so repellent.

PN: Well, she lived with the Blackfeet Indians for a while.
MS: Yes. I mean, she knew about all that. She was probably the first person who opened me up to the subject so that I've never been clean ever since. [*Laughs*]

PN: [*Laughs*] Well, good for her!
MS: Yes, absolutely good for her because I do that now. I've taken on so many of her traits and Ursula's traits. These were my models. And I will not tolerate oblique language. She taught me how to say "fuck you." I never said things like that until Ruth said them, and she said them with such a joie de

vivre. But it's not arbitrary. It was—oh, I don't know what it was—I won't pretend to know what it was. It was that it freed me.

PN: Well, it wasn't just punctuation as it is in popular films or—
MS: No, by no means. On every TV show, on every HBO show, and the endless non-talk, like "you know, you know, you know, you know."

PN: [*Laughs*]
MS: And I can't bear it. And those people on news shows who say, "Well, at the end of the day . . ."—I want to kill them! And they say it as though it were an original thing to say.

PN: Right.

I asked Maurice if Dave and Ruth ever spoke of their earlier lives, but he didn't recall. I spoke of some other friends of Ruth and Dave's, and asked if he knew them. He knew the names, but not the people.

MS: How is it that I never got to met these people? They didn't have—I wish they did—some little salon-type thing on the weekends where artists get together. But I would meet Phyllis—Ruth was out strolling, and I'd walk with her. And we'd meet her in the street. And I'm sure Phyllis came to the house. I don't remember. They didn't have evenings with people to dinner; no, they didn't do things like that, and I don't do things like that either. And that's not because of them. It's because I'm as much an isolate as Dave was. I've grown—I was not influenced by him. It was because my brother was such, too. And, to me, being left alone is the greatest privilege in the world. So, I don't go to New York, and why most of my friendships—with very rare exceptions—are phone friendships. And those people who are intolerant of my behavior, and insist on seeing me, we just stop being friends—I cannot gratify them. I cannot. And I felt that was true of their house, too. It was a pretty closed house. But I could be wrong. I could be wrong.

PN: Well, it's interesting just what side you saw of them.
MS: Yes, exactly.

PN: Because everybody sees something a little different, but also that overlaps with what other people see. And it's Picasso or something: you see it from all different angles, and you start to get the picture.

MS: Yes.

PN: Although, hopefully, it's not written like it's Picasso, or it would be hard to read, but—. So—

MS: Me and Ruth had not a falling out from an argument, but a fading away from each other. She became more elusive. She came to this house. I've lived in this house for thirty years now. I had been very, very, very ill previously—I had a heart attack. And I remember—it was kind of a reunion when I became so ill—of Ruth's concern, postcards. I remember I have numbers of her postcards, with her little doodles, "And I hope, Maury, you're doing better" and such. She was very thoughtful, then.

PN: When was this?

MS: I had my coronary in '67. It was a month before my thirty-ninth birthday. And, I remember Ruth, then. It was like a coming together then. I think she was very worried about me—Dave, too. I know that because I have a joint note from them, somewhere. And she did visit me here, but it was always very stiff, it was very stiff. It was not fun to see her here. And she was restrained or constrained when she came here, as though she had to be an old friend and no longer a collaborator—it was an uneasy feeling.

PN: There was a change in the relationship; it wasn't what you—.

MS: No, no, it was very different. She was very different. I don't know that I was very different. But she assumed I was—I wasn't very different, I just couldn't catch her. I saw her—the last time I saw Ruth, when—not Maureen O'Sullivan, Maureen—

PN: Maureen O'Hara [sister of poet Frank O'Hara].

MS: Maureen O'Hara, thank you, was a very devoted friend, and I never knew her. And she just called me out of the blue to wonder if I knew how ill Ruth was. And I hadn't because I had been that much out of touch. And Maureen wanted to be—she thought I would want to see Ruth, which of course I did, but I wasn't sure if Ruth wanted to see me. But Maureen persuaded me, and I think I went to see her two or three times before she died. But I remember the last time best because I just knew I would not see her again. And she was living with a woman [Joanna Czaderna]—I remember she was at a woman's house [note: actually Ruth's house, but Joanna was living there and looking after Ruth]—and that woman had a child [Bianca]. And Ruth was very difficult or so I was told and felt, but that the child had a magic touch with her. Ruth, then, was shrunken to nothing. She looked like a mummy. She was very small and in a wheelchair. Her hair—I mean Ruth's hair—made a great impression on me. It was like all this sex and so much of it was in her hair. And was still as thick as it ever was, but it was absolutely white. And it hung heavy on her head and then into a very long pigtail down her back, I think. But I know that there was also hair on the side of her head, it was loose and trailing. And I was shocked at her size. And she averted her face from me, and Maureen said there's really no knowing if she recognized me or knew—I didn't know and I still don't know, and if you could tell me the details of her illness, I would be grateful. I never knew, really, what was wrong with Ruth.

PN: I'm not sure. I've spoken with people who've said that, let me think now. I remember that one person told me—and I'd have to go look at all my notes on this—that if she had done the therapy that she was supposed to do, if she had allowed the nurse to help her, she would have lasted longer, and she might not have faded as she did.
MS: What was the source of the illness?

PN: That's what I'm trying to remember. Something to do with the joints stiffening and not being able to move so much. You know she had that hip replacement in the '80s.
MS: Oh, yes, that's right. I do remember that.

PN: I know she was often hurting her ankles, her feet. I remember that. And I've come across a lot in her archives of her being sick for various reasons. Right back from when she was even a small child, she was often ill for one reason or another.
MS: What—what did in Dave?

PN: I beg your pardon?
MS: What did Dave die of?

PN: I believe of lung cancer.
MS: Right. He was a heavy smoker.

PN: Yes. One person suggested throat cancer, but I'm pretty sure it was lung cancer. But it was definitely smoking-related. Did you visit him in his—?
MS: No. I didn't. I felt very excluded. Even when I visited Ruth, it was only

Maureen. Not that I didn't want to see her—I was afraid to. I didn't know where I was in her life. But I did see her; I did see her. I'm very sorry I didn't see Dave. Dave would not have advertised his illness, and I didn't even know when he died.

PN: Well, from what I've learned, it was fairly quick. I mean, I think he was diagnosed in January, and he died by July of '75.
MS: How old would that have made him?

PN: He was sixty-eight when he died. He would have turned sixty-nine that October.
MS: Jesus. I'm older than Dave. It's a remarkable feeling.

PN: Yeah, he—well, it was very sudden, and very unexpected, and too soon.
MS: And he did not oppose it very much.

PN: I beg your pardon?
MS: I don't know why—I'm sure he did not oppose it very much.

PN: Oppose it? You mean fight it?
MS: Yes.

PN: I don't know. Actually, I think he did. One person I talked to said that when she visited him—and this was not long before he died—that he would still try to eat to keep up his strength. And he did oppose it, even though he must have known that it was unopposable.
MS: Well, my brother [Jack Sendak] died of just that.

PN: Of lung cancer?
MS: I'm mixing up the two men because I know my brother did not oppose it, and that's what infuriated me. He just didn't care. And maybe I was doubling up on the men, both very important men in my life.

PN: Yeah, I don't know, I mean one—. The general sense that people gave me was that he tried to oppose it, tried to be strong about. Although, that isn't what everyone says. You know, Sid Landau, who knew them pretty well, says that one thing he remembers about Dave's illness was that he—Dave was angry at being ill.
MS: Angry.

PN: That's what he said. Sid said he remembered that because he had never seen Dave angry.
MS: Angry at dying?

PN: Yes. And that could have just been the day that Sid visited him, you know?
MS: Yes.

PN: It may not have been something that lasted for a long time.
MS: Yes, well you're getting all these irrational reactions, as you know. On the day I—what was memorable about my visit to Ruth was her averting her face, which normally she had such a—. She left such a strong impression on me that she rejected me, that I would be rejected, I wouldn't fight. And the whole dwindling of the relationship had to do with some sense on my part that she was rejecting me. I don't know whether that was true or not. I wish I were wiser and older. I mean that I didn't do for Dave anything.

So, on this day—and let me get this story over with already—I asked, "Where are Dave's paintings?" And she just nodded her head. And I just kept talking to her as though she were answering me. I said, "I hope they're in a safe place, Ruth." And just making conversation with her, and not being afraid to mention Dave to her. Everybody was so nervous about what they were saying. So she had—she really had a fretful expression on her face, and I think it was largely—she was very vain. She was extremely vain, and she didn't like me seeing her this way one bit. And so when I was leaving, I felt extremely frustrated. I felt I knew I was not going to see her again, and even if I did it would be no difference. She was like a little doll. And I needed something, an accord with, and I just went over to her. And I leaned over her, and I asked her if I could kiss her goodbye. And I was only seeing her profile with her eyes half-closed, as I remember. And she didn't actually object, and so I leaned over and I gently took her chin in my hand. I moved it slightly so that I would be closer to her mouth. And I gave her a very, very long big kiss on those yummy lips of hers. And I even, I even had the temerity to put my tongue between her lips. And the result of that—it's hard because it's—the result of that was a giggle and, "Oh, Maury." I can't tell you how much that meant. That she knew it was me all the time and that I had done just what she would have liked me to have done—to not have treated her like a mummy, but to have treated her like the beautiful woman that she was.

PN: Oh, that's great.

MS: It is great. And I have tears in my eyes now because I have, I'm so grateful that I had the sense to do that. And not treat her like a dying person. And putting my tongue between her lips was purely intuitive. I didn't know I was going to do that. I lingered—and just to hear that giggle one more time, and to hear her say may name one more time. And she loved me. I knew she loved me. I loved her. So much time is wasted by people. Can't be helped.

PN: No, no. You know, my stepfather died in January, and I kept thinking of all the things that I wish I had said before it was too late. And, you know, it's too late. So.

MS: We all suffer that. And so many people have died in my life, and I've now become—and I've also learned this from Emily Dickinson, I have just such a passion for her death poems. She was considered a morbid woman because she liked to watch the bodies. She liked to watch the passage, as she called it. She leaned very close and then watched the passage, through the eyes, when life left the eyes and was the end of her.

PN: "I heard a Fly buzz—when I died."

MS: Yes. And I have learned not to waste the death anymore. The most important death in my life was my brother. And it was unbearable to lose such a friend. And I made him talk. I made him. We talked until he couldn't talk about what it meant between us. I held him, and I told him that I love him—.

PN: Well, you did the right thing.

MS: Yes, I did the right thing.

PN: You did the right thing.

MS: We have to learn, you know. We learn everything. It doesn't come naturally to us. It only comes from experience. And there's always regrets, like you have regrets about your grandfather [stepfather]. You learn from that so that you don't regret the next time. It should be done right so they get all of it and you get all of it. It's remarkably wonderful, and it may make you cry for the rest of your life, but so what?

PN: Yeah, yeah. [*Pause*] Well, it feels like any question after this would just . . . It feels like this is a natural closure to this. I don't know if we should—

MS: Yes,—

PN: suspend this or if I should—
MS: well,—

PN: talk to you some other time.
MS: we can talk some other—. It's getting late (I just looked), and I've not been drawing while we're talking. Maybe we should stop. We can go at it again if you'd like.

PN: Yes. I don't have a lot more questions, just one or two, which you may not even have answers to, but this seems like the moment to close the conversation.
MS: That's true. I can't talk now. I've touched all the feelings. I can't—.

PN: I was, I think I was sensing that, which was why I was—
MS: Yes.

PN:—not wanting to ask anything.
MS: I know. I know. The best people in my life except for maybe three people are dead. Are dead. AIDS ate up so many friendships. It was like World War III. And it's still World War III. But everybody—Jim Marshall, my best friends. All my colleagues are gone. There's no one left of my generation. Chris Van Allsburg is a very good friend.

PN: Oh. I'm a big fan of his.
MS: Yes, so am I. And I've saved all his letters, and he sends me proofs of his books. And we have exchanged very—I quite love Chris and his wife. And I love being in touch with people who are so gifted. Another one right now, Jon Agee. Brilliant, brilliant young artist. I save his letters, and I make him some sketches, and we trade drawings. And that's the way it used to be. That's the way it used to be. That's why I have all these little Johnson doodles and Ruth doodles. And I treasure them. And now it's time to figure out where they're going to live.

We talked about where he should leave the work from his collaborations with Ruth Krauss. Maurice wondered if he "should send the Ruth things to Storrs"—the University of Connecticut, where Krauss's papers are. I told him, "I think that makes sense," and he replied, "I think it does too, actually." He said he would send the Krauss-related work there because "I want Ruth's things to be together," and added that he wanted "Dave's things to be together," too. So, we talked about the locations of Johnson's work, most (but not all) of which is at the Smithsonian. We spoke of Johnson's and Krauss's wills, because those documents tell you who was truly important to them. For instance, Johnson left everything to Krauss, but if she were to predecease him, one of the beneficiaries would have been Nina Stagakis.

PN: That suggests how close—
MS: Oh, he adored her [Nina].

PN: they were.
MS: Oh, yes, I think they nourished her.

PN: That's what she says, and that they really took her and her ideas seriously and that Dave—well, for example, when she was going to art school, he and George [Annand] gave her a box of—oh dear, I don't know what the word for it is, but of—art supplies. And I've forgotten, but there's a term for the precise thing he gave her.
MS: Well, when you see her, tell her that they nourished me, too.

PN: I will.
MS: I was a little older than her, but that I was parented by Ruth and Dave. And I was. I grew to understand my parents' difficulties, to have that same mournful feeling that you have about not having done enough about your grandfather, but yes.

PN: Ah, stepfather, actually, but yeah.
MS: I just didn't, I just didn't know.

PN: Yes.
MS: And Ruth and Dave were the parents I wanted. And I'm lucky because I had them. And I had some time to say goodbye to her, but I didn't say goodbye to him.

PN: Well, he went more quickly than—I mean, it wasn't a long illness.
MS: Well . . . my brother went in three months. You sort of galloped to save them, but never overtook . . . They flew away from you.

PN: No, I mean, Jack—my stepfather—it was a month and a half. That was it. It wasn't lung cancer, but it was cancer. So, it was very, very sudden. It really took us all by surprise. He was fine, and then he was rapidly going downhill. It was quite a shock.

MS: Yes. I presume that I pleaded with my brother to not let them do anything to him because it would just postpone the very painfulness of it. And he didn't.

PN: Jack had a living will, too, so when he said it was time, they just took him off what was sustaining him.

MS: My brother's name was Jack, too, so that name rings—. I've just written a new story [*My Brother's Book*]—not to continue this conversation, but I've been struggling for over five years to write a memorial to my brother that would not all be revelatory or autobiographical, but would convey what he meant to me. And I did it.

PN: Wow.

MS: And I did it. The only thing I'm uncertain about is whether I want to publish it. I'm not really interested now in publishing because it's decayed.

PN: Do you feel it's too personal to publish?

MS: No. Everything I've done is so personal. God, if people could read what I've written about myself, it's so—

PN: Do you mean, beyond *Caldecott & Co.* or—?

MS: Jesus, it's so—it reveals everything. But they don't. They don't know how to, and that's just fine. I never wanted them to. And they won't with this one either. This is an homage to Emily Dickinson who taught me how to write, as she would have said, "on the slant."

PN: Right: "Tell all the Truth, but tell it slant"

MS: That's right.

PN: "Success in Circuit lies."

MS: Yes! Precisely. I've learned so much from her. She's been a supreme teacher. I think the past five years of illness and dying, and my mighty teachers are Emily Dickinson and John Keats, Shakespeare, and Herman Melville. They've like lived here in this house with me. I've been reading like my eyes are falling out. But, how many times can you have teachers like that?

PN: Yeah. Can't answer that one.

MS: [*Laughs*]

PN: That's the ultimate rhetorical question.
MS: OK, we'll stop now.

PN: Well, thanks. This has been a couple of hours here. Thanks for—.
MS: Well, I promised you.

PN: And you kept your promise.
MS: Yes, and also because I wanted to do it.

The conversation meandered for a few more minutes. Maurice spoke of watching the eleven o'clock news that night to see "if that fuck-face Bush has done something else," talked of "Serial Baby Killer" (then forthcoming in Art Spiegelman and Françoise Mouly's second *Little Lit* book), and invited me to "call when I like."

In subsequent years, rarely was I courageous enough to phone him. Typically, I'd write and then he'd call me. It was always astonishing to pick up the phone and hear Maurice's voice on the other end. I never quite got over the feeling of *Holy cow, I'm talking with Maurice Sendak.* The several "wows" at the beginning of this interview respond to the serious subject matter (*Brundibár*), but they also reflect what it felt like talking to him that first time (and, to a degree, later on). It was like talking to God or Santa Claus. Sendak believed in neither, of course. He believed in Blake, Mozart, Melville, Keats, and Emily Dickinson. Art was his higher power.

As Ruth Krauss did, Sendak mentored younger artists and was generous to young scholars. He kindly read and offered valuable feedback on an early, partial draft of my Johnson-Krauss biography. But he never saw the finished book. He died three months before it was published.

An Interview with Maurice Sendak

Roger Sutton / 2003

From *The Horn Book*, November/December 2003, pp. 687–99. Used with permission of Roger Sutton, editor-in-chief, *The Horn Book*.

In July, *Horn Book* Editor Sutton talked with the artist in his Connecticut home in a conversation that covered life and death, ego and excavation, dreams and nightmares, Melville and Homer, and . . . plankton.

ROGER SUTTON: Last night on that show *Queer Eye for the Straight Guy*, one of the makeover experts made a joke about how the guy's wallpaper looked like *Where the Wild Things Are*. How does it feel to realize that your work—*Wild Things* in particular—is so much a part of public culture?
MAURICE SENDAK: So you watch trash TV, too. Well, it's been true for a fairly long time now, and, honestly, it doesn't have any effect whatsoever. I see that book almost entirely in personal terms: I think about what I was like at that time; I think about Ursula [Nordstrom]. I'm not very impressed with being a catchword every time someone needs something to be "wild." But then, it's my book, right? So maybe I'm due the right to take it a little bit for granted. I certainly have a right not to be impressed.

RS: I wonder, too, if not being impressed and taking it for granted are both symbols of the same thing: that for you it's also become part of the background.
MS: I do realize that *Where the Wild Things Are* has permitted me to do all kinds of books that I probably never would have done had it not been so popular. I think I took good advantage of that popularity to illustrate books that I passionately wanted to do without having to worry if they were commercial or not. That was a great opportunity. I can *still* do it based on that book. I've always wished that Herman Melville weren't so afraid that he would be remembered for the popular *Typee* instead of *Moby-Dick*. He

said, I just know that on my tombstone it's gonna say, "Herman Melville, the author of *Typee: The Land of the Wild Naked Women*," or something. Well, that's what happened. But the fact is that *Typee* got him through a lot of books; it sold extremely well. You know, his first two novels were terrific boy-on-the-island sex novels. It's only when he met Nathaniel Hawthorne that he decided to allow himself to be driven and passionate and write a serious work of art. His subsequent work, the books we honor him for, were "failures" and cost him his popularity. I don't think *Wild Things* is my best book. But I don't *care* what they put on my tombstone; God knows I'm no Herman Melville, but I've been blessed with having been taken seriously and having profited from my work financially and personally. It's good.

RS: Does it ever feel like it gets in the way? Do you ever wish that like Doris Lessing you could publish something under a different name and see what people would think if they didn't know it was by you?

MS: I fantasize that all the time. I guess most authors do. But I know that when *In the Night Kitchen* came out it was a disappointment to people because it had nothing to do with *Wild Things*. Why couldn't I have just stayed put? The style was different; everything about it was different. The cartoons, the nakedness, everything seemed to be a rebuff of what I had "accomplished." But I had Ursula, who would never have let me do another *Wild Things*. Never. Never. She never suggested it, to her immense credit. And then the other books were notorious in one way or another, but they've all finally settled in nicely, couched on top of the *Wild Things*. When I first discussed *Wild Things*, *Night Kitchen*, and *Outside Over There* as a triumvirate, people said, "What's he talking about, he's just trying to pull his not-so-good books into the good book," but I always knew there would be three. It *was* a triumvirate.

RS: I think that those three books, in lots of different ways, allow people to use them as a lens on you. This is what matters to him. This is what he's about. These are the kinds of things he's afraid of; here's what makes him laugh. Obviously you've done lots of other books, but those three give people a way into the work as a whole.

MS: Everything is in those three books. Over the longevity of a man's life and work you get a sense of where his mind is, where his heart is, where his humor is, where his *dread* is. It's the best thing you could ask, that this kind of understanding of an artist doesn't happen posthumously. What more can you ask? Herman would have settled for a quarter of that.

RS: So what it's like, then, at midlife to have published *Outside Over There*, what you acknowledge as your capstone achievement? What happened after that?

MS: *Outside Over There* was the most painful experience of my creative life. It brought on a catastrophe. It was so hard it caused me to have a break-down. I left the business. I didn't think I could finish it. At that point in my still-young life, I felt I *had* to solve this book; I *had* to plummet as far down deep into myself as I could: excavation work. *Wild Things* was excavation work, but I got up and out in time, like a miner getting out just before the blast occurs. *Night Kitchen* was a deeper run, and that was troublesome. But I did not anticipate the horror of *Outside Over There*, and so I fell down. I lost my belief in it, I didn't know what I was doing, and so I quit; I stopped the book right in the middle, and I stopped work. That's when opera director Frank Corsaro called out of the blue and said he loved my books, especially *Juniper Tree*, and would I work on an opera with him? That was *The Magic Flute*. . . . After that, the books I did were rehabilitation from *Outside Over There*. I was ill. I was just meant to keep working and producing, but the joy and the great passion went into the opera now where I felt as if Mozart were the nurse taking care of me.

RS: What do you think happened?

MS: I think I went over my head. I went into a subject I thought I had some knowledge of or some control over as I did the other two books, but I fell off the ladder that goes down deep into the unconscious. Herman Melville (again I have to refer to him because he's been my patron saint) called it *diving*. I mentioned it in the Arbuthnot speech, that you dive deep and God help you. You could hit your head on something and never come up, and nobody would even know you were missing. Or, you will find some nugget that was worth the pain in your chest, the blindness, everything, and you'll come up with it and that will be what you went down for. In other words, you either risk it or you sell out. In Melville's terms there was only that way. So it was with John Keats, who also believed in the diving. It is my best work, *Outside Over There*. But I can take no pleasure in that.

RS: When did you realize that it was going to be more than you had bar-gained for?

MS: When I did the drawings. I always do a set of accomplished drawings before I get into painting. I did all the drawings for the book, and there was something—Roger, if I knew what happened, I'd tell you, but I don't. Something went amiss in me, a kind of panic, a kind of fear. I had touched on a subject, which is *not* in the book, but which had to be touched on to do the book. I couldn't face painting the pictures. I could not face seeing them all over again and painting Ida. It made me sick to do that. I waited six months between the finishing of the drawing and the very feeble start of that book in paint. I went back into therapy, which didn't help—but by that time I had really lost my faith in therapy. Anything but self-therapy I'd lost my faith in. So I just did it. I could do it, but it was heavy, heavy slogging. This book I'm doing now, *Brundibar*, is twice, three times as long as *Outside Over There*, but I'm just painting pictures and having a good time. I chose *Brundibar* because it's another place in me that needed a solution, but it's not as deep as *Outside Over There*, neither as quixotic nor as potentially lethal. That's not hyperbole; that's just how it feels.

RS: It's interesting to me to hear you talk about *Outside Over There* in that way because the pictures are so light-filled. Even those goblin babies, the planes of their faces. It's art that doesn't seem frightened or in despair.
MS: That's the artist's good luck and grief.

RS: You can link that to *Brundibar*—there's nothing in the story that suggests it was an opera performed by children at Terezin—you aren't leaning really heavily on the context.
MS: No. To have leaned heavily on the context would have pushed the whole thing out of shape, and it would have been a sentimental thrust of no value whatsoever, because the opera was written to amuse the children; it was written to take their minds off the worst elements of their lives, and it was meant to be cheerful. However, if you get to know the work very well, as I have had to, there are elements in the opera that are extremely brave in the face of the circumstances: the tyrant will come down, all bullies will be put away, and we must stick together, brothers and sisters. Who is Brundibar; who is this bully who's been threatening you this way and making you do what you don't want to do? I don't know how the prisoners got away with that. Except it was in the form of a children's opera, the superb music is fairly simple, sweet, Kurt Weill–ish. And you know we can get away with things in children's books that nobody in the adult world ever can because the assumption is that the audience is too innocent to pick it up. And in truth they're the only audience that *does* pick it up. Kids' reaction to all my books has been pretty "for" or very much against. There is a tone, there is a smell, there is some chemical thing going on, and if they don't like that they

go away from it. That's happened in every important book I've done. But it wins the Caldecott, and people think their kids have to love it. *Hello.*

RS: You told Selma Lanes a story about that. "My kid screams every time I read her *Where the Wild Things Are . . .*"
MS: And I answer, did she hate her kid? Is that why she was tormenting her with this book?

Outside Over There brought some hostility from children, but it was a book that made them chew. It works; that's all I know. It just works and whatever that means, that's what you've gotta do. You've gotta make it work. On whatever level, you gotta aim that arrow even though you don't know the target, really, you don't even know why you're so vehement. I hate being this mysterious, but I can't help it because I don't get it; I've never understood this—process, impulse, intuition, subject matter, what pulls me here and not there, what will unleash an enormous excitement in me while other things that I thought would, don't.

RS: Things that you don't think are going to take you as deep or as darkly as they end up doing.
MS: Or as tremendously happily, as *Esau* did. It wasn't just being able to work with Iona [Opie]. That book was cruel in a way that is so human and dear. Kids can be so hard on each other—and you know that these little buggers are just going to be worse when they grow up—but that is the human condition. And the kind of lovingness they still can convey in all of that, and sweetness. I'm reading a new translation of the *Iliad*, and I'm in great pain because I'm finishing. I'm right near the end, and I can't bear it. I chose the *Iliad* because, working on *Brundibar*, I'm so tired I can't see straight. I know the story of the *Iliad*; I'm reading it now for the depth of the poetry. I read two or three pages a night, like reading the Bible. It's exactly what we're talking about, which is the sense of the sheer inanity of life, the stupidity of it—and the gods are worse than the people. Just when Agamemnon thinks they're on his side, it turns out they're on Hector's side. The gratuitousness—I want Troy to win today, says Hera; well, no, says Zeus—and then the rest of it is the killing that goes on and on. I don't know why it touches me this way. There's the point where Hector is coming up behind this young man—say his name is Ajax—and Hector's flashing sword is aimed at his neck, young Ajax who spent his own money to come all the way to Troy; he needn't have, he lived on the rolling plains of Corinth, and he had a farm and his wife stood holding her big pregnant belly as she saw him off, this

young man so promising, so beautiful, so brave—the sword strikes him just under the lobe of his ear, cuts his major artery and the head topples off. And he falls into his smoking foggy death; and he goes clattering on the floor; and everybody grabs for his armor. It's like the cruelty of children. Homer never sits in judgment: Achilles is such an egomaniac, Agamemnon such a cheap bugger. But they don't get chastised; they just get memorialized; that's who they *are*. That's what Esau was like, too. It's that kind of nonjudgmental observation, with a big heart. Who are we to judge other crazy humans? It's like *King Lear*—one of my favorite plays in the whole world. I cannot bear to read it because every time I do it's *got* to end differently. That one brave daughter can *not* be killed at the last minute. It's just too much.

RS: But what else could have happened to her?
MS: Yes, anything else happening would have been false. But during the entire eighteenth century it was performed with Cordelia coming back to life: "Oh, here she is!" Shakespeare, however, understood the need to go to the nth degree. I'm not claiming that I'm one of the nth degree people, but I am claiming that I believe in the nth degree. I believe in going all the way and being so ferociously honest because otherwise it doesn't work; it's contaminated. Why would you bother?

RS: Do you ever question yourself—can I go this far; should I go this far?
MS: No. I see myself as a fairly weak person. I've gotten better with age. Age has really done well by me. It's calmed the volcanoes down considerably. Age is a form of kindness we do ourselves. But I don't feel like I've been misunderstood. Honestly, I don't feel like my work is that important. I have no brilliant conceptual gift for drawing or any really exceptional gift for writing. My gift is a kind of intuitive sense that I often think you would find in a musician, of knowing just what the music sounds like and knowing where to put your fingers. My talent is knowing how to make a picture book. Knowing how to pace it, knowing how to time it. The drawing and the writing are good, but if my whole career counted on that I wouldn't have made it very far. I truly believe that, because I took forever to learn to draw. It took up to *The Juniper Tree* to really *draw*.

I think my work is miraculous in that it has kept me alive and kept me employed. Constantly, since I've been about fifteen. I have to work, that's who I am, that's how I live, that's how I protect myself. I do it for me, it keeps me living, and it's gotten me over the worst of my personal life into a period of time in which I look around carefully and can say, "It's not so bad now."

RS: So it's the *working*, not the work.

MS: Being Jewish in the strict sense is to make your life purposeful. Otherwise, there's no purpose for you to be here at all. I am not an Orthodox Jew, but I was brought up as one and that lingers, the business of making your life purposeful. Actually, you can't make your life purposeful; it just is. And it was from childhood on. Why am I here, all that. But then you get over all that ego crap. I learned so much from Keats when he's writing to his big brother George, who's immigrated to America, about how you have to defeat your ego before you can become an artist who can be considered seriously. Keats says Shakespeare is the only artist who dumped his ego. He's Rosalind, he's King John, he's everybody, but we don't know who *he* is. (Not like Wordsworth, who was brilliant and tried very hard to submerge himself, but if you look very carefully you can see the shadow of his finger in everything.)

RS: Does happiness follow purpose?

MS: I don't know. I've led an unhappy life, but I needn't have. Growing up poor in Brooklyn was just like everybody else. My parents were no better or worse than everybody I saw around me. I had two wonderful siblings, which not a lot of kids had—older siblings who took care of me and protected me and really loved me. There was nothing like what you hear about today, the suffering of children. Yet I did suffer. There was something wrong, always. Why did I spend so many years in therapy? Whatever was wrong was ingested then and only manifested itself when I was becoming a teenager and then going to live on my own in New York. I was permanently frightened. And when you go to the therapist and he says, "Tell me what frightens you," you say, "That's why I'm here. I don't know." I never did find out. What happened was, hey, I got older, and the fear drooped; the fear got Alzheimer's before I did.

RS: Cheap psychology says, Okay, he was this scared and anxious child, and he took this fear and he made art.

MS: Yes, that's way too easy.

RS: So when you allude, as you did in *Outside Over There*, to something that terrified you as a child, like the Lindbergh kidnapping—

MS: Even now. You just said those words, and a little zingo went through me. It's a sickening feeling. Like a lightning strike.

RS:—does it heal?

MS: It helps. I sometimes say I was trying to change history. Ida finds the baby. I refused to let the Lindbergh baby die. I changed history. And that is part of it—but it's a very superficial part because I'm not crazy; the baby was dead, and I don't believe books bring people back to life. There's a stubbornness in me that resists some ways of taking comfort.

I had a recurring nightmare when I was a kid—I must have been four-ish—a nightmare about being chased by a very frightening something, and my heart is beating out of my chest. In the dream I'm desperate to get the cellar door open, but this thing is right behind me. And I finally turn. And it's my father. And his face is hot on my face, and his hands are out: murder. That's all it is: he will kill me. And that went on and on and on. And then just this week, here I am seventy years later, and the dream came back; and even in the dream I was stunned to be dreaming this again! The same thing happened and—this sounds like a TV movie of the week; can't be helped—I did something I never did before. I turned around and there he was, but I stood my ground. And his face was so close to mine; and his nose was pressing my nose; and then I saw that he was laughing—that it was a joke. He wasn't trying to kill me; he was playing with me. Now, does that reach all the way back—like that Gregory Peck movie with Ingrid Bergman, *Spellbound*—and say, "*That's* your answer" (seventy years too late, but what the fuck?). I don't think so. I don't think it's an answer to anything. It's probably just a release on my part. I can't claim now that my father really wanted to kill me and that he really hated me.

RS: But I don't think the dream is an indication that, Oh, all along your father was laughing. He's laughing *now*, when you're seventy-five.

MS: Precisely. Because *I'm* laughing now. Because I've decided these issues don't matter anymore. They cannot be solved. Even more important, they needn't be solved.

My worry, if I have any worry, is am I dodging? Have I found a way to fool myself, to ease myself out of the pressure-cooker life I've always had? Is it too easy?

I want to be plankton. Plankton is so under the radar, and they look real busy. You watch the Discovery channel; and they're bubbling and burbling away; and right behind them is Moby-Dick. Plankton are too small to harbor ego, yet they seem to have plenty to do. You stand on top of the Empire State Building and look down, and everybody looks like plankton. That suits me, to be plankton, not because I'm pretending modesty but because I'm hoping that the big answer is there ain't none, so cut it out.

RS: In her book *Bird by Bird*, Anne Lamott talks about how writers need to turn off the little radio station in their heads—station KFKD, she calls it—which broadcasts endless praise into one ear and infinite criticism into the other.

MS: Yes, you need to get out of the center of attention. You need to stop obsessing. Am I a believer? Am I not a believer? Should I have won the Caldecott three more times? How come? Why not? When you pull out of that orbit—and you can—that's when you're plankton. Then you're just swimming in life. Sure, even if you're plankton you can be afraid that someone you love is going to die. I live in dread of my sister dying; she's older than I am. I don't want to be an official orphan. If that's ego, well . . .

RS: You once said to me you wished you could believe in something—you said you wished your dog Jennie was up there waiting for you.

MS: More poignantly and painfully, my brother. I still can't believe I won't see him again. I can't even talk about it. But death is a comfort because that's what saves you. Suffering, cancer, some horrible disease, I'm terrified of pain. Death will just take you away from that. So what's to be afraid of? It's a cessation of pain. What more could you ask? It's like the good nurse.

RS: Well, since we've established that you're not a believer, there's the basic fear of unconsciousness, intellectual extermination . . .

MS: I think the most graceful thing offered us is sleep without dreams. That is so sensible.

I have a passion for that cable TV show *A Baby Story*. I watch it all the time. People say, "They're all born the same way, Maurice, why do you go on?" But here's the thing: you can see the baby's head; you can see the baby *coming out*. I cannot get enough of that, I cannot get enough of seeing the baby come out. There was one show where it was a C-section, and there was a lot of trouble because the baby was *huge*. And you're right there—you see them slit her belly open, and then they part her belly and grab whatever is there. They get this boy and the doctor is like "My God! Look at his head! No wonder!" And they get his head out, and his head now is just over the slit. He's looking around. His shoulders are stuck he's so big. Just his head out, and he's looking around. It looked kind of like a Beckett play, but it was so beautiful, so moving.

RS: That reminds me of Julie Vivas's book *The Nativity*, which has some really wonderful pictures of the Babe's first look at the world.

MS: It is astonishing. I could look at it over and over. It's that first moment, the uncontrollable gesturing, the legs—you know, babies show us that we're really frogs. A torso, a penis or a vagina, and then the legs bow—it's so basic, so elemental. It's that first moment—we've been talking about mysteries today; you could headline this whole interview "The Mystery." There's nothing to solve. Why am I obsessed with birth? I have to see it, night after night, and obviously there are lots of people like me, because the show is always on. It's the face. And the other moment is when this messy little thing is dried off. And the mother's face is still in pain, and then it dawns on her she hasn't heard the cry. The eyes sharpen; she comes out of herself, and then she looks at her husband whom she hasn't looked at *at all*, that detestable scumbag over there who brought this on her. And he's just standing there taking pictures.

RS: "Look this way, honey."

MS: Almost the first thing she says is "I don't hear the baby cry." Sometimes there's trouble; they have to clean out the baby's lungs; sometimes they die; but oh, ninety percent of the time they cry, and then her face is relieved. And she wants it, she wants it, and they put it in that little blanket; and the baby is struggling with its eyes—and this must be some incredible chemical thing—and the baby looks at her quietly and mostly stops crying, and then the look on her face and the transference of something and then her face just melts. She has given in entirely. It's nature; she has no choice, perhaps. But to see it on a human being's face, see the softness enter and the pact agreed upon; they sign right on the dotted line, the two of them, right at that moment. It's *then* that she looks to her husband. He's allowed to come into the picture. It's so primitive.

All this is corny, right?—*the baby being born*. But I feel about that the way I feel about death. I've seen many people I love die. I was with them for that transference, that look, peaceful, really peaceful.

RS: Coming in and going out?

MS: Yes, you come on a wisp of air and you go on a wisp of air. Emily Dickinson is accused of morbidity because she loved being close to dying people; she loved to be there to *watch*, this little ghoul of a genius. She invested all her energy into looking into the person's face and wanting to see "the Passing"—as she called the moment from life to death. It was almost as though she could see somebody step out and go that way.

RS: Do we know what she believed?

MS: She was basically a nonbeliever. How could she be a believer and be Emily Dickinson? Here's what she believed in: the need to stop calling everything by its name, like when her sister comes out and says, "Emily, it's time to put up the batter for mother's bread. It is Tuesday, you know." I'm making up this conversation, but it's what happened. And Emily would mutiny. "*No.* Why are you calling it Tuesday? How dare you call it Tuesday, that *nails* me to Tuesday. And I don't want to bake bread today. I want to be free; I want to sit here in the garden." The fact that we call it Tuesday drives her crazy. It's *no* day, it's *any* day; if we make it Tuesday that means it came after Monday, which means it's a very short ride to Sunday, and the week is fucked. If we could live that way without saying, Oh, just two more weeks to finish *Brundibar*, gotta go to the dentist next Monday, all of that.

RS: But when you're working away, putting something down on paper, you're saying, here's something that needs to be kept for the future. It's not enough just to have the picture in your head—you're placing it in time as soon as you put it down.

MS: Because I signed a contract, and got money—

RS: Oh, come on.

MS: Listen to me. I am a commercial artist. I told them I would do this work for a certain amount of money by a certain time. My own needs to do this have nothing to do with that. Yes, I need Tuesday. I hope I get old enough to dump it, but I need it. Meanwhile *they* have given *me* the privilege of spending so much time in this *Brundibar* world, where I need to be. I don't know why I need to be there, but that's the joy of all this. The real mystery is, why does this make me so happy? Why does this free me of every inhibition? Why does this allow me to be normal? I know, from experience, that I'm good at this. Really good at it. I'm not ripping it off; I'm not fucking it up; I'm doing it as delicately and carefully as I can.

RS: So the absorption in the creating is the actual reward.

MS: Totally. In that period of time, I don't need the *Iliad*, the baby show, or Ricki Lake. I am stirred to the top of my last brain cell because I'm working. I am stirred into life by my labor.

RS: "Look this way, honey."

Selected Sendak:
Interviews by the Rosenbach

Patrick Rodgers / 2007

From the Rosenbach Museum archives, 2007–2008. © 2015 The Rosenbach Museum and the Free Library of Philadelphia. Reprinted by permission.

Editor's note: The following is excerpted from interviews conducted with Maurice Sendak by the Rosenbach Museum and Library over five sessions between 2007 and 2008, which the Rosenbach has generously provided me permission to print for the first time. Patrick Rodgers, the curator of the Maurice Sendak Collection, was the primary interviewer, and Director of Collections Judith Guston and John C. Haas Director Dr. Derick Dreher were occasionally present as well. The interviews were recorded and produced by Michael O'Reilly. I have selected the fragments not addressed in other interviews, especially those discussing Sendak's often overlooked design work for various national and international opera productions. Patrick Rodgers reviewed the final manuscript and made appropriate copy edits based on the original recordings.—PCK

MR. SENDAK: So this [fascination with] death thing was started very early in my life, and I don't know why. Just recently in talking to people—I was out of circulation for almost three months after Gene died. I just didn't want to talk to or see anybody—and now I'm meeting people who I know and know about it—and they're sorry, and they're very nice. They said, "Have you ever been happy?" And they said, "I know you're not happy now, but have you ever been happy? Because every time we see you, you're upset about something." So I said, "No, I've never been happy." "How could you not have been happy? There must have been something that made you happy." I said, "If there was something that made me happy, I was unaware of it." I was happy when I worked; I was happy when I published a book; I was happy when I was putting watercolor down on a page, yes. But you're not talking about that. You're not talking about the creative act as a form of happiness, which it was.

And I suspect for a lot of people, the act of creation— writing, music, painting pictures, whatever—was the way they were happy. And the rest of life sucked, for the most part. And Mozart, his whole life was writing music. It was a short life, but it was not a good life. I daresay he would never have said, "I was happy." But then I read the obituary of Beverly Sills, and we had worked together. I liked her very much.

And she had a horrible life. Her children, very sick. Her husband, Alzheimer's. And they said to her, "Oh, you must be a very happy woman because you were the prima donna in America. If anyone heard of an opera singer, they heard of Beverly Sills. And you opened up old music to us that we never heard—French opera, German, and all that stuff. And weren't you happy?"

And she said, "How could I have been happy? How could I have been happy?" She said, "The closest I've come to happiness is I'm cheerful." And I thought that was so splendid; that was such a wise thing to say. Because cheerful involves courage, and she's overlooking what was going on and not plaguing other people with what was happening to her. I always saw her laughing. Every time I spent time with her, she was uproariously laughing and telling funny stories.

But this was happening to her at the same time. So I cannot even claim to be cheerful. I don't know how to reach that in myself, and I blame myself for it because look how lucky I am. I've spent my whole life doing books, hiding out from life, not suffering the way most human beings suffer. They have to get married; they have to have children; they have to have jobs; they have to have cars.

Not my life. So it bothers me that I don't know how to be happy. It really bothers me. And then I read this thing just a week ago in a science magazine where a man was in a coma, he came out of the coma—did you read this?—and he was deaf. He could not hear a thing, obviously as a result of the coma. He was in a car accident.

But when they examined him, they could look through all kinds of mechanisms to see how his brain was working, that when somebody talked to him, what made you hear was working in the brain. He should be hearing. He should be hearing. But when he got out of the coma, it was determined by him that he couldn't hear, and he couldn't hear. He wasn't lying.

So what's happened is this disparity between what he thought was wrong with him and what the brain had not informed him of. The brain didn't say, "hey, you're not deaf. I can hear everything they're saying." The brain didn't tell him. Now what that means, I can't be absolutely sure, but I think happiness is like that.

You might be happy, but the brain doesn't want you to know that. So many odd things have happened to you, like the crash that brought this man's deafness about, that the brain says don't tell him. I don't know what I'm talking about, but I get an instinct about it. I do. I get an instinct about it; that even if you were happy, you might not know you were happy.

And I don't know what it feels like to be happy. I can't even imagine what it feels like to be happy. And everybody's happy. You see people at ballgames—they're all drinking beer, and they go to parties; they're all dancing. And are you happy? See, you know you're happy. Damn you.

MR. RODGERS: I can't give you a straight answer to that, either. It's hard to say, isn't it?

MR. SENDAK: It is. It is.

MR. RODGERS: It's hard to say, "Yes, I know I'm happy."

MR. SENDAK: Now I've never had—it's like some people, if you stuck a pin in their finger, they won't feel the pain, and some will. I've never been conscious of being happy, never. I've been envied to death. Oh, you did this book and you did *Wild Things* and blah, blah, blah. I shake my head—and I don't share this with many people, obviously—but I don't know what it feels like to be happy. I don't know what you're supposed to feel like. Can you describe it?

MS. GUSTON: I feel much more at peace than I have when I'm unhappy, and I feel hopeful. I feel a whole lot better than when I'm not.

MR. SENDAK: Say that again?

MS. GUSTON: I feel a whole lot better than when I'm not happy. I can tell you that.

MR. SENDAK: Well, that's putting it well. That's putting it—

MS. GUSTON: In some ways, it is very comparative. You know what you feel like when you're not happy, and it's not that.

MR. SENDAK: Yeah.

MS. GUSTON: But I think it's a combined sense of hopefulness and just being at ease.

MR. SENDAK: I think it's a great shame. It's a great shame to not know happiness. I really do.

MS. GUSTON: Yeah, I think so, too.

MR. SENDAK: A major, major screw-up because I probably have been happy. I must have been happy. I've had this incredible, successful career.

MR. RODGERS: What about all the people in your life, the Mozarts and the Melvilles and the Blakes? Don't you get that from them?

MR. SENDAK: Yes. Only from them. Emily Dickinson. I just have to say her name, and I feel better.

MR. RODGERS: I wanted to ask you about her. You once said that before an interview you were reading her because you were nervous about the interview. What is it about her poems that brings you peace?

MR. SENDAK: Oh, the passion and honesty of this woman's voice. The incredible snatching out of the air the fine point. And this little anecdote that I read somewhere, but I can't remember where, where she's sitting in a garden—she's reading until it begins to get dark, and so she closes the book. She leans back, and she listens to the birds. She smells the aroma of the flowers, and she's just lost in a lovely thing.

Then her sister, Cassandra, comes out angry and says, "What are you doing? Mother's in the kitchen baking. This is Tuesday, Emily. Tuesday is baking day, and you should be in there helping Mother. And what do you do, mooning, swooning out here?" And Emily Dickinson looked at her sister, whom she was very fond of, and said, "Who said it was Tuesday? Who made Tuesday? Off with you. I don't feel like this is Tuesday, so it isn't. Somebody made it up, and I won't go in. And since it isn't Tuesday, I don't have to bake today."

And I thought, ingenious. Ingenious. I thought, that was somebody who's happy, who knows how to dismiss time and dismiss the day, the night, the afternoon, the weekend. Fuck off, she's saying. When I want to feel this way, I feel this way. Now that made me happy because I thought if I could get into that kind of freedom where you dismiss things, that we are enslaved by things, by time, by this, by that, and she wouldn't be. She just wouldn't be. She just wouldn't be. And she wasn't.

• • •

MR. RODGERS: Can I ask you about Shakespeare?

MR. SENDAK: Yeah.

MR. RODGERS: Because you've illustrated some of the covers for the records and things like that.

MR. SENDAK: Yes. They all stink.

MR. RODGERS: You don't talk much about—why do they stink?

MR. SENDAK: You're illustrating Shakespeare?

MR. RODGERS: Well, what do you think about it?

MR. SENDAK: I did them because they had to be little album covers, and they had to be art. I love Shakespeare. So of course, as an artist, I want to do something, to draw something. But every one of them that I did you could dismiss as completely useless. In other words, you don't need to illustrate Shakespeare. You just listen to him; watch him on the stage.

I don't even like going to plays. I do not like going to plays. I don't like seeing elderly men spitting into the first three rows. I can't stand it. And I can't stand poor acting. I love reading him. I love reading him. That's all I ask of him, is to be there for me. But I can't do anything with him. He's useless. Melville also is just about useless, but I had to have something.

I love him, so I got *Pierre*. I chose well because *Pierre* is one of the kooki-est books ever written. Have you read the novel?

MR. RODGERS: I'm three or four chapters into it.

MR. SENDAK: It is weird.

MR. RODGERS: It's really weird.

MR. SENDAK: It makes me look like Walt Disney, God forbid. Well, Schubert is one of the most unhappy people in the whole world, and John Keats, dead at twenty-six and unhappy.

MR. RODGERS: But they make you happy.

MR. SENDAK: They make me want to live. They can't make me happy because they're too unhappy. So my happiness would be grotesque in light of what they were going through. But the fact that art makes me happy—that the artist in the extreme, in the most acute pain, in the most acute circumstances—can produce something like Mozart produced.

Don't forget, Mozart was popular up to a point, and then he was not popular. His stuff was getting too rough and confusing and odd—as the Pope said, "too many notes, too many notes." So these were all people who really did not have the success I had, okay? Melville never had it, except when he was very young. His two first novels were hot stuff. But his real work was ignored and detested, and Mozart got to be too many notes. Strange.

Emily Dickinson, nobody even knew she existed, practically. She wanted to be a success. She denied it, but she wanted to be a success. But she was not. So what do I take from this? I think happiness—it's an interesting point—comes from looking at the work of great artists who are not nourished or praised in any way. Nobody gave them an award, but I have awards up the kazoo. I've won all the major awards. Why aren't I happy?

Because I'm a shithead? Maybe. But that's not what I look for. That's not what I look for. When Emily says it's not Tuesday, I want to laugh. I'm happy. Because that is such a fantastic idea, to destroy time with just a flurry of hands. Who else could do it but Emily?

We've concluded in the ten minutes we had that for me, happiness comes only through art—music, reading, working. That's it. And crappy television. Animal Planet makes me happy. When I see those animals roaming around killing each other, I'm happy. So there you go.

MR. RODGERS: We'll stop it here, then.

MR. SENDAK: You see? You've made me happy, young man, at the end of this session.

MR. O'REILLY: Can I ask a question? Is it a *schadenfreude* kind of thing?

MR. SENDAK: Is it a what?

MR. O'REILLY: *Schadenfreude*? A shameful joy-happiness thing?

MR. SENDAK: It's like a light going on. It's not an emotional thing. I think that part of me is deaf like this guy's hearing. My brain hasn't told me, "this is enough reason to be happy, Maurice, you schmuck. Get going." I don't hear it. I don't get the message. I don't hear it. So I have to eke it out in other ways, and I mostly eke it out not from my work. I don't impress me at all, but Melville, Mozart, Schubert, Goya, Van Gogh, and Dickinson do.

Now I think people say, "oh, poor Vincent Van Gogh—a short, miserable life. Look at those canvases. You know that every one he painted, he was a happy maniac. He had to be happy to paint colors like that and landscapes like that. How do you do that without being extremely happy? But that kind of happiness was like a cancer to him. It ate him up. It ate him up. There was nothing else in his life.

And that's when he was caught off-guard and killed himself—at that moment when there was nothing in his life. It penetrated his brain that he gave up. And that's always a possibility if your work doesn't support you if you're an artist. I depend entirely on whatever cheerfulness, happiness, I get from work and from the work of other artists. I love art, and I know how hard it is to live. I really do.

So all these people we love and praise as great artists—I know how much suffering had to go in to do that. And when there's an artist who's well-known whom I detest—I hate them—like certain composers, I'm not going to name names, who get away with writing crappy movie music or crappy any music, the people who illustrate books are appalling. Are they happy in what they do? Probably.

I think the dumber you are, the happier you can be. Now that's a cruel thing to say because I'm jealous. I'm jealous.

I'm not jealous of you because you earned it.

MS. GUSTON: I feel that way.

MR. SENDAK: I know you a little bit well, so I know that. But it is an earning thing. I think most normal human beings, you just feel it. You just feel it. It should be a normal thing. It's like watching baby tigers tumbling all over each other. They're happy.

MS. GUSTON: They don't know better.

MR. SENDAK: They don't know better, but maybe you shouldn't know better. They're just happy because they're living. They're smelling. They're suckling. They're licking. They're rolling. They're biting. Then they look at their mother and go, oh god, am I going to have to be like her? I guess it's not an answer that can be asked. It's not a question that can be answered in any simplistic way. It just can't. Like you look like a happy man. But what does that mean? I see you as being young, and I envy you that.

MR. RODGERS: Sorry I keep quoting you back at you, but I remember your once saying in an interview, "Everybody says, 'oh, don't you wish you could be young again?'" And you said, "No, I wish I were sixty-nine again."

MR. SENDAK: Well, shows you what a jerk I was.

MR. RODGERS: Really? You don't think that?

MR. SENDAK: No, I would not want to be young again on a bet. On a bet. But if I had to pick an age—that dumb game people play. I would pick fifty. Because by then, you've got to put it together, and you still have the physical energy to do it. You don't have a lame leg, like I have, so I can't go to Europe again. I can't walk down the streets of Rome again. It hurts too much. But at fifty, you're still mostly okay.

I would say sixty, actually, except by then maybe things have started to go. But seventy-nine? It's absurd. It's absurd. What do I do at seventy-nine? Oh, you're going to be eighty years old. We're going to give you a big party. Fuck you.

MS. GUSTON: Kiss that off our list.

• • •

MR. RODGERS: And when you were looking for—you said Blake helped open up some of those sexual elements, particularly of *Pierre.* Was it the same with the Kleist? Can you talk a little bit about Blake's role in the way you envision the characters and the way that he played off of the subtext you saw going into the book?

MR. SENDAK: Well, Blake was a flaming maniac, and that is the best compliment I could give him. He was fearless, totally fearless. His passion for the mystery of the universe. He made up a universe because he rejected what everyone else believed. He rejected the Bible and all. He made up Bible names, and he created a world that he could believe in. You bought it, or you didn't. It's just the way it was. But it was passionately sexual at a time when, I think it is true to say, he was working that was not an acceptable reference or an acceptable way of working or of drawing attention to. Everybody is naked in almost everything he does. Yes, you can see where it comes from Michelangelo, although I don't think he ever made a trip to Europe. I think he only worked from prints. But it's that ferocity in Blake which is under the surface. On the surface it's so simple—the shepherds, the sheep, a light coming over the hill. It's two worlds. It is our world: what we approve of ourselves to be like when we are with other people, and it's what we are really like that we daren't reveal to other people. That makes sense. There is so much more to Blake. I'm feeling as though I'm isolating him into a little corner here.

MR. RODGERS: I think it's hard to kind of get a handle on exactly what is so sexual about some–

MR. SENDAK: [*Interposing*] Yes.

MR. RODGERS: —but it's not just, as I've seen some people say, in the musculature or the references, as you said, to Michelangelo, Roman, or Greek. It's in the curvaceousness of some of it.

MR. SENDAK: His profound love of the human body. He was astonished by the human body. He did the right thing. He covered up most people. Most women are covered up in Blake—I think that's true. He followed some of the rules of his time. But in fact, he was a total failure, and if it weren't for some few people who commissioned work from him—he died perfectly poor. So what he was doing was irritating people. Appealing to something which they did not want to see or comprehend or have anything to do with which I think is probably true of most human nature, even unto our own time.

So that when this sexual thing is released as they say on television or in books that are published, it's gross. It doesn't have the spiritual nudity for want of how to say this as Blake does which is beautiful and—spiritual is the word. It captures your heart. And whether you know what he's talking about or not doesn't matter. I haven't read that much Blake. I don't understand lots of it. I don't understand what the hell he's talking about, so I'm always led back to the *Songs of Innocence and Experience* and feel as though, in my life could I get even half way to expressing something that way and that's—it's so simple. It's so beautiful, it's so limpid, and at the same time it goes so deep down into the soul.

Well, he was a genius, so that's the end of that. It's just not likely you're going to do that again. But that's the best of illustrating. That's what illustrating for me is all about. It's not about echoing a text. You read a text, and then you see a picture. Hello, what's that all about? Most people—I don't like to read illustrated books, adult books I mean. I don't ever. I would hate to read Jane Austen illustrated. Anyone who would show me what so and so looks like, to hell with them. I know what she looks like. I would never illustrate Austen, and mostly all the great novels I would not illustrate which would probably make a lot of people happy to know—that I'll keep my hands off some of their favorite stories.

Children's books are the best way to get this out of your system because of the simplicity of their surface. You could bury anything you like, and you can count on an audience that is so intuitive by nature—so sharp—that they will seek out that "it." They don't even know they're seeking it out. They take it in like air. They write letters that are out of anger sometimes which has nothing to do with the book but has to do with something they smoked out of the book that put them off, made them unhappy. So I succeeded even if I made that little girl in Canada who wrote and said she hated *Outside Over There*, hated it. And what are all those naked babies doing? Why aren't they dressed right? Why is Ida so harsh? Why is the mother looking away? She's picking up all the big don'ts in the book. And she said, "You scared me. This book scared me. The goblins scared me. You never scared me before, but now I never want to read you again. I never want to see any of your work. I hate you, and I hope you die. Cordially, . . ."

Her mother included a note saying she did not like the letter. And she often edits letters that her daughter writes, but she said I would be very interested in the anger that her daughter was conveying. She said, you also should know that I have recently had another child, which would explain why this girl was so pissed off really—that she had to deal with the kid. It was that that infuriated the child. But this mother had another thing to say which was fascinating. It was an insight to me: did you mean that when Ida is dancing in the cave with the babies, then she finds her sister and takes her out, and then all the babies turn to nothing? She said, "It looks like a vast female orifice that Ida has gone into—the vagina, the female part where babies are made—and made sure no more would come out of this place." Okay, she's stuck with her sister, done. But she'd wash out that place. She'd wash out that orifice, she'd come home, and she would know there would be no more babies. I said, "That's fantastic. Does it really look like that to you?" She said, "Have a look. It's your book."

It is. It's a female orifice—that whole section. I loved it. It had passed over me. I had done it. She's right, but I did not know I was doing it. I didn't know, and that's the best fun in all of this—the layers of meaning, the layers of storytelling, the layers of sex and whatever you want but to include them is important. To deny children's sexuality is a crime which we in this county are very guilty of and to presume that they can't bear to hear anything about it . . .

Is that the right way? Is that the wrong way? Most people don't want to hear anything real. How are you doing Maurice? How are you doing? And then you say something like—which happens often as I've had a lot of tragedy in my life, and they'll drive by and they'll say, "How are you?" I'll say, "I'm doing very poorly." They don't want to hear that. That's why I say it. "Oh, I'm so sorry." Well why are you sorry? There's nothing you can do about it. If there was something you could do about it, would you do it? I, I, I, I, well, could I help or do something? No, it's best you don't ask me that question anymore. I leave them totally uncomfortable. It's cruelty. It's cruel. I should be more merciful I've been told. I should just nod my head and go away.

MR. RODGERS: It's interesting you brought up Mickey. You know, sexuality in children's books and Mickey from *Night Kitchen* . . . when I look at the pictures from *Pierre*, the Melville *Pierre*, the changes that you give Pierre's body throughout the book—his genitals change throughout the book, his face changes throughout the book—he is never the same Pierre from one picture to another. His hair changes color, and he is so much more vulnerable than any children in so much of your work. It's more an adult book. It's a book for adults. It's not a book for kids.

MR. SENDAK: You mean Melville's.

MR. RODGERS: Melville's *Pierre*, yeah. I just find that sort of interesting—

when it comes to adult sexuality, that's the anxious piece, that's the vulnerable piece.

MR. SENDAK: Can you imagine him writing this book in Victorian America when the favorite novels were by women, and they were all hobby stories and girls who go falling into the ice? No one dared such a thing. No one dared. And when you think of Hawthorne, and I am. It's curious. I don't know why, but I am so not a fan of Nathanial Hawthorne. I find him so cold and rigid and even when his stories are sexual—like *The Scarlet Letter* is all about sex—it's not about sex. It doesn't breathe sex. It doesn't feel sex. It feels morality. It feels sternness and coldness. And it was a great success. It was the only one of his novels that truly was a great success. Melville adored Hawthorne, adored him—probably literally. Hawthorne and his remarkable wife were the two who read *Moby-Dick* before anyone else saw it and said, "This is it. This is the greatest thing ever." So probably he was satisfied with that—that he could please two people whom he thought so well of. And that did include Hawthorne's wife. She was a most remarkable woman. She loved *Pierre*.

Now, what am I trying to tell you? I kind of lost touch with what I was saying. Well, just the peculiarity of writing such a book and then *Billy Budd* at the end again, powerful sexual thing—unmentionable but it feels like a dark shadow all through the thing. The homoeroticism of that is amazing. And it's known. It's not like I am revealing anything. It's known. That's why Benjamin Britten fell in love with it, and his wife fell in love with *Death in Venice*. Of course, it appealed to him. But where it comes from and in a century which was so basically against such self-revelation is against such discussion of the human body other than the practical way you talk about the human body, like one of those charts in a doctor's office where you see where every muscle, every bone, and everything is. This really leaps past that and insults people. You wonder like watching television, which I do—I work late. I can hear just so much music, and I can't hear music anymore. Then I'll put on whatever is on—usually Animal Planet or someone doing an operation on a guy whose head just split open. I love accidents, and I love operations. So if there's not a good operation thing on, there may be a good animal thing on and vice versa.

I'm very lucky because they put on the most gruesome things they can for crazy people like me. And there's the woman who is the mortician. She is quite an attractive woman. She stands there with her smock and says, "Have nothing else to do? Come on with me, and I'll show you the insides of this guy that we don't know what killed him." And there she is in the mortuary looking down at the corpse, and she's thinking, oh, I don't know what happened to him; bring the saw. And her assistant comes, and they saw his head in half. She says, "Oh my God, this brain is full of blood. Oh, for goodness sake." You know the stink is pretty hard on her. I tell people I watch *Dr. G.*— that's the name of her show. They think I'm mad. But anything to do with the body, anything to do with surgeries, anything to do with the minutia of . . . I love when babies are born—twins and one is perfectly healthy, and look at the other one. They exchange glances, and her blood levels are a little too low or something's a little too high. She's rushed into the NICU, where newborns are, and they start to help her breathe. I'm breathless. I stop breathing myself as I watch a human being being saved from dying just by tubes and things stuck all over. What that tells you about me is that I am morbid.

• • •

MR. SENDAK: To me, [Beatrix Potter] is—she was and is—still the quintessential children's book writer because she didn't write for children. She obviously had no particular feelings for them. Whether she knew that or not, I don't know, but I believe that's how she was. After Jane Austen, she is one of the greatest English prose writers that has lived, and her stories are so concise, precise. She has no wasted words, and her illustrations are the same. They are just perfection. See, these tiny little books which are doomed to be kiddie books are, in fact, brilliant pieces of British writing. It's a shame—the assumption that children are so silly and they don't understand anything, that they have to be written down to. I remember reading her book of letters where she got a letter from her mother, and she said, "How could you?" I don't remember the book . . . *Benjamin Bunny*. She used a word I don't remember. "How did you think a child would understand what that word meant? Why did you do that?" And Potter wrote back and says, "Get off your duff. Go look at the dictionary. Learn something, and then you will know what the word means."

She was incorrigible and absolutely had no patience with these idiot people who said, "Why don't you write easier, easier, easier, stuff?" The same thing goes on now. The same thing goes on now. But she was a wealthy woman, so she could print her own books. She did much better than anybody thought, but then apparently everybody thought she was so wonderful that she became queen of Kiddiebookland. Then I have heard Melville—

who is my great hero and I have almost all his works in the American edition and in the English edition—was much more popular in England. They respected him much more.

• • •

MR. RODGERS: It is something you said about Beatrix Potter and Kiddiebookland.

MR. SENDAK: Yeah.

MR. RODGERS: And Kiddiebookland is the place you have never wanted to be.

MR. SENDAK: No, I don't believe there is such a country.

MR. RODGERS: Did it start with Potter?

MR. SENDAK: No. I'm not so great with dates, but I think she is at the same time as Randolph Caldecott, Kate Greenaway, and Walter Crane, just roughly the same time. She is the only one who—she wrote about animals, so of course she had been in the children's book department. She couldn't be next to Brontë or any of the other great English writers because she wrote for children, which meant a lesser form. She was considered a lesser artist. Just as I am, just as anybody who is employed and doing books for children—we are lesser writers and artists. We don't get invited to the grown-up book parties. I remember I was invited once by Harpers to a grown-up book party and the president who thought he was terribly funny said, "Oh my goodness, I didn't know you stayed up this late." Wretched ass. She was easily matched and perhaps surpassed by Randolph Caldecott, who is my master. He is someone that I emulated and someone who taught me the fundamentals of what a picture book was—not some foolish escapade for children to wander through but a work of art. She was not interested technically—text, picture, text, picture, text, picture—was Beatrix Potter. Nothing wrong with that, but that was her idea of what the book should be.

Caldecott had great open spaces, He let you imagine things, and to me that's what this is all about. You write your story. You draw your pictures, but the fact that you leave those spaces for anyone who happens to be reading. There's one very favorite one of them—and a lot that went to the nursery rhymes. He would illustrate nursery rhymes: "bye baby bunting, daddy has gone a-hunting," and baby is in a bunny suit. It is always wordless, and he or she—rather, the child is dressed in this uniform and is hurling herself around humming the whole time. And the mother takes the child for a little walk. As they walk they pass a hill, and on the hill, looking very solid and quiet, are a group of rabbits. They are all staring at the child, and the child is looking back with first knowledge of where his beautiful coat comes from. There was nothing in it about "don't kill animals" and stuff like that. The expression between the child and the animals makes you believe that the child has made this connection without any words from Mr. Caldecott. That's what it was all about, making those incredible connections through the pictures, through texts, which were ancient rhymes to suggest anything, whatever you made up.

So he was my teacher for picture books—how to tell any number of stories with very few words and by implications and by looks and by body attitudes and stuff like that. So I would put him as king of the form, absolute king of the form. We are not talking about the rest of them, obviously, but I don't think any of them—certainly Kate Greenaway was the bottom of the list, the whole list. There is nothing charitable to say about Kate Greenaway. She is just really a bad artist, a bad writer, and she did the worst thing possible, which was sentimentalize the picture book forever. That became what Americans thought were proper books for children. Little girls in crinoline, pretty little hats, and pretty little dresses; and they run around with bouquets and flowers and no hanky panky.

• • •

MR. RODGERS: I think we're ready to go. Today, obviously, is September 11, and I just—I couldn't let this interview pass anyway without asking a native New Yorker and somebody with as much history as you have a little bit more about the day.

I know that you've talked with Judy a little bit about some things that you heard after September 11. So I kind of wanted to turn this question over to her.

MS. GUSTON: When we first met, you were working on *Brundibar* at the time. I think this was one of the times when we came up here, Bill, Derick, and I. It was around September 11. It must have been sometime soon after that, and you told us this story about the way that children protect their parents.

MR. SENDAK: Yes, yes.

MS. GUSTON: I was wondering if you could talk a little bit about that.

MR. SENDAK: Yes, yes, yes. There was a very good friend of mine. He's a well-known artist, and he lives down in the Village. He then had only one child, a daughter, and she went to a school, a private school, a children's, somewhere near downtown. When it happened, they panicked terribly, the both of them husband and wife, and ran down to where the school was. The school was there, and all the children were outside the school. They saw her and she saw them and they ran together. He picked her up, and they just wanted to get her home as fast as possible.

She said, "Daddy, Daddy, I saw all these birdies, and they were all on fire. Birds were flying and falling down and there was fire coming from all of them." Those were the people who were hurling themselves out of windows. And he was stunned and gratified that she had imagined them as birds. So that's the way she saw it.

That's when he took her home, and then when she went—he put her to bed that night, she said, "Daddy, I know they weren't birds." She didn't say what I imagine she would've said, which is, "I didn't want to scare you." But that's why she said she knew they weren't birds. She didn't want to upset him or her mother.

There's a hundred stories you could tell about that horrible day, but that story is fixed in my memory because it fits with my conception of how children survive, how they make things different, how they look at things differently, and how they manage things. I mean, she apparently knew they were human beings, and they were hurling and flailing in the air. As far as I know, she didn't have any serious affects afterwards. She may have.

I think it made me an old man. Being an American, of course, and not having lived through the Civil War, obviously, the idea of such a thing happening in this country. You know, we would be attacked like anywhere. So that for once, it was like you grow up, and you find out that your parents have to die. You grow up, and you know that you're no longer safe. Anyway there's no way to be safe. There's no place to go to hide.

And the images . . . I don't have to watch anything on TV to know if I could—I've memorized every inch of what happened. I don't want to see it literally. I don't want to see it. And I don't want to hear the cajoling words of the mayor or anybody about strength and determination and stuff, stuff, stuff. I don't want to hear about when the soldiers are coming back when we know it's not now when they should come back. Death just seems to haunt our country, or the specter seems to haunt our country. That's all I can say.

There's no living through that. There are some occasions in life that you are permanently changed by. Obviously that's one of them.

MR. RODGERS: Did that event fuse with your creative process with *Brundibar*? I think of the fiery goose that the children sing about.

MR. SENDAK: Yes.

MR. RODGERS: In the preliminary drawings it's not on fire.

MR. SENDAK: Yeah, I think so. Sure, the burning people. A picture of . . . they were only in silhouette. But it was a man and a woman, and they were holding hands. They plunged holding hands, and I imagine there were flames all around them. I don't know if that's true or if I added that—you know—my imagination added that. But knowing that you're going to die and holding somebody's hands, that's . . .

Brundibár, of course, was that. I am a child of the Holocaust, although I was fortunate to live here by sheer dumb luck. My father was here; my mother was here. Everyone else in the Sendak clan and my mother's clan were wiped out. Just such nonsense why my parents were here.

So the fact that you could die so easily . . . nothing protects you. It was when I lost faith in God, then all religion, and anything, in anything. That my darling brother could die. He was in the invasion of Okinawa in Japan. We didn't know whether he was living or dead. My sister's young, beautiful husband was killed in the invasion of Anzio.

So death, death, death, death stalked all over the place. What more can one say?

MR. RODGERS: That's an important message that kids need to understand, right? That you put into your books. I'm thinking of the coda in *Brundibar* at the end.

MR. SENDAK: Yes. That was not in the opera. The opera ends with we must be together; we must be brothers; we must hold onto each other. But since I can't believe that anymore, I can't believe that. Some kind of Hitler is going to spring up all the time, and that's what the coda means.

Now, okay kids, we hope it's all right, but the devil is here. He can show up anytime. Try to make your life worthwhile and good, and even try to be happy. But you've got to know 1) that you're going to die someday and 2) that there's a certain peril that hovers over all our lives. Your aunt goes out to get you a cheese *blintse* and a Coca Cola. She'll be run over, and she needn't have gone out. You didn't even want it, particularly, but now she's gone. How do you cope with that? Every day in the news there is such a story. A little boy was hit by a truck on the way back from home and this and that.

It's a hard thing to tell children. You don't say you're going to die. I don't know what you say. It's easier to just convey it in the books by that little coda and also by the strength of the children.

Now, the children in the performance in the camp knew they were going to die because after each performance they were sent to Auschwitz. So the next time the production was done, it was a whole bunch of new children. Kids all look alike, right. So nobody worried about who was best in the show. I think there was one kid who played at least two performances, maybe three, before he was killed.

That frightened me so much. So you grow up a different person. You can't believe in anything. I don't wish that for the children, but I was in the hospital yesterday where this friend of mine, whom I adore, is dying, and she's eighty-two. I was crying and sitting with her.

And there was a very sweet woman there whom I didn't know, but she knew who I was. When I was leaving she said, "You know you must be brave, and you must feel good about yourself." And I said, "What makes you say that?" She said, "Because I think every time someone we love dies, we find a reason to hate ourselves or find blame with what we've done or what we didn't do to make it on a high level of meaning. And I have a feeling you're the kind of person who will be very angry with yourself." She said, "I'm angry with myself. I should have done more."

She was right, but my nature is such that my anger goes back to early childhood. Why were Jews being picked on? Why was my father out of his mind? Why was my mother out of her mind? Why did strange things happen?

Well, the Lindbergh kidnapping was terrible, and it destroyed me at the age of three.

MR. RODGERS: You've said *Outside Over There* was sort of an exorcism for you to work through the Lindbergh kidnapping. How successful was *Brundibar* at working through some of this survivor guilt and anger and grief, at that loss?

MR. SENDAK: None, none. It only works while you're doing the work, while you're drawing the pictures, and you're immersed in the book. Then when you're done you know it's just a book. You have just done another book. You did a lot of homework. You looked at pictures. You were in touch with the Polish people in charge of the camp, and Tony Kushner was with you. It was an exciting event. You're both working so hard on this thing. But at the end of it, no.

I always wondered about that. Did art transform the artist? I don't know. It did not to any conscious sense transform me. I'm not aware of being a better person or a wiser person or a more relaxed or happy person. It just doesn't work. And we use the example of Van Gogh painting something. He must have been deliriously happy. He had to be. I'm not just making it up with this farce when he was in the nuthous. The pictures from outside his windows or whatever were glorious. How could somebody be unhappy? But when he was finished, there was just another picture. It didn't make him happy. It didn't stop him from killing himself.

So, I may be so perverted by unhappiness, and I find it so hard to find any reason to be happy, that something's wrong with me.

• • •

MR. RODGERS: I was wondering if you could talk a little bit about the transition from being a book illustrator into opera, and how that was a growing process. Because you've talked in other interviews about how you had to find the nuanced version of a story to add to the text and to add to the images that you're already inventing in your own mind, I'm wondering if you found that that translated into stage designs and costumes or if it involved another way of thinking from the way that you'd worked previously.

MR. SENDAK: Probably the link between the two is music. I've always been passionately in love with opera, as long back as I can recollect. There was a way music helped as an illustrator and as a writer . . . not as a writer. You don't listen to music when you write. You don't listen to anything. You put plugs in your ears. I'm talking about me and these various forms. I can't hear anything when I'm writing, or I'm immediately distracted, so no music.

When I'm illustrating it's always music—always music. Music probably essentially is the most important art form in my life. The irony, of course, is I never could play an instrument. I can't read music. I know all the symphonies of Mozart by heart, but I have to sing them or whistle them. And you have to make sure nobody else is in the house because nobody wants to hear that.

Music as related to book illustration is like a color. It translates itself from music to color. Sometimes it's just black and white, but music as translated to the stage is enormous because the whole opera form is pretty much based on the score. So that someone like Verdi defined the essentialness of a scenario in the music.

Music for an opera is never an illustration. With a poor composer it merely is background music. With the great composers it tells a story that is far richer to the keen listener than merely music being played while somebody is singing. I'll give you an example of—I'll start off, because he just cameto my mind, a composer I have a lot of trouble with now. I didn't when I was younger, and that's Wagner. The most incredible scene in Wagner is when Wotan, the king of the gods, is punishing Brünnhilde, his daughter, because she disobeyed him. All during the dialog between him and her, her acceptance of her fate, and his grievance—he's dying inside that he has to do this, but he has to punish her. What is going on in the orchestra is so drenched with pain, and which also so exalts the relationship of a father and a daughter, that it is just about unbearable. So that when he staged it—not staged it, but when he wrote the libretto himself, and then wrote music for the people, it was the sound of the music penetrating the heart. It sounds very corny, I know, but opera is a glorious form.

You put it together in a way that all the forms are doing their jobs. The libretto is doing its job, the singers, the music, the director of the music. There's nothing like it. There's nothing like it in terms of gratification. You are covering the whole thing. You've got the whole thing. If it's Mozart, if you don't drop dead, I don't know how you're standing after an event like that.

The combination of sound and movement and painting of the sets, all of this is a kind of glorious poem to music. So, I made the shift because I was always trying to copy music into my pictures, and sometimes I would take a Schubert song cycle and merely draw pictures with pen and ink. I've gone into each song, almost like a comic book page, and it was like a juvenile effort to seize the music, capture it. I know that can't be done now. I don't do it anymore, but I feel the music so intensely.

Then you begin to realize how complicated Mozart's thinking was, and his librettist, that they were writing this for the music. There's a real plot going on. The Countess is very upset and says, I don't want to get married, blah, blah, blah. But it's the music that's telling you everything.

So, I finally wanted to be in a profession where I was much closer to the music than ever. I was in it—design and image of a building or a forest or whatever that came from my feelings about the music and not my feelings about the story. Of course, it had to make sense in terms of the story, and that's why there are so many interpretations of operas by various stage designers.

Thus, I became a stage designer, but I always worked from the theory that I'm doing this for the music. I would have to respect the opera very much in order to do it. I couldn't just do an opera. I love Verdi very much, but I can never design a Verdi opera. It's impossible because he has rooms. He has places where people sit down. They have rendezvous, houses, walls, tables. No, because my work is limited—and that's not a bad word, it's a true word—to color, to imagining a background, and having to work. It should work for the opera. *The Magic Flute* is anywhere—anywhere you want it to be. Yet if you listen carefully to what the music is saying, it is very specific as to where he would like you to put it.

Then again, you could say, well, that's how you hear it, and that's how you see it. Who knows if that's how he felt? I believe that the music is telling you what to do all the time. It's got to be serious opera. It's got to be great opera that will talk to an artist that way or help him or give him advice. Unfortunately, like most art forms, there's much more trivial opera, or what I would call trivial opera which I would never bother with. Never, never, never bother with.

I don't like traditional operas, traditional arias, where everybody stops, and they do their thing. Even though Mozart may do that and even Wagner may do that, it's not the same thing. They are unhinged by the music, whereas the other composers are writing music to sing.

I don't know if I'm making it clear. The two different kinds of—one is spiritual, and almost incomprehensible, it's so beautiful, and the other is merely an opera. She's going to sing the jewel song, and he's going to do that. And that's going to do that.

MR. RODGERS: Are you talking about an opera that's written for more of an idea, more of an important, almost philosophical notion, versus an opera that's written as an opera. That's maybe about getting the song across, getting something to—

MR. SENDAK: [*Interposing*] Yes. Opera was an entertainment. It was really a very popular entertainment in the seventeenth, eighteenth, and nineteenth centuries. There was theater, of course. There were concerts, of course, but opera was something that was taken up with a passion in almost all the countries in Europe—especially in Italy and especially in France. It came very late to America.

Of course the great composers offered us something which drove me crazy, even in childhood. When I would hear something, and I wouldn't know why, the story didn't interest me particularly. I remember when I was very young I wanted to do a book of operas—of pictures to operas—and I completed only one opera. It was a strange choice, but I was inexperienced. It was an opera that was played more frequently than it ever has been, and that was called *Louise* by Charpentier—a French opera. I did a whole water-color book of scenes from *Louise* with dashes of color and feeling that she's coming from the bourgeois background to Paris, where she's going to fall in love, of course, with a painter. There was an atelier, and they'll eat in the little—oh, God, just the Paris we all wanted to go to.

It's a terrible job. It's just absolutely appalling because I was literally making a story. It's not a great opera, but it is a very beautiful and poetic opera. I guess I was drawn to it by that—the yearning to be in another country like Paris, to be an artist and free of your family, blah, blah, blah.

MR. RODGERS: But the object wasn't to create a story so much. Is that what you were just saying? Or that was a mistake for that particular opera?

MR. SENDAK: Yes. I was more interested in the story of that opera.

MR. RODGERS: Than in the music?

MR. SENDAK: Than in the music, yes. Exactly. The music is very pretty. It's not great. In order to achieve a set design or costume design, in my way of thinking, the opera must be great. The music must be great, which unfortunately puts you in a very weak position. Rarely you come up to your own expectations. An opera I would love to design, but which I will not because I'm finished with designing operas, is *Falstaff* by Verdi. That was written when he was eighty. I'll be eighty in just a few months. He may have been eighty-one. I don't know. But the miracle of *Falstaff* is—oh, my God, the music is unbelievably beautiful.

There is a recording I have of Toscanini rehearsing *Falstaff*, and he's rehearsing just Act 1. And he's furious, and he says to all the singers, shut up. Shut up and just listen to the orchestra. Listen to what you're doing to the music. In other words, you're killing it. And for about five minutes you hear just the basic sound of the opera. The trombone coming and the clarinet going and the violins going. I was stunned. It was so beautiful. It was like modern music. It was what Verdi heard first, before he imagined what the human voice would sound like in the context of his opera. He wanted them to know that this was a work of such spiritual and passionate nature that it wasn't going to be good for them to just stand and sing. Don't even bother. You hear them all because they're terrified. He was a terrifying man. You hear them all come back into the opera when he decides they should, all having tempered their voices in some way. Having muted their voices in some way so that what he had done musically, which they had heard, probably—they knew what their job was, which was impossible, practically. On top of which he's an old man, and he has moments in that opera of a young girl and a young man in love. Everybody's against them, but it's opera. Parents are always against the shenanigans of their kids.

But what I can't imagine is how he could recollect, in his age, the sound of a young woman and a young man being in love—fresh as a daisy. It's not even as a recollection of an old man going back in time, no. It's like he's right there, and every time that music begins, my skin is crawling. I can't bear the sound of what is beginning as the duet between these three young people. It's amazing. He did not lose anything. He only gained. So to me the attraction of opera was immense. I could paint my backgrounds. I could paint my pictures. I could design the costumes. I could sit in at all the rehearsals and watch the nuances and watch how the director and the producer and everybody worked. Not all of them were good, unfortunately, but the ones that were good—to catch just what I'm talking about so that what you're listening to becomes an experience unlike any other experience you've ever had and where the human voice is more beautiful than you've ever, ever heard it. And everything is being put together—art and painting and costume and lights and music.

So to me it was stepping up into the very next phase, and I couldn't go any further. It always was an unhappy thing in my life, that my parents were so poor that I couldn't take piano lessons nor violin lessons or anything. This was not possible. Not possible. I understood because we were all poor together, so there was . . . they weren't taking anything out on me. It was just the way it was.

The need to have music in my life was almost like it came with my birth. Old age is almost as difficult as childhood, for all the things that are new and terrifying, and you don't know how you're going to deal with it. Music still is, for me, that.

So when I'm working on my book, which has nothing to do with music—

nothing to do with music, I have—I choose the music for my books. I am the director. I am the producer. I am Verdi or Mozart or Wagner.

I carefully have to pick what I'm going to play, and sometimes I'm surprised. Because the book I'm doing is foolish. I don't mean that as a criticism. It's meant to be foolish. But in foolishness there is something that touches; it hurts. So I am in Mahler. There can't be anything different than Mahler, and what I'm working on. And yet there are, in Mahler, moments when the pain becomes almost too intense to bear, and he goes bananas. He starts chirping like a bird. Something is happy. Or in a Mozart sonata it sounds wonderful, wonderful, wonderful, and suddenly dives down into the blackest water. You're stunned, and yet it comes up so fast that you almost missed it. He tells you just how he felt at that very moment. That puts you standing with him, so the more you listen . . . and I'm sure everybody has their own stories to tell like I do. They're all different as to what the passion, the music, is all about and what it does.

That's why I had to change my life and become a stage designer. I had never staged an opera work, and I remember the first day that the Houston Opera producer said to me . . . he was horrified that Frank Corsaro, the director who did it and a great admirer of my books—wanted me to do *The Magic Flute*. The man from Houston said to me, "You do know, Mr. Sendak, that designing a book for children and designing an opera are two very different things." Now, can you imagine what it took me not to hit him? Yes, sir, I get it. The failure is high. I know that. And a number of my operas failed. I failed, and that hurts more than books that didn't work. That's because of the music. You can't fail the music. You can't. That's irreparable. That's terrible. You did a lousy book. . . . Well, you thought it was good. You did your very best on it, and time will tell you that it was an unworthy project. It can't be helped.

MR. RODGERS: There's a particular kind of opera that you feel really drawn to as well, and it's a fantastic kind of opera. It has fantasy elements, mythic elements, and fairytale elements to it. But to hear you describe the difference between sort of foolish operas, or serious operas and non-serious operas, some would criticize fairytale operas as not serious operas. But for you, they mean something very deep. Can you explain a little bit of that?

MR. SENDAK: Well, what I mean is that they are very serious. There's a simple buying the thing out of a fairytale. It's for children, and it's boorish. It's nonsense, but the greatest, greatest things are sometimes so simple. I have to bring in that I mentioned to you guys before—I was reading Chekhov, but before I got to read his biography I was reading short stories, and he wrote endless short stories. I must have read about thirty at this point. You read them, and they're like wisps. The language is so simple, so nondescriptive, so underplayed that you hear the wind. You hear the water. You hear when he's wandering in the woods in Yalta. It's music, and also it is the extraordinarily gifted artist who could tell you in so many simple terms what is beautiful. Even Tolstoy said to him, "You know how to write a short story." Then being Tolstoy, he gave him a list of his best short stories and his worst short stories.

If you read Tolstoy short stories, you can appreciate that's coming from a very great man. Now, what was the point about what I was saying? Oh, another reason why the operas I choose have a magic background is very hard-ass simple: I can't do rooms. I can't do perspective. So like in the Verdi operas, so many of them take place in chambers and cottages. Not for me. That's angular, and no way, I can't. I'm not that kind of an artist. I'm limited. I have to do magic things without borders. Thus the range of operas I can do is limited. I can think now of . . I'd like some Mozart operas to do because you can put them where you like, but I would not do the *Marriage of Figaro*—which is perhaps my favorite Mozart—because that has to be played indoors and in balconies and in outdoor gardens. I can't do that. So there are the great designers who love to draw that, and who can do it, and accomplish everything I said earlier about being part of Mozart. I can't, so my *Magic Flute* is wherever you want it to be. Magic Land.

MR. RODGERS: Speaking of no boundaries in opera, we've got *Wild Things* right here.

MR. SENDAK: Yeah.

MR. RODGERS: I mean, talk about no boundaries!

MR. SENDAK: No boundaries.

MR. RODGERS: This is an amazing opera for no boundaries, no rooms. A room cannot contain this.

MR. SENDAK: That is true, and the room that does contain him is a magic room. There are transformations that take place in the room, so it's only like a regular room for a few minutes. And then—even then, it's not a regular room. It's a book illustration room. So I can't do so many operas. Now it doesn't matter. When I did *Love for Three Oranges* by Prokofiev, that was a dream. I had such a wonderful time, and that's such a nutty, nutty work. That it would take place anywhere, and it could take place in a garden. There is one scene where everything is grotesque. The animals are grotesque. There's a shepherd looking like he's about to rape a poor farm girl, and she's a statue. Who would have such a statue in a garden? It was time for fun. It really was. It really was fun, and you're playing with reality. But if it was real reality, like *Traviata*, forget it, Charlie. I couldn't do it. I wouldn't do it.

Maybe I got to do about as many as I think I could do correctly with my particular gift, and not do the many more I'd like to have done but couldn't have. I wouldn't have accepted it. There are certain books I love, but they can't be illustrated. They should not be illustrated.

One of my favorite novels is *Anna Karenina*. If I pick up a copy and somebody has drawn in it, I want to fling it out the window. How dare anybody draw Anna? Anna has to be the most beautiful woman who ever lived. Everybody who loves that novel knows who Anna is, and what she looks like. And then you draw her? May your hand fall off.

There are rules, but they're rules you make up. You decide what is and isn't and could and couldn't. If anyone gave me an opera list, I could easily check off the ones I'd like to do and the ones I'd like to do but cannot do. I miss that world. I really do miss the world of rehearsing, of watching an artist come up, come up, come up to a great director, when the music becomes more important to the singer, until finally you feel like the music is running through the singer like a river. Of course, if you're with a great singer, mama mia, it's too much.

MR. RODGERS: I want to talk a little bit about the *Wild Things* pictures that you've pulled for us here too. This was a complicated opera because it was a book first.

MR. SENDAK: Yeah.

MR. RODGERS: You didn't have music you were working from, necessarily. Can you talk about what it was like to start from a picture book and create music for it and to start with these characters and turn them full of motion onto the stage?

MR. SENDAK: Oh, that is a daunting question because I was set up with a composer.

MR. RODGERS: Oliver.

MR. SENDAK: Oliver Knussen. My great good fortune is that he is about the best person I could have had. I didn't know it then. He's this big, giant Englishman, bearing down on me, wanting music for this one act opera and me, finding inspiration from Ollie's first sketches. It's a modern opera. I'd never done a modern opera.

Dissonance, strange sounds . . . I had to fit them into my image of my Wild Things—what they look like, now based on what Ollie sounded like. So, you had to make the soup from the beginning, and it's not like doing a Mozart opera. There it is, and you have to match your skill. But this was all of us matching our skills at the same time, and its first production in Brussels was ghastly. We didn't know what we were doing. The costumes were suffocating some of the people inside. The kids who came to see it just loved seeing a Wild Thing fall down. They thought it was part of the fun. A Wild Thing fell into the orchestra pit—even I liked that!

The clumsiness of the creation of it taught me how difficult this form was. Happily, somebody bought it. Glyndebourne Opera, England, bought it, as coarse as it looked. I like to believe that largely because of Ollie's music they began to hear what this could be. Then we redid the whole thing anyway, and it was a great success. It was a very, very charming opera. Then we did *Higglety Pigglety Pop!* together. By then we were inside each other, and it was fun. Our friendship is sustained, right until now, and we always wanted to do a third opera. That's not going to happen. It's too bad.

MR. RODGERS: You spoke about the tone of the music that Oliver and you worked on for the Wild Things, which aimed at dissonance. Other reviewers have described it as having a lot of color in the music. Was this sort of a backwards process from the way that you described listening for colors to create illustrations when you hear music? Here you're working from the colors of the book to create a colored music interpretation. Is that a way of saying it?

MR. SENDAK: I don't know.

MR. RODGERS: It's kind of a weird question.

MR. SENDAK: Yeah, it's a hard question because I'm not hearing.

MR. RODGERS: Sure.

MR. SENDAK: I'm not hearing the question, basically. In a sense I am writing lyrics for the sounds that Ollie makes. Max has to sing about his wish to be free. I've already picked up tempos that Ollie likes and sounds that he likes, and I try to write for those sounds. But he won't give me a piece of paper and say, "I want an aria for Max. I want the first line to be one, two, three, four, that's it. And one, two, three the second line." He drew me a map of what I was to write, and that's just what I did. I filled in what he needed for the orchestra. It worked. There are some things in that opera we got away with. Oh, my God, like we did not want the Wild Things to sing—not to speak English, nothing, just do, fetching, sagging, and . . . there's a whole portion of the opera where they are singing in sounds. I took it from *Boris Godunov*. Who wrote *Boris Godunov*, for goodness sake?

I know it's not part of what has to be put down here right now, but it drives me crazy because he's a great composer—*Khovanshchina, Boris Godunov*.

MR. RODGERS: Mussorgsky.

MR. SENDAK: Thank you. Mussorgsky . . . the peasant sounds of a Mussorgsky opera, where the whole city is chanting, the bells are going, the Czar is marching down the street, and the crowds—the crowds of Russians mumbling against the music. I wanted the Wild Things to sound like they came out of a Mussorgsky opera where they're sounding like they're saying something. What they're saying are terrible things in Yiddish. None of the things my parents said to me or what you say to children—what you should never say to children. I always wondered when somebody is going to figure out what I've done because this is such a vulgarity. I remember at a rehearsal with Beverly Sills sitting right in front of me in the audience—no audience, just us workers—and she wouldn't have heard it except that we repeated it four times. The conductor was doing it over and over and over again, and finally she heard it. She turned and looked at me with such a wild look, "Are you out of your mind?" [*laughing*] And I said, "Well, nobody's heard it but you, Beverly, so I wouldn't worry about it." Thus it remained.

MR. RODGERS: You've talked about the sort of pidgin Yiddish that the–

MR. SENDAK: [*Interposing*] Pidgin Yiddish, yeah.

MR. RODGERS: —Wild Things speak. What were some of the things they said, if I can ask?

MR. SENDAK: No, you cannot ask.

MR. RODGERS: Can't ask? Okay.

MR. SENDAK: No.
MR. RODGERS: Well, one of the things Max says is, "Vildachaiahmima mee-oh!"

MR. SENDAK: Yes. His wolf call, "Vildachaia mommy mia, mia mommy oh." Okay. *Vilde chaya* is literally "wild thing." It's what almost every Jewish mother or father says to their offspring, "You're acting like a *vilde chaya*! Stop it!" Or, you're climbing on the furniture. You're doing all these things. So that was the title of the book.

All the Wild Things were based on relatives that came over from the old country. I think I've told you this before. I didn't want them to be like real people or talk like real people, and my relatives didn't talk like real people. These were all escapees from Nazism. My mother and father worked very hard to bring what was left of her family, and when they got to his there was nobody left.

When they got to the house—they would all stay at our house which I resented terribly. I knew these were my aunts and uncles, but I hadn't known them from childhood. I thought they were awful people. They smoked cigars, their teeth were terrible, and they had hairs pouring out of their noses. What was the matter with them? They would squeeze you until it hurt, press you, and say things about you, "Oh, he looks just like David does. You remember when David was his age?" It was horrible. It was torment. Children are very unforgiving. They didn't look like regular type people in the neighborhood. You took on value what your parents told you—that they were your uncles and your aunts—but you didn't want them. Waiting for my mother to get all the food ready, and her being late, meant these people could eat you. If they got to be hungry enough, they would eat you because they handle you so roughly—by the nape of the neck, by the cheeks, by everything. I remember my sister, brother, and I would go into another room and say, "Horrible, horrible people!"

Then of course you get to know them, and you grow up. You get to love some, and you continue to hate others. They became the Wild Things, and Mussorgsky was the hero of that—or part of—that opera. Also it was such fun with Ollie, who is so knowledgeable musically, and our taste was similar. To sit there and laugh and think who we would make fun of musically, there are a few composers in the *Wild Things* score, and a few that we love, like Ravel.

MR. RODGERS: When you're working on these, . . . I wonder maybe we should spread some of these things out, just to take another look at them. Can you talk a little bit about who these designs are for? Do you give these to a production crew that assembles from your sketches the final stage sets?

MR. SENDAK: This would be a storyboard. That would be for nobody but me, trying to see what the opera was about or trying to see shapes that would work. That would prepare me for doing finished drawings. The opera, thank heavens, never looked like this. My attempt was to sound mysterious and have a silhouette like in a camera, and then it gets larger and larger, until he's in his room. This does start the opening of the opera—a large head which opens, instead of the black, the head opens and the interior of his room is visible.

But this was like how I would do a picture book—a storyboard of what it is going to look like. Elements in this that I really like. Then I would go into how many acts, how long is the first scene. Again based on the music, and the needs of the music, that begins to dictate what's in the picture, what's onstage. When you're working with somebody you respect, it's great fun. Ollie was having fun with setting up timings for me. I was having fun too. We were both taking this very seriously. It was his first opera and my first of two. We were very serious about wanting it to be an important thing. We love music intensely, so we weren't kidding around. But that [storyboard] would be for home use.

MR. RODGERS: Some of these other sketches . . . I can just slide this towards you . . . thinking of that one on top.

MR. SENDAK: This would have been an actual scene from the opera that would have allowed for exits and entrances through the trees. All these portals—main action taking place in the center, of course. That would be like a scene that would last maybe five minutes, and then it would disappear

Then another scene would take its place. Everything had to be considered in terms of exits and entrances—leaving a room.

There was one opera. It was a Mozart opera where I had not enough room for the soprano because I had forgotten how big her dress was, and she was ready to kill me because on the rehearsal stage everything was ready. The door was to open, and she couldn't get through. It made her look like a tub of lard, but it wasn't her problem. It wasn't her fault. It was my fault. We had a lot of strife, me and her. Quite a lot of strife because . . . I was being so dutiful and so—I want this to be exactly right, so I got a Mozart book out to see what the costumes would look like in his version of *The Magic Flute*, and I gave her a beautiful gown. I had an assistant who was a real pain in the butt, and he would come screaming, "Oh, she's making a terrible scene. She's making a terrible scene. She always makes terrible scenes. Don't let her have what she wants. Don't. You must never make it easy for these people," which I thought was a curious bit of advice.

Then I hated her. I avoided her. Then we had a rehearsal, or we took a break. It was a little party, and there she was. She came marching up to me and said, "Are you so and so?" I said, "Yes." She said, "Why are you doing this to me? Look at what I look like. Look, I have no hips. I have a terrible body, and you're making me wear this exquisite dress for a pretty young girl. All I feel as I'm singing is everything is falling off me. Can't you do me the kindness to make me a dress that fits my body?" I realized what a great injustice I unwittingly did. Of course, all opera singers are supposed to be tiresome and asking for this and asking for that, and lots of them are. But she wasn't one of them. She was really realistically suffering. She was afraid to go out and sing because her dress would fall off. I had to redesign her whole thing. It didn't look like the Mozart dress. Then I realized how many contradictions there were in what you were doing and that you had to make sacrifices all of the time. We got to be good friends, and I've learned to stay away from the guy who was giving me advice.

The other side of this are character sketches for *Wild Things*—the hanging of the bear, the toy soldiers in his room. This is a tent that he builds. Most of these things were built and were used onstage. This was the whole first scene of Act 1, of how he goes nuts in his own room.

MR. RODGERS: Is there a picture of the mother character in that stack?

MR. SENDAK: I don't know. There was a mother who I gave up on. Let me look. Yes, here is the mother as she was onstage in the first act when he's making such a mess of everything, and she comes in. The drawing I did for her was a compromise. I wanted it to look like a housedress, which women in the '30s and '40s wore. That's pretty much what they wore, but I also wanted her to have a grotesque shape. I wanted him to be seeing everything—the pulsing through his blood because he's going nuts—so I didn't want him to see a regular mother. The woman I designed for the opera was so grotesque that everybody begged me to let her not be the mother. She was shaped like—what do you call those things? You clean the rug with them—

DR. DREHER: A vacuum cleaner?

MR. SENDAK: The vacuum cleaner. Thank you. That's what happens to your brain after a while. So instead of her looking like a vacuum cleaner, she has a vacuum cleaner. The only way she could get him to knock it off—this is how my mother used it. She would take out the vacuum cleaner, and the minute I saw it I was finished. I was done. I'd collapse into a corner. I was so afraid of it. I still think it would have been great fun to see the vacuum cleaner come out as though it were a person, go after Max, and attack. But that was not to be. I couldn't convince anybody that that was worth doing. She still wins the battle, but then here is the room changing. When she puts him in his room and punishes him for the raucous mess he's made of everything, he attacks his dog. He's broken the soldiers. He's done everything that a normal child would do.

This is how I first envisioned the opera. This was changed also—that it would have a background of the endpapers from the book. This would open like a camera, getting bigger and bigger and bigger. You see the interior of his life, his dog, and the mess he was making.

You see how many times you go over it and over it and over it. Sometimes you think you have it. Then you put it onstage, and everybody starts carrying on. I can't wear this. I can't get through that doorway. There's no way I can deal with that rope. I have had a rope thing since I was a child, just like I've had a vacuum cleaner thing.

You're dealing with a lot of *meshuggenahs*, a lot of people who have various problems. You keep placating them by trying to take out as much as—I was much more lenient here. You get harder as you continue. Like some guy, one of the young heroes in *The Magic Flute*, is very fond of his hair—the blond hair—and he had to wear a cap. He said—before he even met me, he says, "Oh, if you know Mr. Sendak, tell him I cannot wear a cap. I cannot wear a hat. It will just make a mess of my hair." I thought, "You pig. You won't wear the cap I designed for you because of your bloody hair?" And that's how I treated him—as the vain pig that he was. Then of course, I felt like, "oh, you're really turning into a designer. You're really knowing how to be mean to people." No, I was defending myself because they all wanted something changed. All of them. There's only a limit to how much you can bother with that.

Now, here are two very nice scenes. This is one—I say modestly—of his room where he has his toy cannon, and he's shooting off his toy cannon, killing all the soldiers. Max was sung by a soprano. She was great. She went on to sing Max everywhere the opera was set. There she is coming on to the island.

• • •

MR. RODGERS: Maybe we'll start with these from *Hansel and Gretel*.

MR. SENDAK: Okay.

MR. RODGERS: This was a very different period in your opera career. This is—

MR. SENDAK: [*Interposing*] This is late.

MR. RODGERS: This is late, and this is after you've done *Pierre*. You've finished with the intense opera period in the 1980s, and now it's the late '90s. You've gone back to it. Did you approach this one any differently, having had that break and having gone through the soul searching that it took to do Melville?

MR. SENDAK: Well, it freed me to do Humperdinck because I had long not wanted to do this opera. I thought, what could be more commonplace than the kiddie book illustrator designing *Hansel and Gretel*?

Fortunately, I fell in love with the opera. I've heard it often enough, but I did a lot of homework. I read the Grimm tales. I've read analyses of this particular story. I realized that the culprit was Mr. Humperdinck's sister, who wrote the libretto. She took out everything that made the story rich and frightening. She wanted it to be sweet and lovely. The director and I both felt that we had to put back, in some way, the horror.

Why is this one of the most popular fairytales in the whole world? It isn't because it makes you happy. It isn't because it has a happy ending because in order to get there you have to go through hell. It's because children are abused, and it's one of the very few stories that tell you that there are such things as parents who abuse their children, who don't love their children. In this case a stepmother who hates her children and a father who's too weak to defend them. It's well known, according to literature, that if you wanted to portray a bad mother you called her a stepmother. It's a cover-all so that no child would feel pointed at aggressively.

So stepmothers were usually just mothers—real mothers—and you know of this fairytale. Obviously everyone knows it—that this, what's out here—is . . . I know this storyboard of events in the fairytale, and how I might convey them on the stage. Because again this is a fairly short opera, and the progression is really short—from the house they live in, to them being driven out of the house, to their time in the woods, to the witch's house where they nearly get eaten, to their murder of the witch, escape and home, and forgiveness of their father. They bring all this money and gold back that the witch had in her house.

What discomforts me is that they ever forgive the father. But children do that. They forgive their parents—one of those strange things about kids. I guess they have to. I think kids are better people than regular people. They have bigger hearts.

So that's the storyboard of *Hansel and Gretel*.

MR. RODGERS: Do you sense that horror in the music as well? How well did he reach that in the music?

MR. SENDAK: Not at all. He backs the sister's libretto. Don't forget; he was not a major composer. He wrote other operas which we do not listen to. I've heard one other, which was really quite terrible. *Hansel and Gretel* is a masterpiece. It's just a masterpiece. It is absolutely beautiful. It is faithful to miss—what's his name? The composer? Humperdinck.

DR. DREHER: Humperdinck?

MR. SENDAK: Engelbert Humperdinck. This is the show curtain which would be the first thing you would see when you came in and sat down. It's a vision of how hunger is the major issue in this opera. If they fall asleep and dream, it's of food because they are utterly deprived. They are sent out in the woods by their angry mother—stepmother—to collect stuff for them to eat tonight. When the father comes home, he says, "Where are the children?" She says "Well, I've sent them out. I've been working all day, and I sent them to get berries and food for us to eat." He sings this big aria which is "Oh, are you out of your mind? Don't you know that a witch lives in the woods and that she eats little children?" And that's how Act 1 ends.

MR. RODGERS: Another favorite of yours reappears in this, too That's the goblins from *Outside*–

MR. SENDAK: [*Interposing*] Yes.

MR. RODGERS: What connections did you see between that book and this Grimm?

MR. SENDAK: Only that it was Grimm—it has the same characters that a Grimm fairytale has, and *Outside Over There* was my attempt to produce a Grimm fairytale.

These are variations on what Gretel looks like, what kind of costume she wears, and there are costumes for the witch. Now, the witch is a bother because for some strange reason, maybe Humperdinck felt uneasy about conveying the witch, but she is snappy. She does a fandango almost, which is such a silly thing. It's wonderful music, but a happy witch? What is she doing? It's like he's really afraid to touch the darkest place in the story, but it wasn't in the libretto. If he had done it, it would have been out of keeping with what his sister had done. This was meant as a home entertainment piece. It was never made to be on an opera stage. He underestimated himself. This was to be a Christmas fun thing—you come around, and you sit around. The family, like those pre-TV entertainment families . . . imagine how fun that would have been.

Like Charles Dickens would write eighteen chapters in the morning, drive forty-four miles to see his girlfriend in the afternoon, come back, have a glass of tea, then write a masque or a little playlet for all the children that were—that he was producing in the evening. He wrote nine thousand novels and walked forty miles a day. Forty miles a day. I hate him.

DR. DREHER: Uphill both ways.

MR. SENDAK: I don't hate him. I love him.

MR. RODGERS: It's really unforgettable that you try to inject some more of the, as you say, horror back in the gingerbread house.

MR. SENDAK: Yes. The house really is a spider's web of how to seduce children who are hungry. They're all hungry. My original idea for this was that the children would be seen right from the beginning of the opera wandering in the woods, helpless. Hansel and Gretel would be little kids that would lead [other children] to the witch, and how they will survive her by killing her.

For me the opera was wonderfully about Gretel because she's a little bit older than Hansel, and he'll eat or do anything. He's just a dumb little boy, which she watches, and she saves his life. She gathers the gold, and she takes him home to papa. She is a great heroine. I really love Gretel very much, and I wish the opera made it clear that she was the heroine of the whole thing, and Hansel is just anybody's dumb kid brother.

MR. RODGERS: That's a theme that you've found since Mozart. I remember reading that you once said Mozart had these incredible, strong, clever women characters.

MR. SENDAK: Yes.

MR. RODGERS: That his structuring of the heroine is what you've tried to capture in a lot of your work.

MR. SENDAK: Yes.

MR. RODGERS: Is that something you found in the Humperdinck as well?

MR. SENDAK: I find in life that the longer you live, the clearer it becomes—at least to me. I don't want to make any theories about anything—that women are so much stronger than men. So much stronger, in every way. Really, in every way. Read Henry James. Read any of the great novels. *Moby-Dick* don't read. There are no women in *Moby-Dick*. But on the whole the great works of life have—like *Anna Karenina* and even *War and Peace* and these little Chekhov stories—the girls or the women hold up what's going on. They have the strength. Society deprives the privilege, the rights, and the congratulations, but they do it sneakily. They do it anyway. When you finish with Chekhov, all you want is a Russian wife, if you're so inclined that way.

I just think culturally it's true. They hold up. They live longer than we do. I'm thinking of what operas I really love . . . even in Wagner, who I have a lot of problems with personally. He and I just don't get on. I don't know what the question was.

MR. RODGERS: I was just asking about Mozart's influence on some of your–

MR. SENDAK: [*Interposing*] Yes. Yes. Well, like the Countess in the *Marriage of Figaro*. . . the Countess is betrayed endlessly by the Count. He's just a sexual pig. Because he is a count, anyone who marries on his grounds, he gets first shot at the girl in bed. Not a bad situation—it's Susanna, who is the girl in this particular place, and Figaro—the whole opera is about how to avoid the Count and how to give up her virginity to him when she wants to give it to Figaro, who will be her husband. She outwits him, and the whole opera is about the outwitting of the Count, to a large degree, by a simple country girl.

The Countess, who knows what her life is like—we've met her first in *The Barber of Seville*. She was a lovely, innocent, charming girl who fell in love with the Count. By the time she's in the *Marriage of Figaro*, she's already burnt. She knows what she's married. In the very last scene, and I think it's one of the best scenes in any opera, is the mystery in the garden. Everyone's in disguise. Nobody knows who anybody is. The Count thinks his wife is Susanna the maid, and he's trying to get her to make love. Then only at the last minute when the disguises are thrown back does he see his wife standing in front of him. His betrayal was clear, and it's obvious what she's going to do. He sinks to his knees, and he pleads with his wife. It's some of the most beautiful music ever written. He begs her pardon and will she—*perdono*—will she forgive him? There's this long pause, and she forgives him.

Which means she knows him in and out—she knows that by taking him back now it'll all happen again. There's no changing because he's a man. He just can't control himself, and that's the message. This is what is plain to me, that the heroines are tremendous heroines. They're not just mealy-mouthed sufferers. She loves him, so what's she have to do? She loves him.

Her *perdona* at the end is—if you don't cry you're dead. Then it all breaks up into a happy tune. That's what Mozart always does. He'll hit you in the back of the neck until you can't stand it, and then, just when you're gonna stop standing it, he'll—something else—a fairytale play, beautiful music, everybody starts dancing in the garden. So only for a second did you look into somebody's heart and see it get broken.

I can't say Gretel is up there with Susanna. She's only a little girl, but she knows her job already, which is to take care of her little brother, make sure the witch doesn't eat him, make sure that they escape from this place, and if possible get rid of the witch so that no child ever has to suffer this fate again. So that's what I [audio cuts out] the opera. I made it for her—the costumes for her, everything. I wanted her to be up front in the whole production. The boy is just a nice kid, but one who never understood the larger business of what was going on—of life and death. There's no harm in that because if he's a little boy then he can . . . he's not ready to see that yet.

But that's the excitement of doing a production—reading into it. I've read all of Grimm, so I know where you could go with these things and where a German child in the eighteenth century, hearing the story told, will be frightened and captivated and excited. That's why when the English translated Grimm for the first time they eliminated all these things.

So Fraulein Humperdinck was just doing the same thing. She wanted to have a fun evening. She didn't want anything serious going on, like dead kids. But you get in trouble, like when those kids wanted to meet the dead girl at the end of the production. The little girl who dies—did I mention that? In our version of *Hansel and Gretel*, since I tried so hard to bring back some element of the original story, we did make the mother an alcoholic, which would account for the bitchiness, and we made the father a grumpy, dumpy, non-interesting or concerned man.

The children get kicked out of the house for making a mess, and they get lost in the woods. Then they meet other kids who are lost. Lots of children are kicked out by their parents or just get lost or run away, and they all hang out in the woods, having to figure out how to eat, how to live, how to go on. Somehow Hansel and Gretel become their leaders. It doesn't say so, but somehow she takes care of them. They all go to sleep and the wood nymphs sing an unbelievably beautiful prayer that is the most famous thing from that opera. They were angels that come down to protect the kids, but angels and I just don't get on. So I changed them to wood nymphs—beautiful preadolescent girls in filmy, gauzy gowns—coming to take care of the children. I saw a production where the angels had big yellow wigs, and their bodies are top heavy with wings. They all looked like Bette Midler, each and every one of them. I thought I was going crazy. What is Bette Midler doing in a German forest? So these were not Bette Midler. At the end of the prayer, the lights get lighter, dawn comes up, and the children yawn and stretch. They're getting up, and there's a little girl who's just lying there. They all gradually, slowly begin to be aware of her. Why isn't she stretching? Why isn't she getting up? The wood nymphs exchange looks. Despite their watching over them during the night, a child died.

It was an experiment. The opera company was terrified that this production would fail because of that, but that was the only way to get something of Grimm into the opera. The wood nymphs pick up the little girl—I'll always remember—with her hands dangling, and they take her off stage. The children stand silently, grieving for one of their lost friends. Then the opera picks up again.

Of course, you could hear a pin drop in the opera house. People were never expecting to see this. Then after the opera was done—and of course it was filled with children, everybody takes children to all these things, like *Nutcracker*—kids ran upstage. They wanted autographs. They always want autographs, but not from me and not from Frank. "We want the dead girl. Where's the dead girl?!" They knew perfectly well she wasn't dead, but she was acting dead. That's what I've always said about kids. You can't really scare them. They know this is an opera. But to see them running, "Have you seen the dead girl? Do you know where she is?!" "Hello, I designed it, don't you want my autograph?" "No. No, whoever you are."

But I think I'd like to imagine that they were grateful for the reality of that moment, and they know that children die.

• • •

MR. RODGERS: Can I ask about this? Do you miss doing dummy books?

MR. SENDAK: Yes. The one I'm working on now . . . *Bumble-Ardy* is the name of the new book I'm doing. It's had three dummies now—three dummies. It's a simple book, but it's turned into something else. I don't know what it's turned into, and I am a different person now than I was when I first played with this idea back in the '90s. It's going its own way. It's becoming very strange. I am letting it go wherever it wants to go. It's a kind of different confidence than I've had before, where I am very pedantic about doing it right. If you experiment, okay, but you experiment within the right of that work. You can't just go all over the place like Julie Taymor does, which is why I can't stand her work. She is so gifted—and she is—but she goes wild and loses contact with what she's doing. Anyway, I'm sure she's had enough crap from critics without needing mine. But this is a different thing. *Bumble-Ardy* started out with a very definitive little plot. When I started doing it, it was to take some consolation from my friend's illness and just work on anything that was there. And it was there.

But as I went on, and he died during the procedure, which must have had a big effect, although I don't know how. That simple story began to take on, I guess, sort of ominous tones or a different tone. Yet I stuck to the plot. I followed the text. I was still as pedantic as I ever was, and yet something had filtered into the work which I had not been aware of. Instead of taking it out,

I let it grow like a mushroom, until now, as I'm coming towards the end of the book in pencil. . . . I still have to do the whole thing over again in color, which will change it again, but now it's haunting. Now it's strange. It strikes me that this is what a book should be. As long as you're not stupid and as long as you're not vain, you're trying to make people sit up because of what you're doing. Most of the people I know can't sit up anymore.

I like that it's taking this course. I really like that it's going its own way, which is of course my way, but it's unconscious. I've never experienced that before. I've never experienced working on a book where I'm in control of a matter and a situation, but something else has come in which I have no control over. Nor do I wish to understand or control, and I think it has to do with old age. I think it has to do with some other part of me which is oddly free because I don't have to do books anymore. I don't have to sit and be belittled by the idiot people who run the publishing business.

So if I'm doing this, it's for me. If it's a successful book, I'm glad for the publisher, but that's all. I do worry about what I'll do next. I don't know what I'm going to do next, but I know it has to include William Blake and—oh, God, I'm so bad with names. I can't believe I'm forgetting—Emily Dickinson and maybe Chekhov right now, because I'm so hot with Chekhov. I doubt if he'll stay in the grouping when the time comes. I do have a book I've written which I'm very proud of, but it's the first book I've written in my whole life that I don't know how to illustrate. Whether I ever get to do it or not, I don't know. I just don't know. I hope I do.

This Pig Wants to Party:
Maurice Sendak's Latest

Terry Gross / 2011

From *Fresh Air*, aired on 20 September 2011. © 2015 NPR. *Fresh Air* is produced by WHYY in Philadelphia and distributed by NPR. You can hear the complete interview and other Fresh Air interviews or the Fresh Air podcast at www.npr.org/freshair.

TERRY GROSS, HOST: Maurice Sendak is like part of the extended family for those people who grew up reading his books or who have read those books to their children. Books like *Where the Wild Things Are, In the Night Kitchen*, and *Outside Over There*.

I was slightly too old to grow up with those books, but I came to love them as an adult. I try to talk with Sendak whenever he has a new book, which he does now—it's called *Bumble-Ardy*.

On Sunday, in the back page essay of the *New York Times Book Review*, Pamela Paul wrote, "Sendak, Shel Silverstein, and Theodor Geisel, a.k.a. Dr. Seuss, are so much a part of the childhood vernacular today that it's hard to imagine their books were once considered to be wholly inappropriate for children. They brought a shock of subversion to the genre, defying the notion that children's books shouldn't be scary, silly, or sophisticated. Their books encouraged bad or, perhaps, just human behavior."

Maurice Sendak is eighty-three now. It would have been difficult for him to get to a studio, so we called him at home.

Maurice Sendak, congratulations on your new book. It gives me this opportunity to call you up, see how you're doing, and say "hello" and talk with you about your work. So, how have you been?

MAURICE SENDAK: Well, it's been a rough time. I've gotten quite old, Terry, since you've seen me last, which is not very unusual. I'm working very hard, but I feel that I'm working for myself at this point because everything

I'm doing is, if it's publishable, fine. If not, it makes not too much difference because I claim that this time is for me and me alone.

GROSS: Do you have a secret stash of work that you've never published?
SENDAK: Yes. Oh, sure.

GROSS: You do? Yes?
SENDAK: A lot of it is junk which should not be published. Some of it is good, and some of it is just fits and starts of things. I'm writing a poem now about a nose. I always wanted to write a poem about a nose. I thought, "Gee, it's a ludicrous subject." That's why when I was younger I was afraid of something that didn't make a lot of sense, and there was not. There's nothing to worry about. It doesn't matter.

GROSS: In your new book *Bumble-Ardy*, the main character is a pig who is orphaned and lives with his aunt.
SENDAK: Yes.

GROSS: When his parents were alive, he never had a birthday party because his immediate family frowned on fun. Then he turns nine. His aunt buys him some gifts to throw him a quiet party for two. But then he decides to throw a costume party for himself, and he invites some grubby swine.
   The party begins after his aunt leaves for work and then mayhem ensues. When his aunt returns, she throws everyone out and says, "OK, smarty, you've had your party, but never again." And then Bumble-Ardy says, in tears, "I promise, I swear, I won't ever turn 10."
SENDAK: Right.

GROSS: So when the aunt says never again, which people say about the Holocaust—when she says that in reference to never having a party again, that's really, really loaded.
SENDAK: I don't know what to answer to that. You've just picked the two lines of the book that are my favorite lines. There's something so poignant and extremely funny, if you could say that's funny about his answer, I'll never turn ten. In fact, it sums up my life. It sums up my work. Whether it's mad or ludicrous or funny and odd, it's true.
   What you just said is extremely insightful. Nobody has said anything like that, but I always expect that from you. Those two lines are essential. I'll never be ten. It touches me deeply, but I won't pretend that I know exactly

what it means. I only know it touches me deeply, and when I thought of it, I was so happy I thought of it. It came to me, which is what the creative act is all about. Things come to you without your necessarily knowing what they mean.

GROSS: Let me ask you, those two lines where she says, "OK, smarty, you've had your party, but never again." And he says, "I promise, I swear, I won't ever turn 10." What a bargain that is.

He has to promise to never have boisterous fun again, to not get older, to just stay in that moment, the nice little boy.

SENDAK: That is correct. I will do as you say.

GROSS: Did you have to make that bargain with your parents to get love?

SENDAK: I had somewhat the same problem. I had a brother who was my savior. He made my childhood bearable. He was older by five years, Jack Sendak. He wrote a number of books. He was very, very, very gifted. More importantly to my life, he saved my life. He drew me away from the lack of comprehension that existed between me and my parents. He took his time with me to draw pictures, to read stories, and to live a kind of fantastical life.

My sister occasionally joined in, but mostly after all, she was a girl. All that was expected of her was that she should grow up and be very pretty and marry a decent man. So she had to concentrate on what my parents expected of her. She didn't have the creative insanity that existed between me and my brother to go further with that. I wish she had. I loved her very much.

But that life with him contradicted the prosaic life that I was expected to be a decent child. I was expected to be with my brother and help him and to shut up and just be a quiet kid. I hated them for a long time. But I don't anymore because, God knows, it's a blessing to have a quiet kid. I don't have kids at all, and I thank God that I never did.

GROSS: Yes, but isn't there a part of you that wishes you had a son or a daughter to come help take care of you and shop for you and bring you things. And . . .

SENDAK: Yes, I would infinitely prefer a daughter. If I had a son, I'd leave him at the A&P . . . or some other big advertising place where somebody who needs a kid would find him, and then he would be all right.

GROSS: Why? Isn't that stereotyping what a son would be?

SENDAK: I suppose it is, but I'm just an ordinary human being. A daughter would be drawn to me. A daughter would want to help me. Girls are infinitely more complicated than boys and women more than men. There's no doubt about that. We all know it. We just don't like to think about it, and certainly the men don't like to think about it. But a daughter would—oh, God, I've fantasies [of] a daughter! I have lived my whole life with a dream daughter.

GROSS: Well, let me ask you this: You came out a few years ago.
SENDAK: Correct.

GROSS: If you were able to be out in a period like we live in today where it's socially acceptable in lots of circles to be gay and have children—it's so much easier to be gay and have children now, would you have had a child?
SENDAK: No. No.

GROSS: But you just said you fantasized all your life about having a daughter!
SENDAK: But that sucks. There's too much hard work involved. I am devoted to being an artist and a person who reads books for the rest of my life, however long I have.

GROSS: That takes a certain amount of self-absorption to be able to do that.
SENDAK: Well, I think so, and I think it has to do with time spent trying to understand what it means to be an artist, to get under the skin of what is happening as best you can. To have a real child—a real daughter—would've been hard work—work I would not want to do: changing clothes, fixing, taking her to school, putting up with her anger, putting up with her indifference, and praying all the time that she grows up to be a good woman and take care of her poor ole dad. It is typical of a male. It doesn't make a difference what kind of male you are. You are a selfish pig in very, very complicated ways. I would fantasize a daughter full-grown. She would have to be in her late thirties, early forties, and be all over me, taking care of poor, ole dad.

GROSS: Do you have someone to help you?
SENDAK: Yes, she is a youngish lady who puts up with my oldness that I'm fighting and struggling against. She puts up with my bad behavior. She loves me, and I love her.

GROSS: Is she a friend? Is she a nurse?
SENDAK: She's a friend.

GROSS: Oh, that's great.
SENDAK: I've known her since she was a little girl.

GROSS: Oh, wow, so it's kind of almost like a daughter.
SENDAK: Yes, she belonged down the road, and her mother was a saint in the best sense of that word, the best sense of what I imagine Christianity is all about. I adored her mother, and I adore her. Her name is Lynn, and I adore her brother. His name is Peter. They both have grown up and are attached to me. I might as well have had them for my kids. They put up with everything.

GROSS: Oh, that's beautiful. Plus, you didn't have to do the work . . .
We've talked before how you've been in therapy. Your late partner who died in 2007—you were together for about fifty years? Do I have that right?
SENDAK: Oh, about fifty years, yes.

GROSS: He was a psychoanalyst, right?
SENDAK: He was a psychoanalyst.

GROSS: Okay, so here's the thing: when you're in therapy, you have to decide if you're going to tell your spouse, your friends, your family about things that happen in those sessions—things you learned about yourself, things you said about other people—or not, whether you can confide in people about that or not. Since your partner was a psychoanalyst, did you talk to him about your therapy sessions?
SENDAK: About my therapy?

GROSS: Yes.
SENDAK: With him. No, it just seemed like, "why?" I don't know why. It just seemed inauthentic and incorrect to burden him with that. My therapies went on forever. My being gay was something of not great interest to me—you just have to believe that. The person I lived with—we lived together for all those years so that we could make trips to our favorite places in Europe, so that we could read our favorite books, so that we could—and this is most important—listen to music. Now I couldn't deal with 9/11 the other day. I just couldn't bear it.

GROSS: The tenth anniversary of 9/11?

SENDAK: Yes, that evening of 9/11, they conducted Mahler's *2nd Symphony*, the *Resurrection Symphony*, which has never been a great favorite of mine, but Mahler is a great favorite of mine. I sat there and cried like a baby listening to the music. I'd got through the day—the whole day had not gotten through to me. I just couldn't deal with the whole situation. But sitting there and listening to music that was written almost now a hundred years ago, it had nothing to do with 9/11, except that it had to do with the life and death of human beings, which takes me back for some reason to *Bumble-Ardy*, "I won't turn 10."

The fragility of life, the irrationality of life, the comedy of life . . . my tears flow because two great, great friends died close together—a husband and a wife—who meant everything to me. I am having to deal with that. It's very, very hard.

GROSS: Did they die very recently?

SENDAK: Yes, she died two months ago, and he died the day before yesterday. I was, except for his son, the last person to speak with him. He was my publisher. I loved him, and I loved her.

GROSS: Are you at the point where you feel like you've outlived a lot of people whom you loved?

SENDAK: Yes, of course. Since I don't believe in another world, in another life, this is it. When they die they are out of my life. They're gone forever. Blank. Blank. Blank. I am not afraid of death. I begin to—as maybe a good many elderly people do. Who knows?

When I did *Bumble-Ardy*, I was so intensely aware of death. Eugene, my friend and my partner, was dying here in the house while I did *Bumble-Ardy*. I did *Bumble-Ardy* to save myself. I did not want to die with him. I wanted to live, as any human being does. But there's no question that the book was affected by what was going on here in the house.

GROSS: We've talked before about how you're Jewish, but you're very secular. You don't believe in God. You don't . . .

SENDAK: No, I don't.

GROSS: I think having friends who die, getting older, getting closer toward the end of life tests people's faith, and it also tests people's atheism. It sounds like your atheism is staying strong.

SENDAK: Is what?

GROSS: Staying strong.

SENDAK: Yes, I'm not unhappy about becoming old. I'm not unhappy about what must be. It makes me cry only when I see my friends go before me, and life is emptied. I don't believe in an afterlife, but I still fully expect to see my brother again. It's like a dream life. I'm reading a biography of Samuel Palmer. It was written by a woman in England. I can't remember her name.[1] It's sort of how I feel now, when he was just beginning to gain his strength as a creative man and beginning to see nature. But he believed in God, you see, and he believed in Heaven and he believed in Hell. Goodness gracious, that must've made life much easier. It's harder for us non-believers. There's something I'm finding out as I'm aging: that I am in love with the world.

I look right now, as we speak together, out my window in my studio, and I see my trees and my beautiful, beautiful maples that are hundreds of years old. They're beautiful. I can see how beautiful they are. I can take time to see how beautiful they are. It is a blessing to get old. It is a blessing to find the time to do the things, to read the books, to listen to the music.

I don't think I'm rationalizing anything. I really don't. This is all inevitable, and I have no control over it. *Bumble-Ardy* was a combination of the deepest pain and the wondrous feeling of coming into my own, and it took a long time. It took a very long time, but it's genuine. Unless I'm crazy—I could be crazy, and you could be talking to a crazy person.

GROSS: I don't think so [*laughs*] .

SENDAK: I don't know anymore, and I don't care.

GROSS: What are your physical restrictions like? Can you walk okay? Can you get around?

SENDAK: No, I can't walk okay. I'd love to walk. That's why I've been doing that since the '70s when I had my first coronary. I have heart trouble, and I've had a very bad time after Eugene died. I was very sick, and they thought I would die. I came back to do *Bumble-Ardy*. I have nothing but praise now, really, for my life. I mean I'm not unhappy. I cry a lot because I miss people. I cry a lot because they die, and I can't stop them. They leave me, and I love them more. I'm in a very soft mood, as you can gather because new people have died.

GROSS: Yes.

SENDAK: They were not that old. It's what I dread more than anything—the isolation.

GROSS: Yes.

SENDAK: But I have my young people here, four of them who are studying, and they look at me as somebody who knows everything. Those poor kids. If they only knew how little I know. Obviously, I give off something that they trust because they're all intelligent. Oh God, there are so many beautiful things in the world, which I will have to leave when I die, but I'm ready, I'm ready, I'm ready.

GROSS: Well, listen—

SENDAK: I have to tell you something.

GROSS: Go ahead.

SENDAK: You are the only person I have ever dealt with in terms of being interviewed or talking to who brings this out in me. There's something very unique and special in you, which I so trust. When I heard that you were going to interview me or that you wanted to, I was really, really pleased.

GROSS: I'm really glad we got the chance to speak because when I heard you had a book coming out I thought, what a good excuse to call up Maurice Sendak and have a chat.

SENDAK: Yes, that's what we always do, isn't it?

GROSS: Yes, it is.

SENDAK: That's what we've always done.

GROSS: It is.

SENDAK: Thank God we're still around to do it.

GROSS: Yes.

SENDAK: Almost certainly, I'll go before you go, so I won't have to miss you.

GROSS: Oh, God, what a . . .

SENDAK: I don't know whether I'll do another book or not. I might. It doesn't matter. I'm a happy old man. But I will cry my way all the way to the grave.

GROSS: Well, I'm so glad you have a new book. I'm really glad we had a chance to talk.

SENDAK: I am too.

GROSS: I wish you all good things.

SENDAK: I wish you all good things. Live your life. Live your life. Live your life.

Note

1. Editor's note: *Mysterious Wisdom: The Life and Work of Samuel Palmer* (2011), written by British art critic Rachel Campbell-Johnston.

Further Reading

Editor's Note: Maurice Sendak was a generous interviewee, and a complete collection of his interviews would inevitably fill numerous volumes. Here is a selection of prominent interviews worthy of further consideration. They could not be reproduced here because of space, permissions, or cost of reprinting, yet many are available online or through libraries. Patrick Rodgers provided a preliminary list that was invaluable in the preparation of this appendix.

Braun, Saul. "Sendak Raises the Shade on Childhood." *New York Times Sunday Magazine.* 7 June 1970. 34+.

Brockes, Emma. "Maurice Sendak: Author, Illustrator." *The Believer.* 10.9 (November/December 2012): n.p. http://www.believermag.com/issues/201211/?read=interview_sendak.

Ciotti, Paul. "The Dark World of Maurice Sendak." *Los Angeles Times Magazine.* 16 September 1990. 24+.

Cott, Jonathan. "Maurice Sendak, King of All Wild Things." *Rolling Stone.* 30 December 1976. Web. http://www.rollingstone.com/culture/news/maurice-sendak-king-of-all-wild-things-19761230.

Eggers, Dave. "*V. F.* Portrait: Maurice Sendak." *Vanity Fair.* (July 2011): n.p. http://www.vanityfair.com/news/2011/08/maurice-sendak-201108.

Esmonde, Margaret P., and Priscilla A. Ord, eds. "Picture Book Genesis: A Conversation with Maurice Sendak." *Proceedings of the Fifth Annual Conference of the Children's Literature Association.* Villanova, Pa.: Villanova/Children's Literature Association, 1979. 29–40.

Groth, Gary. "Maurice Sendak Interview." *Comics Journal* 302 (January 2013): 30–109.

Kopley, Richard. "Sendak on Melville: An Interview" *Melville Society Extracts* 87 (November 1991): 1–6.

Marcus, Leonard S. *Show Me a Story!: Why Picture Books Matter: Conversations with 21 of the World's Most Celebrated Illustrators.* Somerville, Mass.: Candlewick, 2012.

McAlpine, Julie Carlson. "Sendak Confronts the 'Now' Generation." *Children's Literature* 1 (1972): 138–42.

McPherson, William. "Maurice Sendak in Profile." *Washington Post.* 10 May 1981. Web. https://www.washingtonpost.com/archive/entertainment/books/1981/05/10/maurice-sendak-in-profile/c85246cc-1134-4ef6-b5f6-52a04e105c76/.

O'Doherty, Brian. "Portrait of the Artist as a Young Alchemist." *New York Times Book Review.* 12 May 1963. 22+.

Otten, Charlotte F. "An Interview with Maurice Sendak." *Signal* 68 (May 1992): 110–27.

Spiegelman, Art, and Maurice Sendak. "In the Dumps." *New Yorker.* 27 September 1993. 80–81.

Tell Them Anything You Want: A Portrait of Maurice Sendak. Dir. Spike Jonze and Lance Bangs. Perf. Maurice Sendak, Lynn Caponera, Catherine Keener. Oscilloscope Laboratories, 2010. DVD.

Zarin, Cynthia. "Not Nice: Maurice Sendak and the Perils of Childhood." *New Yorker.* 17 April 2006. 38+.

Text and Illustrations

Kenny's Window (1956)
Very Far Away (1957)
The Acrobat (1959)
The Sign on Rosie's Door (1960)
The Nutshell Library (1962)
    Alligators All Around
    Chicken Soup with Rice
    One Was Johnny
    Pierre
Where the Wild Things Are (1963)
Hector Protector and As I Went Over the Water (1965)
Higglety Pigglety Pop! or, There Must Be More to Life (1967)
In the Night Kitchen (1970)
Fantasy Sketches (1970)
Ten Little Rabbits: A Counting Book with Mino the Magician (1970)
Pictures by Maurice Sendak (1971)

Really Rosie, Starring the Nutshell Kids with music by Carole King and design by Jane Byers Bierhorst (1975)

Some Swell Pup, or Are You Sure You Want a Dog? with Matthew Margolis (1976)

Seven Little Monsters (1977)

Outside Over There (1981)

Caldecott and Co.: Notes on Books and Pictures (1988)

We Are All in the Dumps with Jack and Guy (1993)

Maurice Sendak's Christmas Mystery (1995)

Frank & Joey Eat Lunch with Arthur Yorinks (1996)

Frank & Joey Go to Work with Arthur Yorinks (1996)

Bumble-Ardy (2011)

My Brother's Book (2013)

Illustrations

Atomics for the Millions by Maxwell Leigh Eidinoff and Hyman Ruchlis (1947)

Good Shabbos, Everybody by Robert Garvey (1951)

The Wonderful Farm by Marcel Aymé (1951)

A Hole Is to Dig by Ruth Krauss (1952)

Maggie Rose: Her Birthday Christmas by Ruth Sawyer (1952)

The Giant Story by Beatrice Schenk de Regniers (1953)

Hurry Home, Candy by Meindert DeJong (1953)

Shadrach by Meindert DeJong (1953)

A Very Special House by Ruth Krauss (1953)

I'll Be You and You Be Me by Ruth Krauss (1954)

The Magic Pictures by Marcel Aymé (1954)

Mrs. Piggle-Wiggle's Farm by Betty MacDonald (1954)

The Tin Fiddle by Edward Tripp (1954)

The Wheel on the School by Meindert DeJong (1954)

Charlotte and the White Horse by Ruth Krauss (1955)

Happy Hanukah, Everybody by Hyman and Alice Chanover (1955)

The Little Cow and the Turtle by Meindert DeJong (1955)

Seven Little Stories on Big Subjects by Gladys Baker Bond (1955)

Singing Family of the Cumberlands by Jean Ritchie (1955)

What Can You Do with a Shoe? by Beatrice Schenk de Regniers (1955, new ed. 1997)

The Happy Rain by Jack Sendak (1956)

The House of Sixty Fathers by Meindert DeJong (1956)

I Want to Paint My Bathroom Blue by Ruth Krauss (1956)

The Birthday Party by Ruth Krauss (1957)

Circus Girl by Jack Sendak (1957)

Little Bear by Else Holmelund Minarik (1957)

You Can't Get There from Here by Ogden Nash (1957)

Along Came a Dog by Meindert DeJong (1958)

No Fighting, No Biting! by Else Holmelund Minarik (1958)

Somebody Else's Nut Tree and Other Tales from Children by Ruth Krauss (1958)

What Do You Say, Dear? By Sesyle Joslin (1958)

Father Bear Comes Home by Else Holmelund Minarik (1959)

The Moon Jumpers by Janice May Udry (1959)

Seven Tales by Hans Christian Andersen, translated by Eva Le Gallienne (1959)

Dwarf Long-Nose by Wilhelm Hauff, translated by Doris Orgel (1960)

Little Bear's Friend by Else Holmelund Minarik (1960)

Open House for Butterflies by Ruth Krauss (1960)

Let's Be Enemies by Janice May Udry (1961)

Little Bear's Visit by Else Holmelund Minarik (1961)

The Tale of Gockel, Hinkel and Gackeliah by Clemens Brentano, translated by Doris Orge (1961)

What Do You Do, Dear? by Sesyle Joslin (1961)

The Big Green Book by Robert Graves (1962)

Mr. Rabbit and the Lovely Present by Charlotte Zolotow (1962)

Schoolmaster Whackwell's Wonderful Sons by Clemens Brentano, translated by Doris Orge (1962)

The Singing Hill by Meindert DeJong (1962)

The Griffin and the Minor Canon by Frank Stockton (1963)

How Little Lori Visited Times Square by Amos Vogel (1963)

Nikolenka's Childhood by Leo Tolstoy (1963)

Sarah's Room by Doris Orgel (1963)

She Loves Me . . . She Loves Me Not . . . by Robert Keeshan (1963)

The Bat-Poet by Randall Jarrell (1964)

The Bee-Man of Orn by Frank Stockton (1964)

Pleasant Fieldmouse by Jan Wahl (1964)

The Animal Family by Randall Jarrell (1965)

Lullabies and Night Songs edited by William Engvick and music by Alec Wilder (1965)

Zlateh the Goat and Other Stories by Isaac Bashevis Singer, translated by
   Singer and Elizabet Shub (1966)
The Golden Key by George MacDonald (1967)
Poems from William Blake's "Songs of Innocence" by William Blake (1967)
A Kiss for Little Bear by Else Holmelund Minarik (1968)
The Light Princess by George MacDonald (1969)
The Juniper Tree and Other Tales from Grimm translated by Lore Segal and
   Randall Jarrel (1973)
King Grisly-Beard: A Tale from the Brothers Grimm translated by Edgar
   Taylor (1973)
Fortunia by Madame d'Aulnoy, translated by Richard Schaubeck (1974)
Fly by Night by Randall Jarrell (1976)
Nutcracker by E. T. A. Hoffmann, translated by Ralph Manheim (1984)
In Grandpa's House by Philip Sendak, translated by Seymour Barofsky
   (1985)
The Cunning Little Vixen by Rudolf Těsnohlídek, translated by Tatiana
   Firkusny, Maritza Morgan, and Robert T. Jones (1985)
Dear Mili by Wilhelm Grimm, translated by Ralph Manheim (1988)
Sing a Song of Popcorn: Every Child's Book of Poems selected by Beatrice
   Schenk de Regniers, Eva Moore, Mary Michaels White, and Jan Carr
   (1988)
I Saw Esau: The Schoolchild's Picture Book edited by Iona and Peter Opie
   (1992)
The Miami Giant by Arthur Yorinks (1995)
Pierre: or, The Ambiguities by Herman Melville (1995)
Penthesilea by Heinrich von Kleist, translated by Joel Agee (1998)
Swine Lake by James Marshall (1999)
Brundibar by Tony Kushner (2003)
Bears by Ruth Krauss (2005)
Mommy? by Arthur Yorinks (2006)

Index